THE SNAKE-DANCE OF THE MOQUIS OF ARIZONA

*Being a Narrative of a Journey
from Santa Fe, New Mexico,
to the Villages of the
Moqui Indians of Arizona*

JOHN G. BOURKE

The University of Arizona Press
TUCSON, ARIZONA

About the Author

JOHN GREGORY BOURKE (1846–1896) was one of the last in the tradition of humanist-scientific military officers who recorded the American West. He left home at age sixteen to join the cavalry and eventually became aide-de-camp to General George S. Crook and rose to the rank of captain. He participated in most of the campaigns against the Apaches and in the 1876–77 war against the Sioux and Cheyenne Indians. He spent his spare time methodically recording the customs of the Indians he observed and was granted a year's leave in 1880–81 for that purpose. Bourke wrote several other books, including *Medicine Men of the Apache* and *On the Border with Crook,* which have brought him recognition as an observant, a vivid, and sometimes even a humorous writer.

Copyright 1884 by John G. Bourke
THE UNIVERSITY OF ARIZONA PRESS
First Printing 1984
Copyright © 1984
The Arizona Board of Regents
All Rights Reserved
Manufactured in the U.S.A.

Library of Congress Cataloging in Publication Data

Bourke, John Gregory, 1846–1896.
The snake dance of the Moquis of Arizona

Reprint. Originally published: New York:
Scribner, 1884. With new foreword.
1. Hopi Indians.   2. Snake-dance.   3. Serpent
worship—Arizona. I. Title.
E99.H7B7   1984   979.1'3500497   84-16379

ISBN 0-8165-0872-0

CONTENTS.

CHAPTER I.

CHAPTER II.

CHAPTER III.

CHAPTER IV.

CHAPTER V.

CHAPTER VI.

CHAPTER VII.

CHAPTER VIII.

CHAPTER IX.

CHAPTER X.

CHAPTER XI.

CHAPTER XVIII.

CHAPTER XIX.

CHAPTER XX.

CHAPTER XXI.

CHAPTER XXII.

CHAPTER XXIII.

CHAPTER XXIV.

CHAPTER XXV.

CHAPTER XXVI.

CHAPTER XXVII.

CHAPTER XXVIII.

CHAPTER XXIX.

CHAPTER XXX.

CHAPTER XXXI.

CHAPTER XXXII.

LIST OF PLATES.

FOREWORD

by Emory Sekaquaptewa

THE HOPI SNAKE DANCE was photographed and
sketched perhaps more than any other Indian ceremony ever perfomed. By the last quarter of the
nineteenth century, people from the four corners of
this country had discovered the Hopis, or Moquis, as
they were called by the Spaniards, and their spectacu-
lar dances, undoubtedly because of vivid reports by
early visitors to the American Southwest such as
Lieut. John G. Bourke. By the turn of the century,
photographs taken with the earliest picture-taking
contraptions filled ethnographic reports and popular
magazines. The idea of dancing with snakes in a religious ritual outraged some Americans for whom this
practice conjured up vestiges of satanical worship.
The original title of this book leaves no doubt that the
author intended to reveal the ritual as offensive.* But

*The full title of the original book published in 1884 was *The Snake-
Dance of the Moquis of Arizona: Being a Narrative of a Journey from
Santa Fe, New Mexico, to the Villages of the Moqui Indians of Arizona,
with a Description of the Manners and Customs of this peculiar People,
and especially of the revolting religious rite, The Snake-Dance; to which
is added a Brief Dissertation upon Serpent-Worship in General with an
Account of the Tablet Dance of the Pueblo of Santo Domingo, New
Mexico, etc.*

for some other people, and perhaps with equal impact, the snake dance of these far-off Indians in remote Arizona struck a note of fascination and promised an exciting pioneer adventure on the last frontier in America, the West.

By the first decade of the twentieth century, the non-Indians almost outnumbered the indigenous population as spectators of the Snake Dance. Some photographs of that period show the dancers in the plaza completely encircled by photographers with their cameras focused from all angles at the ritual—quite a different picture from what was supposed to be a solemn ceremony, and certainly a different scene from what Lieutenant Bourke must have encountered.

Indeed, the author describes some unusual privileges accorded him in his attempts to understand the Snake Dance in all its elements of ritualistic, spiritual, and historical meanings. They included going into the kiva of the snake priests to observe the kiva activities before the public dance, having certain Hopi informants who volunteered to explain some aspects of the ceremony, and acquiring some ritual objects. These privileges are not even accorded to nonparticipating Hopis.

The author made no claims for being an official agent on a mission to document this ceremony, but neither did he disavow the Hopi rumors about his being a representative of the Great White Father in Washington, which his informant probably assumed that he was. Under these ostentatious circumstances the Hopi informants chose to oblige him rather than to confront him with their own reasons for forbidding strangers to enter the kiva. At the time, the Hopi people failed to realize the eternal nature of the printed word that produced this document. By this unwitting error, they left us with a written account of some esoteric knowledge that weighs upon present-day members of the Snake Ceremony as they try to maintain its ritual dignity.

Outside spectators to a Hopi ceremony today are not only prohibited from photographing or sketching the ceremony, but in some cases may even be barred from the ceremony itself. These restrictions are consequences of past excesses on the ceremony by the outsiders with their cameras and curiosity. These excesses, along with others, such as simulated performances of the ceremony, have been rationalized as a public right and as having redeeming value toward preservation of Hopi lore. But the question is who has the right, morally, to preserve the cultural ways of the Hopis. The Hopis have always felt that they are preserving the things of Hopi life through their oral tradition and ritual symbolism, although for those who demand more graphic encapsulation of history, these are not an adequate preservation. On the other hand, we may view photographs and sketches and read the most careful and professional descriptions of events such as the Hopi Snake Ceremony, and still perhaps be unable to comprehend the meaning such longstanding practices hold for the people to whose culture they belong.

Even so, from the standpoint of the preservation of things Hopi, the illustrator of this book, a military companion of Bourke, accomplished a remarkable rendering of the choreographic setting of the Snake Dance (Plate II at the back of the book), complete with the festive character of the spectator crowd and the ever-present wandering dogs. It is understandable, however, that even the most observant person would find great difficulty noting every detail of this dramatic and intricate ceremony, especially upon the first viewing of it. The sketches were done after the Walpi ceremony of 1881. They show a picture-perfect formation of the snake dancers, the antelope priests, and the clan women in the ceremony. But according to the ceremony as it is performed in the 1980s, the antelope priests who provide the chants remain in place in front of the "sacred lodge" instead of dancing around the lodge as the illustration portrays them. The sketch, therefore, is not accurate based on twentieth-century Hopi performance of the ceremony.

Interesting also is the placement of the turtle

shell rattles on the right leg of the snake priests, hanging to the side and front of the shins (Plates VI, XII–XV). It would not take long for the rattles to bruise the shins if worn in that manner while dancing! In all ceremonial uses today, the turtle shell rattle is worn so that it hangs to the back of the leg where it clacks against the calf. Another inaccuracy pertaining to accessories is the wearing of the sash by the dancers around the waist with the fringes falling down the left side as shown in Plate XV. Traditionally, the sash is worn with the fringes hanging along the right leg, as accurately depicted in Plates XII–XIV.

The moccasins in some of the sketches seem to have furry fluffs around their tops. The furry fluffs were probably meant to represent the fringes that normally fall straight down from the ankles to the heels all the way around. These anklets are usually made from a piece of buckskin that is dyed ochre and cut into narrow strips to make the fringes and tied around the ankles over the moccasins. They are worn by many other Hopi ceremonial dancers as well, including kachinas.

On the whole, however, this account of the author's visit to the Hopi country and the sketches of his companion add to other historical accounts that give a verifying effect to the Hopi people's own oral traditions.

PREFACE.

It is a matter of deep regret to the Author that circumstances have compelled him to prepare this little volume in a remote military outpost.

Only those who have assumed the burden of authorship can appreciate the fatigue and labour of research demanded, when exactness of statement is aimed at. This fatigue and this labour increase ten-fold at outlying military stations where libraries are of insignificant proportions, and where books bearing upon special topics are not to be had for love or money.

The author has endeavoured to present a truthful description of religious rites, the very existence of which is known to but few of our people, and a narrative of incidents which may serve to entertain and amuse, if they do not instruct, those into whose hands this book may fall.

The illustrations, by Sergeant A. F. HARMER, U. S. Army, a student of the Philadelphia Academy of Fine Arts, may be relied upon as true to Nature and to Art alike. They speak for themselves.

The Author has had much difficulty in deciding where to expand, where to condense, and where to reject.

In a work intended for popular perusal he was afraid that by giving too much attention to topics interesting to himself he might fail to retain the interest of persons not so well acquainted with them ; and he has accordingly preferred to make his allusions as succinct as possible, consistent with intelligibility.

The Moqui Indians inhabit seven different villages, situated a few leagues apart. In treating of them all, it has been impossible to avoid a seeming repetition of description, where the same apparel, food, arms, and ceremonies were to be explained.

They are known to have lived in their present location since the Spaniards first entered this portion of America, which was about the middle of the sixteenth century.

As they were then, so they are in our own day, one of the most interesting peoples in the world.

Their religion, system of government, apparel, manufactures,—no less than the romantic positions of their villages, appeal to the curiosity or sympathy of almost every class of travellers, archæologists, divines, men of letters, or ordinary sight-seers. The various railroad systems penetrating Arizona and New Mexico have brought the hitherto isolated Moquis to the doors of the scholars and men of leisure of our eastern cities and of Europe. If the author has succeeded in demonstrating that our South-Western Territories contain much that is fully worthy of the attention and study of people of intelligence, he will feel amply repaid for the time and labour devoted to this volume.

J. G. B.

Whipple Barracks, Arizona Territory,
March 1, 1884.

SNAKE-DANCE OF THE MOQUIS.

CHAPTER I.

En route—Uniformity of customs—The start from Santa Fé—
La Bajada—The arrival in safety.

ALTHOUGH vague rumours had from time to time
reached me of the peculiar ceremonies to be noticed
among the Moquis, I had paid but slight attention to
them, as they came from mining prospectors and
others of the same genus, who delight in the marvellous; and I first heard with certainty of the rattlesnake-dance of this strange people from my old friend
Mr. William Leonard, then trader at the Navajo
Indian Agency, Fort Defiance, Arizona.

Mr. Leonard's account was so exact and circum-
stantial (although given at second hand from the
Navajo Indians), and his desire so earnest that I
should be the first white man to carefully note this
strange heathen rite during the moment of its celebration, that I made up my mind that, come what
would, I should make the effort to reach the village
of Hualpi by the full moon of August, the date set for
its commencement.

B

It was by this time almost the middle of May, and to perform in the intervening weeks the amount of work assigned to myself would, I saw plainly, tax my physical powers to the utmost. Nevertheless, after much calculation, I concluded that I could carry out the scheme already outlined, and still have the narrowest margin of time left in which to make the trip upon which I had set my heart. May, June, and July flew rapidly by, every moment occupied in something of an intensely interesting nature. I witnessed the sundance of the Dakotas at Red Cloud Agency, Dakota, early in June, under exceptionally favourable circumstances.

Dr. M'Gillicuddy, the agent, an old friend, rendered me every assistance, and many of the Indian chiefs and head men—" Red Cloud," " Red Dog," " American Horse," " Young Man Afraid," " Little Big Man," " Woman's Dress," and many others whom I had known with more or less intimacy during the months when they were serving as scouts under General Crook in 1876-77, gave me points of information extremely curious and valuable.

The month of July was devoted to an examination of the Pueblos north of Santa Fé. Many of these Pueblos —most of them, in fact—belong to the tribe known as the Teguas, one of whose bands lives among and forms part of the Moquis. Those on the Rio Grande are fairly familiar with the Spanish language, and my hope was to learn from them all possible relating to their congeners in Arizona, and, if such a thing could be done, persuade one of the Rio Grande Teguas to accompany me in the capacity of interpreter upon the trip I had in contemplation.

I obtained much new and singular information, and shall always look back upon that tour as one of the most valuable and interesting in a chequered experience. But I found that the Rio Grande Teguas had in their sympathies grown so apart from their relatives to the west that I determined not to embarrass myself with one of them as an interpreter, but to trust to luck for coming across a Navajo or Moqui, with whom communication could be carried on in Spanish or English.

I supposed, too, when I began the tour, from what I had previously known, and from what Indians coming into the city of the Holy Faith had assured me, that all the sedentary Indians of New Mexico and Arizona would be found to possess many attributes in common ; or, to express the idea with even greater force, that their lives were moulded in a common pattern, and that any divergences of manners and customs would be clearly ascribable to Spanish intervention.

Investigation demonstrated the accuracy of this surmise. Taking the present condition of Zuni and its people as a datum line, the advancement beyond or deterioration below this is very small, the different Pueblos adhering tenaciously to old-time ideas, except in the cases of such almost extinct communities as Nambé and Pojuaque, where foreign influence has made an appreciable impression upon the surviving aborigines.

In religion, the Pueblos on the Rio Grande are suspected, with very good reason, of practising in secret that which the Zunis and Moquis openly avow.

In government they retain the same usages, and in such matters as food and dress differ less from the Moqui standard or Zuni standard than the same number of little villages separated by the same distances would among ourselves differ from any given one we might assume as a criterion.

In their apparel the women on the Rio Grande make a more general use of underclothing than do those of the Moqui family, who go about with the left arm and the upper half of the left breast entirely exposed, and the right arm nearly so. This innovation, a step in the direction of modesty, as we understand it, is due to the Spanish missionaries.

The women in the Pueblos north of Santa Fé very frequently wear a bottine, or legging, shaped somewhat like a Wellington boot, which is at least more graceful than the cumbrous and unwieldy footgear of the Zunians, which, however, is also to be seen very generally on the Rio Grande. The light "drop-over" boot of which I am now speaking, can be found more commonly in San Juan than in any other community.

The ordinary use of valuable necklaces of globular silver beads, having the double or archiepiscopal cross

as a pendant in front, will at once attract comment :
these are also to be seen in Zuni, but with nothing
like the frequency noticeable on the Rio Grande,
where no Indian woman is so poor as not to be possessed of this beautiful and highly-prized ornament.[1]

With the first days of August I was back in Santa
Fé, and up to my eyes in preparations.   It was at first
intended that General Edward Hatch and Captain
C. A. Woodruff of his staff should be of the party, an
arrangement I was sorry to see broken by a sudden
outbreak of the Apache Indians in the southern part
of the district, necessitating General Hatch's presence
in command of the troops.   I had also contemplated
inviting Mr. S. B. Evans of Illinois, an experienced
archæologist, then in New Mexico, but he did not
return in time from his visit to the interesting ruins
near Cochiti, so I was compelled to go without him.

Mr. Peter Moran, the artist, the last of the party
as at first organised, still remained, and together we
determined to start at once, fearing that unexpected
obstacles might frustrate our plans.

Those who are not familiar with the fearful type
of thunder-storms which arise in the Trans-Missouri
region can form no conception of the havoc wrought
by those which assailed the vicinity of Santa Fé in
the first week of August 1881, and taxed to the utmost

---

[1] The introduction of these rosary necklaces dates back to the re-
conquest of New Mexico by Espejo in 1692-94, when the natives were
required to wear them as a mark of subjection to the crown of Spain,
and to the religion of which it was the champion.   *V.* Davis' *Conquest of New Mexico.*

the engineering ability of the managers of the Topeka and Santa Fé Railroad to keep their trains running with anything like regularity. The worst storm of the series (that of the early morning of August 2), although spasmodic in its nature, was phenomenal in the amount of water falling during the time it lasted. It seemed as if the bottom had fallen out of an immense tank, and the noise made by the descending torrent was so great as almost to drown the sullen growls of the thunder, which added a terrible majesty to the grandeur of the tempest.

Consequently we were not astonished to learn, as we did at breakfast, that the railroad track had been washed away, and that there was no probability of trains running on schedule time for several days.

There was but one thing for us to do, and we did it. I obtained an ambulance from Colonel Lee, the chief quartermaster of the district, and in company with Mr. Moran left the quaint and ever-curious town of Santa Fé on the afternoon of August 3, intending to go as far south as the important Pueblo of Santo Domingo, where we should be in time for the grand annual celebration of the Dance of the Tablet and its attendant ceremonies ; and this witnessed, could strike the Atchison, Topeka, and Santa Fé Railroad below the " wash-out," and readily reach Albuquerque, the initial point of the Atlantic and Pacific Railroad, then just building in the direction of the Arizona boundary, and the shortest line of approach to our goal, the Moqui villages.

Six or seven miles north of Santo Domingo is "La Bajada" (the grade or descent), a fearful grade cut out of the face of a precipitous hill of black columnar basalt. The total descent is, in round numbers, about 600 feet, and the difficulty of ascent or descent is much increased by abrupt curves and by the presence in the roadway of large blocks of lava. In former days it was the most dangerous spot on the road between Santa Fé and El Paso, Texas, and many are the reminiscences of the rough experience of passengers who were obliged to leave the stage and even to assist the drivers in "chocking" the wheels and supplying them with iron shoes and lock chains.

With brake firmly applied, wheels locked and shod, and a passenger at the head of each "leader," the driver of the "Great Southern Overland" would cautiously pick his way down from the crest of the precipice to the little valley below.

In my own experience, when I first became acquainted with this classic spot (in 1869), I was aroused from a sound sleep, and told by the gruff-voiced Jehu to "light," which I did, in a half-dazed kind of a way, landing in the middle of a cactus bush, which did much to bring to the surface all the latent eloquence of an impulsive nature.

"La Bajada" was the scene of the story told against Mr. O'C., a gentleman who worthily represented the Emerald Isle in the years immediately after the war, when the railroad was still undreamed of on the Rio Grande. O'C. was one of the best-hearted fellows that ever lived, but extremely eccentric and very absent-minded.

He left Santa Fé one bright winter's morning to go to one of the small posts, a couple of hundred of miles down the Rio Grande in the immediate vicinity of El Paso.

Right in front of him, not more than a mile ahead, was the conveyance of Colonel Pratt, the U.S. Marshal of the territory. When Pratt reached the crest of " La Bajada" he and all his party, except the driver, got out, locked the wheels, and walked down in front of the mules, according to the most approved formula.

About the moment of reaching the foot of the grade Pratt heard a fine round Irish voice close behind him saying, "Shure she'll git down oll roight, I dunno ;" and turning, he saw at his heels O'C. and his man-servant, while far up the dizzy ramp was the O'C. carriage, in which sat, unconscious of danger, the lovely and accomplished Mrs. O'C. There was no brake, no lock, and no shoe to the wheels ; the mules every now and then turned their heads in a lazy sort of a way, as if undecided whether to kick the old carry-all to pieces or haul it quietly to the bottom. Mrs. O'C. chirped to them cheerily, while O'C., from his station at the foot of the grade, looked up complacently, and again remarked, " Shure she'll git down oll roight, I dunno." Pratt was fearfully disgusted and frightened, and cried out, "Why, my good heavens, man, *I* wouldn't drive down La Bajada *myself!*" " No,' rejoined O'C., unconcernedly, " nor oi."

But the same kind Providence which watches over the sparrow in its flight guarded Mrs. O'C. on her perilous journey, and brought her safely to the foot of the precipice.

Looking south from the crest of La Bajada, a very fine view is obtained of the Sandia (Watermelon) Mountains, while below is the valley, on the left or east bank of the Rio Grande, thirty-two miles south of Santa Fé, and about two miles from the station of " Wallace," on the Atchison, Topeka, and Santa Fé Railroad, is the Pueblo of Santo Domingo, where we soon arrived.

CHAPTER II.

In driving through the Pueblo the irregularity of its arrangement was noticeable ; it seemed to be composed of two distinct villages, a quarter of a mile or more apart. The houses are nearly all of adobe, and mostly of two stories.

The great number of windows glazed with selenite astonished me very much. This mineral is found in this region in great slabs, often as much as one and even two feet square, and, being fully as good as cheap glass, has not been superseded by that material.

We hunted up the house of the Lieutenant-Governor, who met us at the doorway, and presented himself as Bautista Calabaza ; said, the Governor being absent, he had charge of the Pueblo, and after inflicting upon me a long and prosy account of how he had received a severe injury to his chest by being kicked by a mule in Kansas City, forgot his ailments so far as to conduct us to a small but new, and therefore comparatively clean, house of adobe, where we were to make our quarters for the night.

The single room was almost full of the debris

of a primitive carpenter's shop, for which it had served.

A half-hour's hard work on the part of Moran and myself, assisted in a rather listless way by a couple of Indians, put one end of the apartment in ship-shape by the time that Baxter, our driver, had unharnessed and watered the mules and gotten ready to make us a bite of supper.

The Lieutenant-Governor was very officious and voluble in his talk—in promises great ; in performance he was nothing.

"Could we have hay for our mules?"

"Oh, certainly, gentlemen, ahorita" (presently). But "ahorita" had become an hour and a half, and still no signs of hay for our poor famished animals, which were braying together in dismal solos and choruses outside.

"Where is that hay, Governor?"

"Oh, the hay! Is it possible that the Captain don't know that to-morrow is a great 'fiesta,' and that all the young men of the Pueblo are to take part? It is impossible to get hay to-night."

"No ; I am going to have it to-night, and if *you* can't get it, I'll get it myself."

A few of the young boys standing close by were soon hired at a good figure to go to a neighbouring "cienaga"[1] and cut all the hay their "burros" could carry. The burdens brought back were almost as small as their consciences, not much over a good

[1] Cienaga means a swamp or low meadow-land.

mouthful for each of the four mules, but they helped wonderfully with the supply of corn we had brought along from Santa Fé, and silenced the serenade which, without the hay, would certainly have lasted all night.

A similar arrangement brought us firewood in tiny bundles, water for cooking, a few eggs, and a small jug of milk. In each case the small boy was brought into acquisition, and his services remunerated so satisfactorily that, in eggs at least, a " corner " was formed to bull the market, the boys judging that when we wanted them so badly we would, in the lapse of an hour or so, be only too glad to pay still higher figures. In this they were disappointed. After the first dozen had been purchased the youngsters were told that we had all we could eat, and that we didn't want any more. This announcement broke the market, and had the ludicrous effect of bringing out many more than we had any need for. Every little boy and every little girl seemed to have two or three, which he or she was most anxious to sell, while a sore-eyed old crone, who had perversely sat in a corner and listened unmoved to our piteous appeals for "hueros" (eggs), now hastened up to make some kind of a sale for the twelve or fifteen which she had kept stealthily concealed in the folds of her garments.

We told the boys : " We have paid you just twice as much for your eggs as you would have received had you taken them all the way to Santa Fé ; you know that. Now, we don't know whether we shall remain here very long or not ; but if we need any more, after eating what we have on hand, we'll pay you the same price we have been paying, and no more."

To this the boys and girls said, "Bueno," and many of them wandered off to their homes ; but a contingent of respectable proportions remained to watch us preparing supper. This was composed of fried bacon, a can of baked beans warmed in the ashes, hard tack, coffee, and boiled eggs.

The Lieutenant-Governor "happened in," and was invited to take pot-luck with us. His decision of character made itself manifest in the promptness of his acceptance. He made excellent use of his opportunities, and, without any exaggeration, ate as much as Moran, the driver, and myself put together.

We had no table conveniences ; the can of baked beans was set down in the centre of a circle, and each one dipped in his spoon and lifted the food to his mouth ; the eggs were boiled hard and needed no dishes ; and the hard tack could be consumed direct from the box.

The coffee was excellent ; we were hungry as wolves, and gulped down our meal with eagerness, that we might hurry out to examine the Pueblo, and witness the celebration going on in the old church.

We managed to extract from the Lieutenant-Governor the statement that his Indian name was Yashté-tiwa, that he belonged to the Aguila or Eagle clan, and that his wife and children were of the Kuta or Shípi clan. (From his explanation of the meaning of this word I made out that it was an herb of small size and strong smell,—either the sage-brush or sun-flower. Bautista's Spanish was not of the best, and his speech so interfered with by coughing, that it was not always easy to maintain a conversation with him.)

The whole subject of clan or Gentile organisation by which our Indian tribes, with scarcely an exception, are governed, is one of the most interesting to which the student of ethnology can devote his attention. In no section of our country is it better defined than in New Mexico and Arizona; but for reasons best known to themselves the Indians of the various tribes are averse to imparting information upon the matter or anything concerning their system of civic polity, which is so largely based upon it.

During many years' experience with the native tribes I have been enabled to gain, little by little, much that is important upon this head, and hope at an early day to have it in shape for general dissemination. As the general reader may not perhaps take much interest in the subject, I will restrict my remarks in this place to the broad statement that the clans themselves closely resemble the Septs of the Ancient Irish, and that the management of the tribes is mainly in the hands of the clan-heads, or chiefs of bands as we call them. Children belong in nearly all cases to their mother's clan, which, in the event of their father's death, assumes, with rare exceptions, their care and maintenance. Later on I shall have more to say upon this subject.

Bautista gave me the names of four clans—those of the Sol or Sun, Aguila or Eagle, Cayote, and the Shípi or Kuta before mentioned. Although I was more than half satisfied that he wasn't giving me one quarter the truth, yet to extract any information at all upon this head was a gratifying advantage which I hoped, with some reason, to be able to turn to account in interviews with more communicative persons.

He also told us that the inhabitants of the Pueblos of Santo Domingo, Santana, San Félipe, Zia, Laguna, and Acoma speak one language, and are of one stock —the Querez. The same information was also given by an old man whom we met at the church door a short time afterwards.

The house in which Bautista had placed us was so dark and unwholesome-looking, scarcely lit up by the flickering flames of the fire over which sputtered our bacon and coffee, or the still feebler parody upon illumination afforded by the forlorn piece of candle which the driver had stuck in the wall, that Moran and I lost not a moment in freeing ourselves from such disagreeable surroundings and making our way along with the multitude progressing towards the old church.

The venerable edifice, of which the outlines of the façade only were traceable against the sky, was filling rapidly with devout worshippers.

An energetic performer upon one of the oblong drums peculiar to the Pueblos had taken his stand at the main entrance, there to emulate the doleful performance of the band inside, the strains from whose racked and untuned guitars rent the evening air. The congregation assembled before the chancel rails numbered anywhere from 100 to 125, a fair proportion being men, nearly all Indians, with a slight sprinkling of Mexicans.

They were chanting the rosary in a manner so strange and odd, so thoroughly Indian, that, taken in connection with what I had seen outside, the impression was hard to shake off that I was listening to refrains which ante-dated the introduction of Christianity, refrains which were the original music this people once sung in honour of the sun or other deity, and so thoroughly engrafted upon their affection and reverence that the early Spanish missionaries, with the astuteness and knowledge of human nature for which they were noted, had quietly deferred to popular prejudice and allowed their retention, taking care only to change the object of the application.

This suggestion I advance with much diffidence. Not having any knowledge of music, I cannot pretend to speak critically, but I am sufficiently familiar with Catholic Church music, as well as with that (so to call it) of our Indian tribes, to feel confident of the exactness of my assertion, that while this music bore no resemblance whatever to the former, it was almost identical in type with the latter.

From the roof of the church near the belfry

blazed five different fires of asphaltum which from moment to moment increased in brilliancy and were answered by the flashes from similar but smaller pyres kindled upon the flat earthen roofs of the houses.

What all this meant the Indians were unable or unwilling to explain, but the same idea occurred at once to Moran and myself, and found vent in my friend's exclamation, "Well! don't this beat all ? It's just what Stephens describes as done in Yucatan, where the people burned copal in honour of the sun."[1]

To come back to the refrain : the voices were not musical, and individual execution was poor, but the accord was perfect, and the general effect weird and touching.

The statue of Santo Domingo, in one corner behind the altar rails, is looked up to by the simple-minded aborigines as something but little short of miraculous. It is a coarsely-painted wooden image of the cigar-sign order of sculpture, but so much superior to the other sacred crudities of the Rio Grande Valley that my sympathies went in unison with those of the poor old women who unmistakably regarded the statue as a work of genius too peerless to be approached save on bended knees. As each got close enough, she took in her hands the hem of the garment of faded gold brocade and kissed it with fervour.

---

[1] Bancroft, H. H. (*Native Races*, etc.), vol. ii. p. 231, mentions the Mexican priests as burning an incense made of copal, and again on p. 234, same volume, he includes copal in the list of articles paid in as tribute to Montezuma. *See* also Tylor, *Anthropology*, p. 137.

The orchestra next favoured us with an instrumental selection while the singers were resting.

Over the merits of this let us draw the veil of charity. It was rendered as well, perhaps, as could be by performers whose home-made violins and guitars were in an execrable state of repair, and who had but a vague and incoherent idea of the divine art which "soothes the savage breast."

From a distant quarter of the Pueblo, as we retired to rest, came the sound of drumming and singing, strangely like that with which the Apaches and Sioux begin their dances.

CHAPTER III.

OUR sleep was broken between one and two the next
morning by a procession of Indian youths who slowly
moved past our door and all around the Pueblo,
singing in a measured cadence a song or hymn which
the Lieutenant-Governor, later in the day, informed
me was a notification that the feast was about to
commence.

" But why was not this notification entrusted to
the ' pregonero' (town-crier) who discharges this duty
at other festivals, and why did they sing a hymn, and
what were the words they sung?"   Upon these heads
Bautista was discreetly silent.

The remarkable thing about this vocalisation was
the absolutely perfect time maintained throughout.

Bautista afterwards said that Santo Domingo keeps
up the practice remarked in all the other Pueblos of
sending out a patrol or " grand rounds " every night.

The day opened cloudy, but without indications
of a storm.   With the first dawn Indians tapped at our
door, bringing fresh eggs for sale—the number was
inconsiderable, but amply sufficient for all our needs.

Some of these visitors wore nothing but a shirt.

These shirts, as all other garments worn this day, were fresh and sweet, and, so the Indians told us, donned in honour of the feast.

Breakfast over, I took a promenade around the town with Moran. The Pueblo, as has already been stated, consists of two divisions, the new one in which we were living, and the "old," a quarter of a mile nearer the river, but now almost depopulated on account of danger apprehended from the caving in of the bank. In the new town the houses are almost all of two stories, built of adobes, and in a number of cases surmounted by small wooden crosses.

There are very few doors opening out from the ground-floor, the mode of entrance in all, or nearly all, houses being by ladders to the first roof or terrace, and thence by other ladders down into the rooms of the first-floor.

The windows are almost invariably filled in with slabs of translucent selenite; there are not half a dozen windows of glass in the whole Pueblo.

In each house we saw great haunches of mutton freshly killed, and enormous piles of snowy bread, newly baked for the coming feast.

Hospitality, open-handed, uncalculating hospitality, is a characteristic of all the American Indians; one, indeed, which may well be placed in the list of their vices.

Bushes of cottonwood were planted in double rows along the streets through which the procession of Santo Domingo was to march from the church to the receptacle prepared for the statue in a cool niche, built of boughs, from which floated all that was beautiful or quaint in the way of Mexican or Navajo blankets ; and there were many of both kinds in the Pueblo.

There are two Estufas[1] in Santo Domingo ; each is circular, built of stone and mud, plastered within and without, about 25 feet or 30 feet in diameter and 12 feet in height, half below and half above ground. A broad and well-constructed stone stairway leads to the roof, from which the descent to the interior is by a wide, strong ladder.

The busy hum of voices within told of unusual commotion and preparation. Every moment or so Indians, singly or in squads, of both sexes, and in a more or less complete state of ornamentation and attire, would appear above the companion-way and dart back again with the air of persons who had something of importance on hand. Peeping through small rectangular openings, at the level of the ground, I saw that the edifices were *stuffed* with humanity, old and young. A half-dozen old men in the centre of each Estufa were quietly smoking, while the other occupants were arranging their dresses and putting the finishing touches to the patterns of paint covering their bodies and limbs.

It was evident that whatever *secret* ceremonies were connected with the festival had been held at dead of the previous night, and, as I supposed, had terminated with the chorus heard chanted so early this morning.

[1] Houses used for public ceremonies, and as meeting-places.

As it might be a good thing to obtain a correct description of the little that was transpiring within the Estufas, Moran and I laid our heads together, and concluded that an attempt should be made to penetrate the larger edifice.

Our note-books were gripped tightly in one hand, and our sharpened pencils in the other, the theory of our advance being that, with boldness and celerity, we might gain an entrance and jot down a few memoranda of value before the preoccupied savages could discover and expel us.

My pulse beat high as we reached the roof and passed the sacred standard floating from the top of the ladder.[1] Everything looked propitious, and I had gotten down four rungs of the ladder, within two of the bottom, when a yell was raised, repeated from point to point in warning tones, and from every conceivable spot—from out of the earth as it seemed to me—Indians fairly boiled.

The Estufa itself buzzed like a hive of bees. Before I could count ten I was seized from above by the neck and shoulders, and from below by the legs and feet, and lifted or thrown out of the Estufa, the Indians yelling at the tops of their voices, " Que no entres, amigo, mañana bueno "—" You mustn't enter, friend—to-morrow (will be) good (or proper for that)." They reiterated: "To-morrow, to-morrow; you can come in to-morrow; it isn't good now."

There was no disguising the fact; I was " fired

[1] See Plate IV.

out," as the slang phrase is, and had to make the best of a bad bargain. My tailor had left too much "slack" in my pantaloons, and thus gave the Indians so much the better purchase when they seized me.

I laughed very heartily at my discomfiture, and the Indians, seeing that I was taking the affair good-naturedly, became very much appeased, and joined in my hilarity.

The good-humour of the Indians was, however, I am persuaded, in no small extent induced by the presence of a large delegation of robust miners from the gold and silver leads of the " Cerrillos " district, who had arrived in a body about this hour.

Moran's face was very red, as if from violent exertion of some sort. He stoutly averred that he had walked down from the roof of the Estufa, a statement which keeps me from even so much as intimating in these notes that he too had been "fired out"; but, to record faithfully all that transpired that morning, I must say that one of the horny-handed miners above alluded to, addressing me in a husky stage whisper, asked if Moran was my "pardner," and then informed me confidentially that he had "see'd him h'isted, biggod."

During the momentary glance I was able to cast around the interior I saw that there was no fire, although the ashes in the hearth had been carefully swept and arranged apparently in readiness to have one kindled there at any moment.

One of the Indians who " escorted " me up the

ladder said that there would be a fire there in a
"ratito" (little while), which might mean any time
from ten minutes to as many hours.

A bed of corn fodder lay on the floor close to the
fireplace, but I am certain that there was no fire in
that Estufa excepting the small amount in the
ancient and odd-looking pipes smoked by the group
of old men in the centre.

This smoking struck me as invested with a certain
religious, or at least ceremonial, significance, since
pipes are no longer to be found in ordinary use among
our sedentary Indians.[1]

The reappearance of farming implements, clothing,
tools,—anything, in fact, which, having had a former
connection with the life of a people, had been superseded by later inventions,—testifies to the sacred
character of the dance or ceremony in which they are
employed, and has an important ethnological bearing in
determining the exact former status of the tribe, and
from that the amount of its advancement in civilisation.

The Indians who seized me from below were nearly
naked, their bodies and limbs daubed with white, and
their hair tied up at sides of head with corn-shucks.

A fuller description at this moment is unnecessary,
the costumes of the dancers as they moved about the
plaza being minutely described and carefully sketched
at a later hour in the day.

---

[1] "Smoking is, throughout America, closely connected with all
religious ceremonies, just as incense is used for the same purpose in the
old world."—Lubbock, *Origin of Civilisation*, p. 157.

From the pole projecting above the Estufa lazily
floated a very curious and beautiful banner, which
merits minute delineation.   A rough drawing was
made for me by Mr. Moran.   The standard itself was
of coarse white cotton cloth, much in texture and
colour like our unbleached canvas ; or, more strictly,
like the material known as "Marseilles."   At the
borders were tasteful designs in bright red wool upon
a dark blue ground.

Parrot and eagle feathers, singly and in clusters,
were attached to it, and also a crown of sea-
shells.[1]   "Where did they get the sea-shells?"
"From California" (the name given by the Indians
of the Rio Grande to all the land lying along the
Pacific Ocean).

The banner, they said, was made long ago by the
Zunis, but the Moquis also made them.   The shells
came from the sea in California.

"Were they brought here by the Zunis?"

"Sometimes we get them from the Zunis, sometimes from the Moquis, and sometimes we have gone
with our own beasts over there to get them."

The shells are of the variety called, I think, the
olivette.

The skin of a fox was pendant from the top of the
staff, and a small gourd encrusted with blue beads and
filled, as my informants asserted, with kernels of corn,
were conspicuous portions of the standard.

[1] See Plate IV.

CHAPTER IV.

SANTO DOMINGO has been seriously threatened with
destruction by freshets in the Rio Grande. The
inhabitants of the Pueblo have made much laborious
and expensive revetments to protect the bank, but
many have taken counsel with their fears and
constructed new houses farther inland, making the
Pueblo a double town.

A youngster named "Trinidad" told me that
there were parrots kept in cages by his people.
"There is one in my own house; come and see it."

There it was in a little cage of willow saplings.
The poor bird was in a fearful state of demoralisa-
tion, nearly every one of its fine blue, red, and yellow
feathers having been plucked to make wands for the
dancers or to decorate the sacred standards.

There were several other parrots in the Pueblo
utilised for the same object. The value ascribed to
the plumage of the eagle and parrot by all the
sedentary Indians of Arizona and New Mexico is
doubtless based upon some considerations graver

than those of commerce. The feathers of the parrot, which have to be brought up from the interior of the neighbouring Republic of Mexico, are treasured by all the Pueblos as far north as Taos and Picuris, and west to Acoma, Zuni, and Oraybe. They will always be found carefully preserved in peculiar wooden boxes, generally cylindrical in shape, made expressly for the purpose; with them is invariably associated the soft white down of the eagle.[1] Eagles are still raised in cages in Picuris, San Ildefonso, Santa Clara, Zuni, Acoma, and the villages of the Moquis farthest to the west; but in no Pueblo except Santo Domingo have I ever come across live parrots.

We had the pleasure of meeting Padre José Romulo Ribera, the priest under whose spiritual charge this Pueblo lies. His place of residence is at Peña Blanca (White Rock), a Mexican town on the Rio Grande, five or six miles distant; and I should imagine that constant work kept time from hanging heavy upon his hands.

The Padre was a bright and good-natured young gentleman, a native of Santa Fé, and thoroughly familiar with our language, and he expressed a desire to show us every attention.

The *old* church of the Pueblo, he said, is one of the oldest in this country, while the *new* one dates

---

[1] " The parrot was a sacred bird among the Zapotecs of Mexico, and as such worshipped."—Bancroft, H. H., vol. ii. p. 212. The same authority tells us that eagles were furnished as tribute to Montezuma, one town alone sending in forty each year (vol. ii. p. 234).

back so far that the Indians have no tradition as to the date of its erection.

Inside the old church is a very small statue of Saint Dominick; it is very old, very homely, and very dirty. Good authority says that it came from Spain with the first missionaries penetrating to this part of America.

The newer and larger figure, mentioned a few pages back, also came from Spain, and, if without any pronounced claims to beauty in an absolute sense, looks perfect in contrast with its uglier and more venerable brother.

On the main door of the old church are carved— on one leaf the arms of Spain, and on the other a globe surmounted by a crowned cross, with two human arms, naked, passing each other, and having the hands nailed to the horizontal bar. This, the Padre conjectured, represents the armorial bearings of the archbishop under whose administration the sacred structure was completed.[1]

In front of the main portal of the *new* church is an arabesque pavement, very neatly and compactly laid, and dating from the erection of the building.

Ascending to the roof of the new church we enjoyed an expanded and picturesque view of the valley of the Rio Grande.

The bell in the tower dates only to 1858, is heavy, clumsy, and poorly cast. It is of Mexican manufacture, and from El Paso, or the city of Chihuahua.

---

[1] See Plate III.

The rafters of the new church are painted and carved in quaint, archaic patterns.

Having now walked over the whole Pueblo, we were in a position to form an opinion of its hygienic condition. Whether on account of the festival or not, it was fairly clean, and by no means badly built. The roofs were—in nearly every street—provided with small walls, with stone coping, thus affording the younger children a safe place upon each terrace in which to play.

Gutters of cottonwood carried off the summer rains.

Continuing our walk, we saw half a dozen men and women trying to induce vomiting by titillating their throats with long feathers. This remedy is much in use among Zunis and Moquis. Nearly every indisposition is attributed to a disordered stomach, or else is supposed to be complicated by such an abnormal condition ; consequently this organ is cleared at once, either in the way just indicated, or else by an emetic of lukewarm water swallowed in copious doses.

Other Indians, determined to look their best on this grand gala day, were kneeling before their wives, who patiently examined their heads, hair by hair, for vermin.

By the use of an infusion of "aurole" (soap-weed or yucca root), followed by a vigorous brushing with bundles of sun-dried hay, these Indians succeed in giving to their chevelure a rich blue-black gloss which many an American belle would be glad to impart to her own tresses.

When the bell clanged for mass I took my place

inside the church.   The congregation was mainly composed of Indians, with some Mexicans and a very few Americans.   There was no attempt at uniformity in dress; many of the Indians were gorgeous in Navajo blankets of royal hues, others—the little boys especially — had no clothing whatever beyond buckskin moccasins, and clean white shirts which did not reach much below the waist.

The altar attendants were arrayed in white cotton knee breeches, made loose, and slit up for several inches along the outer seam, white cotton shirts, worn outside the breeches, and girt at the waist by red and green woollen cinctures of Navajo manufacture.

At the elevation of the Host guitars twanged, drums rolled, and rusty old shot guns added a volley in honour of the occasion.

Thirty-five candles were burning as votive offerings on the floor in front of the altar.   New corn, in considerable quantity, also covered the floor; a retention of the old church custom of the " pinnicia," or offering of the first-fruits of the harvest.

A bridal party knelt at the chancel rails.   The bride and groom, as well as the attendants, being in their best raiment, and having their coarse shining hair freshly brushed and banged square across the eyebrows.

The young married couple (for such they already were, the nuptial benediction having been pronounced before mass) were tied together by the priest's stole passing loosely around their necks, and each held in the right hand a burning candle.[1] The bride was attended by a maiden friend who knelt at her left, and the groom by his best man who knelt on his right; while to the right of the whole party, and also on their knees, were the aged, snowy-haired parents of the two young people whom the blessing of the Church had just made one.

The Navajo rugs upon which these eight persons knelt were of the most beautiful description.

To the music of an orchestra of cracked fiddles, squeaky guitars, bell, drums, and rusty shot-guns, and of voices cracked worse than the fiddles or guitars, the new statue of Saint Dominick was carried in solemn procession through the streets, which were now a surging mass of Indians from all the neighbouring Pueblos, Mexicans from as far north as Santa Fé and as far south as Albuquerque, and Americans from the mining districts close by.

Slowly the procession made its way, chanting with an extremely nasal intonation the litany of the saints. In front of the statue was carried a little plaster cast of a dog, from whose mouth projected a flaming torch. This recalled the dream of the mother of Saint Dominick, who, shortly before his birth, imagined that she was to bring into the world a dog as herein depicted. Her fears were soothed by the interpretation that she was to bear a son who should be eloquent and bold as a barking dog, and the fire of

[1] " The Aztec bride knelt on the left of her husband, and the dresses of the pair were tied together."—Bancroft, H. H., vol. ii. p. 257.

whose words should spread a conflagration throughout the universe.

After the congregation had begun to leave the church the bridal party entered the chancel, advanced to the altar, knelt and kissed it reverently, kissed the copy of the Gospels, and then passed completely round behind the altar, the men going by the right and the women by the left, and re-uniting in front, when they marched down the nave to the main door, and there turning together, made a profound obeisance back towards the sanctuary. As soon as they had emerged from the building the bride fell behind and followed docilely in the footsteps of her liege lord, who paid no further attention to her.

Padre Ribera told me that the newly-married pair would some time during the day give to all their friends a grand feast, part of which had already been sent over to his house for his breakfast after mass.

He ended his remarks by cordially inviting Moran and myself to eat with him and judge for ourselves what the cooking was like, an invitation promptly and gladly accepted.

The procession made a very complete circuit of both the old and the new Pueblos, neglecting no street or avenue, until it reached the booth prepared for the reception of the statue early in the day, and which was now gorgeous and fairly ablaze with the dazzling colours of the choicest productions of the Navajo looms.

The procession having deposited the statue of

Saint Dominick in its niche, abruptly dissolved, a few only of the more zealous and devout remaining on their knees to implore the advocacy of their patron for some desired object. Most of the men, women, and children hurried to their homes to dress or undress for the dance, the main feature of the day's work.

Clowns were already running about from house to house, giving warning to those who were to enact parts of any prominence.

We now took another glance through the small rectangular windows on the ground-floor of the Estufas.

Each was almost full of young men, women, and children. The men were nearly naked, their bodies painted white, hair done up at the sides in horns, wound with corn-shucks; bands of cedar sprigs encircled their bodies from shoulders to waist, and rattles of tortoise-shells and sheep's toes were pendent from the rear of right knee. A number of old men were haranguing them, but upon what topic I could not discover.

All—old and young, and of both sexes—wore curious head-dresses of thin boards, painted pea-green and sky blue, with tips of red or yellow, and with incisions in shape of the crescent, cross, square, or letter T.

Small white flecks of eagle-down floated from the corners of those worn by the squaws.[1]

---

[1] For Head-dress, see Plate IV.

The garments worn by the women were the same as those in general use among those of the Zunis and Moquis, that is, a single garment, woven of dark blue wool, reaching to the knees. The left arm and shoulder and the upper half of left breast were exposed, and the right arm almost so. But the Santo Domingo women wore, under these, clean white petticoats with ruffled and scalloped edges, which were allowed to project an inch below the woollen skirts, producing a very pretty effect. Their long hair, smooth and polished as jet, was carefully brushed over their shoulders and down their backs.

They were all barefooted and barelegged, but so neat and clean was each and every one that I can say never before or since have I seen so pleasing an assemblage of what might in all fairness claim the title of savage beauty.

The men were arrayed uniformly with regard to the kilt of white cotton cloth, made by the Zunis and Moquis, and evidently preserved in the same family for generations.

Each dancer of either sex carried a little sprig of cedar in the left hand.[1]

Just as we passed they began to sally out from the Estufas. Down the stairs filed an even hundred, not counting the standard-bearer, but including a chorus of a dozen men, who worked themselves into a frenzy, keeping time to the thump, thump, thumping of an oblong, keg-shaped drum, made of a hollow cottonwood

[1] See Plates V., VI., and VII.

log, covered with skin, the body of the instrument
being yellow and the "trimmings" blue.

For a long time I found it impossible to catch the
refrain, but by persistent effort I at last made out
the concluding words of each verse,

"Wi-ka-tolli-ná-mashé-é-é-é-é;"

which were repeated over and over again in excellent
time and with increasing vehemence.

While the dancers were arranging themselves in
proper order we had plenty of time to hunt up Padre
Ribera and sample his breakfast.

We were welcomed with cordiality, and introduced
to all the cooks and attendants.   To frame an opinion
from what I saw that morning Padre Ribera must be
held in high repute by his flock.

Three young girls had been detailed to cook, wash
the dishes, and set the table; as many old women
chaperoned, superintended, bustled about, and made
themselves general nuisances, under the impression
that they were rendering invaluable service; and half
a dozen old men, more or less lazy and decrepit, did
what might be called "the heavy standing around."

The young girls were models of neatness, modesty,
and decorum; their hands and faces were clean as
amber; their hair freshly washed with "aurole,"
brushed and tied up; their dresses new and bright,
under each the crisply starched petticoat and a cotton
chemise covering arms, neck, and bosom.

While cooking, washing dishes, or setting table,

they wore white cotton cloths tied round the neck and covering the dress in front.

The Padre invited us to be seated, and then gave the signal to bring in the repast. A big Indian grabbed in one hand a saddle of mutton roasted over the coals and cut it into large " gobs," any one of which would have been plenty for a small family.

To each guest one of these was handed by the attendants, who accompanied it with a correspondingly great hunch of bread and a bowl of rich goat's milk.

The centre of the table was reserved for a pile of melons and two platters, one containing boiled, the other fried, eggs. During the meal there was the greatest confusion ; Indians kept running in or out, on business or pleasure intent. The business was largely comprehended in falling over each other's feet and over a pack of mangy curs which the appetising odours of the roast meat had attracted inside the house ; while the pleasure seemed to consist in scratching their heads, or in gazing at the strangers with open mouths and open eyes.

There was enough confusion to drive a saint mad. Padre Ribera, however, never lost his good-humour, and indeed infected us with a fair portion of his own joviality.

" Captain," he said, turning to me, " did you ever know that in olden times the Spanish priests who lived among these Indians used to keep journals of their daily lives, in which were narrated all that the

Indians had done or said ? It would be a great thing for you to get some of those journals, would it not ?"

"Yes, Father Ribera, I appreciate fully the wonderful labours of those devoted men, and I regret extremely that some plan cannot be devised by our Government, or by private associations interested in the early history of our country, to get back those books, or copies of them, from the city of Mexico, Simancas in Spain, or wherever else they may be stored. I think they would be almost priceless."

Our conversation was here broken off abruptly by the sound of the approaching procession, and sallying out, we took our places in the shade of the church to see it pass. The first division of the dance was now moving slowly and sedately into the church "plaza," the formation being in column of twos, the men on the right, the woman on the left. The men were all bareheaded, hair flowing loose, and with parrot feathers tied to front of crown. They were naked, except that Scotch kilts of white cotton Zuni cloth reached half-way to the knees, the lower edge of the kilts being generally fringed with a narrow border of black. Their bodies were painted a reddish pink with, in occasional instances, streaks of white. This same pinkish white was applied to the legs from knees to ankles, but above the knees and the forearms were a dead white.

Above the elbows were broad green armlets holding sprigs of cedar in place.

Hanging from the rear of the waist-belts were

coyote or fox skins, tails downward.[1] No leggings were worn, but around the calves were green, black, or yellow garters, with small shell pendants, which rattled in unison with the music of tortoise backs and sheep's toes tied to the right knee, or of small painted gourds, filled with corn, shaken in the right hand.

These men wore moccasins trimmed around the ankles with goats' hair.[2]

The women and girls carried on their heads painted tablets, already mentioned: they were bare-legged, bare-footed, wore no garters or tortoise-shell rattles, and carried no gourds, but each bore a fair-sized bunch of cedar in her left hand.

The necklaces of the women were of hollow silver spheres, strung like rosaries, and having pendant from them double or archiepiscopal crosses of silver.

The departures from this uniformity of decoration were not numerous, and consisted altogether of necklaces of fine shells, malachite or coral, of home manufacture, bored out by the bow-drill with flint tip, in the use of which the Indians of this Pueblo are unusually dexterous. I also noticed, as a pendant, a crescent of solid silver, outlining the man in the moon.[3]

---

[1] "The Totonac priests of Ceuteotl (Ceres) were always dressed in the skins of *foxes* or *coyotes*."—Bancroft, H. H., vol. ii. p. 214.

[2] See Plate VI.

[3] This ornament is to be found among the Navajoes, who occasionally make it, and who say that it has some connection with their worship of Ah-sun-nuth, or the Woman in the Western Ocean. While I was among the Navajoes, in April and May 1881, my old friend

The management of this division of the dance was under the care of three or four clowns, who were naked excepting the breech-clout, and wore no moccasins; their bodies, limbs, and faces were striped black and white; bands of otter fur crossed their bodies diagonally; tortoise-shells clanked at their right knees, cedar sprigs encircled ankles and waists, and corn-shucks tied up their hair.[1]

With this first hundred were numbers of tiny children not counted in the aggregate.

The step of the dance was a " mark-time," something between a shuffle and a goose step; in advancing slowly the body was bent forward.

Thus the procession worked its way round the plaza, the clowns prancing hither and thither, waving small wands of cottonwood branches.

When in front of the church and Padre Ribera's position, the fun grew fast and furious; the clowns darted hither and thither, bellowing orders; the drummers and choristers gave us another dose of

" Wi-ka-tolli-ná-mash-é-é-é-é ; "

while the dancers, now facing each other, but preserving the same step, turned round and round in place for several moments, ending in a series of terpsichorean evolutions, rather too complicated for my descriptive powers, at the termination of which they

Mr. Leonard obtained for me, with much difficulty, a couple of these ornaments; one of the pair is at this moment in the private collection of Lieutenant-General P. H. Sheridan, U.S. Army.

[1] See Plate VII.

marched away rapidly in single file, each woman or
girl falling in behind her male partner as he passed
her, and the orchestra and clowns giving a farewell
howl ere they joined their comrades.

The dress of the dancers evidently perpetuated the
pre-historic costume of their forefathers. Not a few
of the kilts were worn threadbare, although all were
clean. There was also to be seen a number of the
Moqui and Zuni girdles of cotton, terminating in a
string and ball fringe. These are so highly regarded
by all the Pueblos that it is a matter of extreme
difficulty to obtain one of them.

CHAPTER V.

A BRIEF interlude followed, and then the second division entered the plaza, headed by a standard with a border varying only slightly, if at all, from that upon the banner borne by the first division. In advance of this division was borne another oblong drum, with white body, black heads, and red "points." In this division there were twenty - four choristers, eighty dancers, twelve clowns, and twenty-six children. In attire they were almost the counterparts of their respective predecessors, but the bodies, arms, and legs of the male dancers were painted *blue*, and the bodies of the clowns streaked with the same colour. The wooden head-dresses of the women were painted bluish green, tipped on the upper corners with red and yellow, and perforated with crescent or square holes.

The modest deportment of the gentler sex attracted general comment. During the whole dance numbers of them never raised their eyes from the ground. The beauty of the women was in a few cases enhanced, but in most impaired, by patches of vermilion painted on each cheek.

The second division of dancers went through the

same evolutions as their comrades of the first, whom they soon followed to the shrine of Santo Domingo, whither Moran and I also proceeded under a broiling sun.

The two bodies of dancers, massed together, made a scene resplendent with gorgeous colouring ; the dark blue blanket-skirts of the squaws, girt with red and green worsted sashes ; their long, black, glistening hair ; the vivid green of the head-dresses, and the darker hues of the cedar sprigs ; the dangling feathers of eagle and parrot ; the painted legs and arms of the men, or the glistening white petticoats of the women, heightened the barbaric splendours of Navajo blankets and the sheen of silver necklaces.

Each Indian in turn filed into the shrine of Saint Dominick, and presented an offering of a candle, or else the first-fruits of his melon-patch or corn-field,— the donations swelling into a grand pile of loaves of bread, candles, and Apache baskets filled with plums and melons,—all of which the stolid attendants upon the shrine apathetically deposited at one side.

The clowns made the most of the chance now given to display their wit ; they approached the shrine with mock obeisance, addressed the saint with simulated humility and deference, affected to hand him their offerings, called him " Tata" (father) in a very familiar way, and perpetrated jokes which must have been coeval with the veteran witticisms of the American circus, if the impassive serenity with which the grown men and women received them could be accepted as an indication.

The melons and other presents tendered by the clowns and dancers were handed to them by friends and relatives in waiting as they drew near the statue.

One of the clowns offered a melon to a miner, who accepted it as a bona fide gift; but the Indian snatched it out of his hands, and darted away through the crowd to the unrestrained delight of the youngsters, who, it should be said, were giggling heartily at everything said and done for their diversion.

Elbowing my way about in the closely-packed mass of spectators, I had abundant opportunity for seeing all that was prized in the way of personal decoration in Santo Domingo. Nearly every old squaw in the Pueblo wore one of the silver rosary necklaces already mentioned. It then occurred to me that somewhere I had read that when the Spaniards reconquered New Mexico, in 1692-94, their commanding general, D. Diego Vargas, imposed upon the Rio Grande Pueblos the condition that each full-grown man and woman should habitually wear round the neck a rosary as a mark of subjection to the Crown of Spain and the true Church; and at same time insisted upon the discontinuance of the dance in honour of the idols, called by the Castilians the Cochino or Pig, from its ugly snout, but known among the Zunis, who still practise it as the dances of the Coyamashé or Shalacu.[1]

[1] Consult Davis' *Conquest of New Mexico*, p. 337. The incident mentioned occurred, but the officer was named Cruzate. He entered New Mexico about 1690. I am confident that Vargas, who came after him in 1692-94, imposed the same badge of subjection.

When the rosary ceased to be a badge of subjection it might have been refined into an ornament, and its use continued long after the tradition of its introduction had faded from the minds of the Indians themselves.   The Cochino dance never was openly revived so long as the Spaniards could prevent it; yet it is possible that the Dance of the Tablet may have afforded a satisfactory substitute.   And, further, may not these exercises have been a compromise between the prejudices of those who tenaciously clung to the old heathen rites and the inclinations of others whom fear, venality, superior intelligence, or hidden sympathy attracted to the doctrines of the conquerors ?

Certain it is that every symbol seen here this day has been seen at other times among the Zunis, Moquis, and Jemez people, with whose heathenism they are linked, and if heathenish in those Pueblos, they can scarcely be Christian in Santo Domingo.

These remarks apply, of course, only to such of the Indians as have not accepted the teachings of the Spanish missionaries.   It must not be forgotten that there is a very respectable percentage seemingly imbued with Christian fervour, and humbly and devoutly following in the footsteps of the Master.

The dancers, after depositing their gifts, resumed their places in line, and continued without intermission, until the sun had sunk to rest, their performances in singing, drumming and shuffling.

The amount of the offerings was considerable ; the quality was not very good.   It looked to me as if this part of the proceedings was more complimentary than otherwise, since no man in his sound senses would think of eating the immature melons and plums unless he had his life insured at a high figure.

The monotonous drumming and the nasal intonation of the singers grew wearisome after a while, and as there was still much to be seen in the Pueblo itself, we sauntered leisurely through it, examining everything in a deliberate manner.

One of the first things attracting my attention was a meeting between a pair of lovers; they had evidently only lately had a quarrel, for which each was heartily sorry. He approached, and was received with a disdain tempered with so much sweetness and affection that he wilted at once, and, instead of boldly asserting himself, dared do nothing but timidly touch her hand. The touch, I imagine, was not disagreeable, because the girl's hand was soon firmly held in his, and he with earnest warmth was pouring into her ears words whose purport it was not difficult to conjecture.

It was at this stage of the proceedings that I came upon the scene. They detected my presence, and manifested no particular pleasure at my company; as I did not wish to embarrass them, I at once took my departure.

The young man was unusually good-looking, with a countenance expressive of fine attributes; the maiden was quite pretty, of good figure, and modest, gentle demeanour, and dressed in the full agony of

Pueblo fashion. I hope that by this time they are married and happy. So much stuff and nonsense have been written about the entire absence of affection from the Indian character, especially in the relations between the sexes, that it affords me great pleasure to note this little incident, in which the parties acted with perfect freedom from the restraint the known presence of strangers imposes. Padre Ribera gives these people a high character for virtue.

On our return we found that the Lieutenant-Governor had sent to say that he would like to see us down at our house ; as we suspected, upon the subject of our rent. The room we occupied was the ordinary apartment of the poorer classes of the country, without furniture of any kind, and worth, as rents go there, about 25 c. a day. The hay, wood, water, eggs, and everything received had been paid for at prices so liberal that I suppose the cupidity of our esteemed friend had been aroused, and he had come to look upon us as a couple of perambulating silver-mines, or perhaps thought that we were Jay Gould and William H. Vanderbilt out on a picnic.

He began his remarks by blandly expressing his gratification that the great father in Washington had sent out two of his best men to give an account of the Pueblo and the dance ; that his heart was very " content " to have us there, and that he had given us his best room to sleep in and stay in while we remained in the Pueblo ; and as he had such a high opinion of the great father and ourselves, he would

charge us only ten dollars for the day. This generosity overwhelmed us. An abundant charge would
have been 50 c.

Moran called out, " Confound the man ! Tell him
I was here last year and occupied this very room with
General Hatch, and then he charged us only $1.50,
and we thought that *that* was extortionate enough.

I quietly communicated Moran's views to Bautista,
and also laid three bright silver half dollars upon the
floor.

He shrieked in well-feigned horror ; he was a sick
man, we were rich officers, we came from where money
was plenty. But as he considered us his friends and
didn't want to quarrel with us, he would say, give
him $5.50 for the love of God, and say no more about it.

I remained impassive, and the money lay upon
the floor untouched. He had a wife and children ;
he was also the Lieutenant-Governor of the Pueblo,
and had not any time to lose from the dance ; " Make
it $3, amigo, and let's stop quarrelling."

I replied, " I'll not give you another cent. I wish
to pay the very highest prices for everything obtained
here for our mules or ourselves, but I'll not be swindled.
You're an embustero" (cheat).

" Two dollars and let me go," said our worthy
Governor.

" No, here are seven quarters; that's at least one
dollar more than you are entitled to, and two shillings
more than I first intended giving you. Take it or leave
it, and take it quickly, or I'll put it back in my pocket."

"Your mules have eaten much hay."

"You old pirate, we paid the boys for the hay last night."

"Your driver has had firewood and water and eggs."

"That is none of your business ; we have paid for every stick of wood, every drop of water, and every single egg brought into this room, and that's all the money you're going to get."

He took it, making a great fuss, but secretly delighted to get so much.

We were glad to be rid of the old fraud, as we did not care to be delayed in our further examination of the town, and observation of the manners and customs of its inhabitants.

The Indians of Santo Domingo are experts in the use of the bow-drill,[1] of which I saw more than a dozen at work during my ramble through the town. With this clumsy tool they manufacture the perforated beads of chalchihuitl, or impure malachite, and sea-shells, which they send to the Navajoes of the west at a great enhancement upon their value in the raw state. Coral necklaces are more rare, but by no means infrequent. They are made of the deep red *stone*, not of celluloid, and were originally, it is said, brought from the South Sea.

It would be an interesting point to determine whether or not at the date of the advent of the first European explorers the Indians of the Rio Grande,

[1] See Plate XXXI.

and the sedentary Indians generally, were familiar
with coral; it would, in my opinion, serve (in conjunction with other facts we now know relative to
their use of sea-shells, sea sand, etc., in their religious
ceremonies) to demonstrate pretty conclusively that
they had reached their present location from the
Pacific.

There were very few arms of precision, and none
that I saw of any value; the principal weapons were
bows and arrows in small numbers, and shields of
raw hide, without any pretensions to beauty.

In one of the houses we made the acquaintance
of a man past middle age, who conversed with much
intelligence.

His name in Spanish was Sebastian Aguilar; his
Indian name was "Pajarito Amarillo" (Little Yellow
Bird), or in his own language, A-chee-á-ya. The
little Yellow Bird, he told me, was the young Huaca-
mayo or Macaw.

He asserted that he was a member of the Chamisa
or Sage Brush clan, his father was of the Maiz or
Corn clan, his wife and children of the Coyote, and
his wife's father of the Aguila or Eagle. The Governor of the Pueblo belonged to the Eucina or Evergreen
Oak, and the Lieutenant-Governor to the Aguila or
Eagle.

With a very little persuasion and a small sum of
money we extracted from this intelligent and communicative man the following list of the clans of the
Querez people, every one of which is represented in

E

Santo Domingo, although the representation is. in some cases reduced to two or three persons :—

1. Aguila,	Eagle.	10. Palmila,	{ Yucca or Soap-weed.
2. Agua,	Water.		
3. Sapo,	Toad.	11. Chamisa,	Sage Brush.
4. Huacamayo,	{ Macaw, Parrot.	12. Tejon,	Badger.
		13. Cibola,	Buffalo.
5. Culebra,	Snake.	14. Coyote,	Coyote.
6. Sol,	Sun.	15. Berenda,	Antelope.
7. Oso,	Bear.	16. Tortuga,	Tortoise.
8. Leon,	Mountain Lion	17. Eucina,	Evergreen Oak.
9. Grulla,	Crane.	18. Maiz,	Corn.

The cool breezes of evening blew in from the river, driving before them the radiant fervour of the day. Excitement and curiosity had made us unmindful of the torrid rays which had been beating down upon us since early in the morning, or the scarcely less torrid air which had burned our necks and faces; we had these recalled to mind by the refreshing contrast of the night wind, which the young Indians apparently enjoyed fully as much as we did.

Preparations for a grand horse-race were completed by sundown, and at a given signal, not far from fifty or sixty riders started. The course was not, as well as I could understand, from a given starting-point to a given goal and back, but was rather in the nature of a chase. A first detachment having been allowed certain headway, a second detachment started in brisk pursuit. It was permissible to dodge in and out, around and through every obstacle within certain limits, always providing that the two parties kept constantly moving.

The struggle became extremely exciting, and served to show off the excellent equestrianism of the young men of Santo Domingo and their Navajo friends, who cheerfully joined in this rough amusement.

Soon this was succeeded by the ever-popular sport of charging down at break-neck speed upon a poor, forlorn fowl imbedded up to its neck in the sand.

The old barn-yard rooster did not like its share in this amusement, and stretched its neck in a vain attempt to extricate itself from its living grave. This action gives all the better chance to the horsemen, who rush down at full swoop, and, when at proper distance, lean from the saddle and grasp at the fowl's neck.

If the bird sees one approach it shrinks back; the odds are largely in favour of a miss, and sometimes, when the cavalier is not especially alert and active, he may sprawl upon the sand, to the delight and amusement of his comrades.

At last some one bolder, more skilful, or more fortunate than the others, succeeds in reaching the rooster and drags it out to the air. Away goes the lucky horseman, pursued by a shouting mob of reckless, dare-devil riders, whose one object is to dispossess him of his capture.

The upshot of the whole business is that the poor fowl is torn to pieces before the struggle is ended.

No one cares for the pain inflicted upon chanti-
cleer, and, indeed, it has never occurred to me that
the pastime was devised for the bird's amusement. It
serves only to display some exceptionally fine feats of
horsemanship from which I should be glad to disso-
ciate the elements of brutality. A pretty good sprinkling of the youth and beauty, or, to speak more correctly, of the old age and homeliness, of the Pueblo,
had gathered in front of our door with specimens of
home-made pottery for our inspection.

We purchased all for which we could find room in
our ambulance, and with these pieces half a dozen or
more of the chalchihuitl.

The squaws again surrounded us with fresh objects
of their ceramic skill, hoping to persuade us to make
further investments. We closed our ears to their
syren song of "Muncho wally ese, do'peso" ("this is
very valuable for two dollars"—two dollars meaning
anything in silver coin), and mounting into our ambulance, which stood ready hitched-up, drove three miles
to Wallace Station (Atchison, Topeka, and Santa Fé
Railroad) in time to catch a "wild" train for Albuquerque. The station agent had kindly notified us the
train was expected, a courtesy which saved us much
trouble and annoyance.

We had not a day to lose, if we hoped to get to
the Moqui villages in time for the snake-dance, and
much as we should have liked to remain in Santo Domingo for a week or two longer, we felt it prudent to
leave by the first, which, in the frightful weather then

damaging the railroad, might be for some days to come the last opportunity.

When we reached Albuquerque Moran and I took such accommodations as the indifferent but really overworked clerk of the "Armijo House" deigned to bestow upon us.

The room had altogether three occupants; my comrade and myself bunked together in the double bed, leaving the single cot to "the entire stranger."

In another room, a trifle larger than ours, seven poor unfortunates were huddled, and this was called first-class accommodation, or rather accommodation for which first-class prices were exacted.

With all its disadvantages the apartment in the Armijo House was much superior to the den we had occupied while in Santo Domingo, or to the bed we should have had to share on the seats of the ambulance had we not sent that back to Santa Fé with our driver.

CHAPTER VI.

AUGUST 3, 1881.—Greatly to our delight we learned
that the Atlantic and Pacific Railroad was open, and its
trains running on time. We left Albuquerque at 8
o'clock of a bright and beautiful morning, and ran
down on the Topeka and Santa Fé's track for twelve
miles to the bridge crossing to the west bank of the Rio
Grande at the Pueblo of Isleta. On our train were
several Indians from the Pueblo of San Felipe, one of
them an *Albino*. The Atlantic and Pacific was at that
date a brand-new road, with much still lacking in the
way of equipment. The promoters of the enterprise
had from the commencement used only the finest and
heaviest steel rails, and many of the engines were
models of power and beauty. The cars were new and
clean, but of the class known as " combination," the
front half given up to mail, baggage, freight, etc., and
the other portion provided with seats for passengers.

The people about us were mostly miners, ranchmen, and labourers,—a good-natured set, indifferent
as to personal appearance, but accommodating, generous, and whole-souled.

Our route from the Rio Grande lay almost due west up the valley of the Puerco of the east, keeping under the shadow of Mount Taylor, one of the highest and most imposing peaks of the south-western country. There was much to attract our attention; in fact, everything seemed worthy of note, either by reason of oddity or loveliness. Certainly, nowhere in the world can there be found air more balmy and exhilarating than that which puts new life into the lungs of the traveller in New Mexico.

A soft, sensuous haze of blue half hid, half disclosed the square, hard outlines of bold escarpment of sandstone which for league after league bounded the horizon on the right and left, while, closer to the track, a river of lava, rough, black, and repellent, recorded a primeval convulsion of nature.

The accommodation along the line of the road was as yet of a primitive character, and travellers were constantly reminded of the fact that they were on a new road in a new country. At a small station called El Rito we took dinner, a very well-cooked meal indeed, taking everything into consideration. The table service was of a really beautiful description. The sugar-bowls, salt and butter dishes, bread and potato plates, were of Indian pottery from the Pueblos of Laguna and Acoma, a few miles to the west, for be it understood that the valley of the Puerco of the east, up which the Atlantic and Pacific runs, is studded with Indian towns. Laguna, Acoma, and Isleta, with their outlying dependencies, take up all

the arable, or I should say irrigable, land in the valley
itself or adjacent to it. As it is now demonstrated
that water can be found not many feet below the surface, the capacity of this valley for supporting population is increased tenfold. Here will yet be one of
the most flourishing seats of the American wine trade ;
the warm, sheltered terraces of the Rio Grande and
Puerco, from Albuquerque to Laguna will soon be
purple and green with the fruit and tendrils of the
royal grape, yielding a most generous wine. May the
Good Lord speed the day when Americans shall be
able to make a good wine and be proud to drink it.
Mines of gold and silver there are without number in
Arizona and New Mexico ; success or failure may
attend their development, but long after the very
names of the most promising of them shall have been
forgotten, the great bonanza of grape culture and wine
manufacture will exist to pour its constant dividends
into the treasury of the south-west.

Were it within the scope of this volume there could
be transcribed from my notes and memoranda much
to show that the capabilities of the Rio Grande and
its tributary valleys have not been over-rated, and
much, too, might have been said of the quaint and
archaic attractions of Santa Fé and Albuquerque, and
the old-fashioned home life and manners of the Spanish-
American civilisation, receding so rapidly before the
aggressive American. All references to such matters,
however, have been carefully excluded, lest the bulk
of what was commenced as a modest description of

a summer's ramble be swollen to the dimensions of a pretentious volume of travel.

The cook at the El Rito station admitted that his life at this time was quite lonely, and that his only moments of pleasurable excitement were those attending the arrival and departure of the freight and passenger trains : " And yet," said he, " I have plenty to do, and don't get lonesome. Bi'me by, the road will be finished, and this will be a favourite route of travel between the two oceans ; it can't fail to be that. And lots of people are beginning to come in now. Besides, I've some pets—come and see them."

He displayed an aviary, containing three eagles, two hawks, and a crow, all caught in the hills near by.

The warning cry of " Lolebore " from the conductor, which was as close to " all aboard " as any conductor ever gets, caused us to rush, in the pell-mell fashion of our country, to the seats vacated a few moments previously ; a tap on the bell, a toot of the whistle, and we were speeding up the valley.

Indians, alone or in groups, working in the fields or trudging to distant markets, bearing upon their backs blankets filled with heavy burdens of sweet apples, apricots, and plums from their own orchards, or driving donkeys freighted with pottery, could be seen at any moment from the car windows.

On the different " sidings " were construction and repair trains of freight-cars, fitted up with windows, doors, tables, and beds, the homes of bands of labourers working upon grades and bridges.

At Crane's, the terminus of the first division, we were informed, to our great dismay, that our train would lay over for the night, and that nothing would run out on the western division before five the next morning.

Mr. Brown, the division superintendent, listened with courteous attention to what we had to say about the snake-dance, and when we told him that we hadn't a moment to lose if we were to reach the Moqui villages by the 9th, the night of the full moon, when the dance was to commence, he replied that a locomotive was going out very soon as far as Wingate Station, and to oblige us he would have it take a car out in which we could ride.

For this courteous and kindly act I have no words sufficient to express my grateful acknowledgments.

A throng of fine-looking Navajo Indians surrounded the engine, watching it with a curious interest they vainly tried to conceal under the mask of stolid indifference. These witnesses, as such I learned they were, had come down from their own reservation to give testimony against a fellow caught in the act of selling whisky to members of their tribe.

This villainous-looking wretch, fettered hand and foot, stood a few feet farther back in the custody of Deputy U.S. Marshal Dye.

By a fatal defect in our laws for the preservation of peace with the native tribes, the rascals who sell them whisky and ammunition, or who rob them of their ponies, are practically screened from punishment for their villainy.   Cases must be tried before Courts at a distance from the scene of the crimes ; witnesses cannot always afford the time and expense involved in attendance, and dodge the responsibility; and as soon as the accused has secured the services of one or two of those fledglings of hell,—the frontier Jack lawyers,—the machinery of the law is set in motion, not to assist justice but to defeat it.

Our engine moved out very slowly, at a rate not over four miles an hour, the engineer being very much afraid of the track, which was new and badly undermined by water from recent storms.   In approaching bridges or culverts we stopped altogether until the fireman had gone ahead with his lantern and made a close inspection.

The heavens suddenly darkened ; brown and inky masses of clouds palled the horizon, the lurid glare of lightning disclosed in all its majesty the bold outline of the approaching tempest and the solid sheet of rain falling on all sides of us.

The storm drew very close to the track, but its full force was wasted without doing us the least damage.   It was not until we drew up at Wingate Station that we received a drenching, at which we did not grumble, feeling thankful that the full fury of the elements had not been visited upon us.

Moran remained in the car to guard our valises and baggage, while I set out to reach Fort Wingate, three and a half miles to the south.   The rain was still falling with irritating persistency, and the road had been converted into a vast quagmire of muddy sloughs, alternating with deep ponds of very respectable area.

I trudged and splashed, covering myself from head to foot with slimy ooze, and several times had narrow escapes from sprawling at full length.

The darkness was almost tangible, and yet the lightning was so frequent and so vivid that no other difficulty than was due to the deep and slippery mud was experienced in pushing ahead. An hour's hard work brought me to the summit of a small knoll, and while resting at this point I discerned through the murky haze the twinkling lights of the officers' quarters, which assured me that the post was almost under my feet.

Wet, bedraggled, muddy, tired, and cross, I made my way to the house of my friend General Bradley, the post commander, who, without regard to my wretched plight, insisted that I should accept his hospitality and remain in his house until rested.

Most comforting assurance of all received from him was one to the effect that the rattlesnake-dance would not occur until the 11th, and that Mr. Tom Keam was now in the post, where he was to stay all the next day and then start back for his home at Moqui Agency, reaching there in plenty of time for seeing this strange ceremony.

Late as the hour was, a table was immediately spread with a warm supper, of which I partook with zest.

General Bradley then sent after Moran. The storm had broken, and the mud, deep and tenacious as it might be, would offer no impediment to a driver and mules familiar with every inch of the road. So General Bradley thought; but the mud was deeper than he supposed, and Moran did not reach his house until half-past two on the following morning.

Then both Moran and myself began to show very pronounced symptoms of something like nervous exhaustion.

We had been on the go without cessation for a number of weeks, working hard in a red-hot sun or in driving rain and chilly evening air, going without proper food, clothing, or rest; and the attack which now set in was nothing but Dame Nature's quiet but emphatic mode of notification that the drafts upon our physical powers had used up the amounts to our credit in her treasury.

Nothing could have been kinder than the treatment we received from General Bradley, of whose goodness I shall always cherish a grateful remembrance.

Every attention our cases demanded was rendered by Dr. Matthews, the post surgeon, with whom it was my good fortune to hold several long conversations. He is an officer who has devoted much of his leisure to the study of American ethnology, and he kindly gave me a number of important hints derived from his own enlarged experience.

CHAPTER VII.

AUGUST 7, 1881.—Mr. Thomas Keam, Mr. Moran, and myself, left Fort Wingate at eight o'clock of a morning whose exhilarating loveliness we accepted as a harbinger of success. A half score of miles out from the fort we met a Navajo Indian on horseback carrying the U.S. mail.

Our course lay about north-west through a picturesque country, in whose many gentle little dales grew in abundance the wild potato, a favourite food of the Apaches, Zunis, Utes, and Navajoes; and Moran kept us laughing by his amusing descriptions of his experiences while sketching among the Pennsylvania Dutch, and so made us unmindful of the swarms of flies which attacked us during the day.

At Fort Defiance, the agency of the Navajo Indians, my old friend Mr. William Leonard extended his usual cordial reception, in which he was assisted by his clerks, Sinclair and M'Donald.

The cook Francisco, a full-blooded Navajo Indian, soon called out "chiniago" (dinner), and we seated ourselves before a plentiful and well-cooked meal, our enjoyment of which was, however, greatly impaired by the attacks made by clouds of flies.

There were at this time not many Indians about the agency, but those we saw were typical representatives of their race—square-shouldered, sinewy, compact, and well-proportioned figures, with straight limbs, square jaws, flashing eyes, and intelligent, good-natured faces.

The next morning, after a most refreshing sleep, we were aroused by what I at first thought was the sound of heavy rain beating against the window-glass; it proved to be the buzzing of myriads of flies warmed to renewed vigour under the genial rays of the early sun.

Mr. Leonard was the proud possessor of ten or fifteen cats, which amused themselves in scampering across our bed-clothes, and completed the awakening the buzzing of the flies had begun.

Francisco cooked a good breakfast, but informed his employer while we were at table that he was going away at once to attend to his brother, who was very ill. This illness, Francisco had been advised, was due to witchcraft, his poor brother's body having been shot full of beads by some malignant or envious Indian. It would be necessary to do a great deal of singing and rattling over him; and, in case the worst came to the worst, to have the "medicine men" suck the beads out from the invalid's shoulders or breast.

Were I so disposed, I might fill many pages with

accounts of the Navajoes, one of the most powerful tribes now remaining in the United States.

Every facility was granted me earlier in the year by Colonel Frank L. Bennett, 9th Cavalry, who had been in charge of the tribe at various dates since 1868 ; who had studied their habits, knew something of their language, and was well acquainted with their prominent chiefs and head men.

The hundreds of pages of notes and memoranda gathered together while on this duty are full of interesting details of the daily life of the Navajoes, and were it not for their bulk, I should be greatly tempted to condense them as much as possible and incorporate them in the present narrative.

Keam, Moran, and myself, joined by Mr. Sinclair and two soldiers, Gordon and Smallwood, who had preceded us from Fort Wingate, started for the Moqui villages. Our drive of yesterday had been over forty miles ; that of this day was to be over thirty, so it became necessary to leave early.

Our road followed up the Bonito Cañon, and then through a rugged country of red sandstone bluffs, plentifully covered with pine, cedar, and piñon of good size, much of the pine being suitable for lumber.

The road in places was quite steep, but generally excellent, and much of the scenery from the hill-crests was of great beauty.

Keam, with whom I was riding, told me that among the Navajoes there was one family of Albinos, numbering three girls and one boy, who at present live

near Barney Williams' ranch, on Pueblo Colorado
Creek, where we expected to remain for the night.
No other Albinos are known among the tribe of
18,000 souls.

Before the sun had reached the meridian we entered a "park" country, where tall, straight pine-trees
encircled lovely swales matted with fresh, green grass.

The sky, up to this moment of an immaculate
blue, almost immediately filmed over with gauzy
clouds, and a smart shower of rain fell, wetting us
through, but, fortunately, lasting only ten minutes.

We remained in a "park" country the greater portion of the day, but the interminable emerald of the
juicy grass was succeeded by the enchanting enamel
of wild-flowers, which in every hue—yellow, scarlet,
white, purple, and blue—matted the ground with the
effect of a Persian carpet. We were certainly in a
most enchanting section of Arizona (we had crossed
the boundary line between New Mexico and Arizona
seven miles on the other side of Fort Defiance).

In these charming flower-fields dainty little humming-birds sought refreshment, and, by the rapidity
of their flight, added animation to the scene.

We dismounted from our conveyances, and the
whole party of prosy, commonplace men devoted
themselves to the poetical occupation of culling nose-
gays : never did buds more lovely grace the bosom
of lady fair.

We were upon the summit of a plateau of considerable elevation, the soil, to my great surprise,

F

being covered in numerous spots with "wash," gravel, and other drift.

Since leaving Fort Wingate, we had been inhaling the life-restoring, balsam-laden breezes of pine-clad mountains, and our spirits and feelings—I am alluding, of course, more particularly to Moran and myself— were wonderfully exhilarated; while at Santo Domingo we breathed so much that was offensive and even putrid, probably dead meat and other effete matter accumulated on account of the feast, that until this morning we were certain we could taste the foulness each time we opened our mouths.

Thirteen miles north-west of the Navajo Agency are the rock-tanks, called by the Navajoes Tzi-tá-ni-salán, or "the holes in hard rock."

Sixteen miles out the road began to descend from the plateau by an easy grade. On the lower flanks of the mountain pine gave place to piñon, which presented itself in compact groves. There was also an abundance of cedar, with much sage-brush of considerable size and Spanish bayonet, upon which hung clusters of the hosh-kow, a favourite food of the Navajoes.

Grama grass, in thick bunches, filled all the ground not covered, or too deeply shadowed, by other vegetation.

Down in the valley the sage-brush and Spanish bayonet obtained the mastery, while piñon disappeared, except as isolated bushes not large enough to be called trees. The grass still remained excellent.

Twenty-two miles out were the "Cloo-hallone" tanks, filled with curious four-legged reptiles (axolotl). The sun was yet several hours high when we drove up to Barney Williams' ranch, on the banks of the Pueblo Colorado, a stream at this time ten feet wide and four or five inches deep, whose slow and tortuous current crawled over a bottom of red clay and sand, and between vertical banks of crumbling clay, twelve or fifteen feet high.

With genuine western hospitality Mr. Williams insisted upon our taking up our quarters with him. Why he should be called Barney Williams instead of George Williams is one of the mysteries of the Arizona nomenclature it would be useless to attempt to unravel. We made no effort in that direction, but accepted his proffered courtesies with the more alacrity because the reputation he had established for his kindness to all travellers extended for many miles.

While talking with Mr. Williams and his partner, Mr. Webber, I felt a nibbling at my boot, and looking down saw a prairie-dog, one of the family pets. These little animals are not very common in Arizona, where they are to be found only along the eastern boundary.

Mr. Williams' ranch is of the Arizona order of architecture,—a single-storied, long, low building of "jacal" or palisade, filled in with mud chinking, and roofed with a covering of earth and brush.

He had surrounded himself with many of the creature comforts, not the least important of which were one hundred chickens. In this secluded spot, away from the lines of ordinary travel, and almost cut off from communion with white men, Williams has built up for himself a thriving and lucrative wool trade with the Navajoes, over whom, in common with Keam and Leonard, he wields great influence.

To improve our appetite for supper, we walked over to the ruins of the old Pueblo from which the creek takes its name, and which I do not describe minutely, for the simple reason that they differ in no essential from better examples to be adduced farther on in the course of my narrative.

The tracings of the inner and outer walls are perfectly distinct, and the material of construction blocks of friable sandstone of all shapes and sizes, from six to ten inches long, three to six wide, and one to four thick.

The stones were uncut or unpecked, and placed in position just as they were taken from the adjacent mesa. The mud or clay which had once held them together was now washed away, and the walls reduced to piles of rock, but the general plan of the Pueblo could still be made out. It had evidently been shaped like a hollow square, the "placeta" in the centre reserved for movements of religion, festivity, or public business. Two circular depressions marked the sites of Estufas, both within the square.

We had an excellent supper or dinner of beef-steak, canned fruit, bread, butter, pie, and tea. I make mention of the kind of food we receive and the

style in which it is served because I am of the opinion
that the best index of the progress of a new country
is its domestic economy.

To one as familiar as myself with the unsavoury
aspect of Arizona tables in 1869 - 70 and there-
abouts, the sight of a neatly-arranged supper or
dinner is a gratifying demonstration of the rapid
approach of railroad connections, of increasing wealth
and commerce, and consequent refinement of manners
and sentiment.

Having eaten very heartily, we assembled outside
the house, in the pure air of Northern Arizona, and
whiled away the evening hours in pleasant converse.

Dr. Elbert, the physician at the Navajo Agency,
got in after dark, having come on horseback by a
rough trail. The worthy doctor was unusually cor-
pulent, and, in the language of Shakespeare, had a
" belly with fat capon lined," only, in more prosy
terms, it must be confessed that sheep meat and Government bacon have been the inciting causes of his
obesity. Many a sly laugh had been indulged in at
his expense by the leaner or more practical riders who
accompanied him, who, I strongly suspected, instead
of taking a " cut off," had purposely added an extra
five or ten miles to the journey.

While we were talking old " Ganado Mucho "
(Heap of Cattle), a prominent Navajo chief and head
of the Tûtsoni (Heap of Water People or Water Clan
of his tribe), joined the party. Mr. Williams had
just presented me with an ancient stone axe. Ganado

Mucho, seeing this, said that in old times, before the white man came, these axes were very valuable, and each one would buy a squaw. The old man went on to tell us that a Navajo husband never looks his mother-in-law in the face. Were he to do so he would go blind.

One of the items of Mr. Williams' commerce with the Navajoes was *crucibles,* for use in silver work ; they also make many for themselves out of the impure kaolin found in their country, the clay which they eat with the wild potato.[1]

---

[1] The Navajoes, to a very marked extent, and the Apaches, Moquis, and Zunis to a smaller degree, may be classed among the clay-eaters. Bancroft, H. H., tells us that the Mexicans were very fond of edible earth (vol. ii. p. 267).

CHAPTER VIII.

THE next morning (August 9, 1881), we were up and ready for the onward march at a very early hour. Our party had now attained swollen proportions. Mr. Williams and Mr. Webber concluded to come along, confident of a cordial welcome from their "neighbour," Mr. Keam. Their ranches were not more than fifty miles apart, and as no one lived between, they were neighbours in the strictest sense of the term.

We were a large party to impose upon Keam's hospitality, but the matter seemed not to give him the slightest concern. " If you fellows 'll take what I've got, without growling, why, you're welcome, and that's all there is about it;" and he added : " I've got lots of grub and dishes, and a pretty fair cook, and plenty of blankets. What more do you want? You don't expect to find a Crystal Palace down at my place, do you?"

Our line of travel this day ran west by a trifle north, and towards evening nearly due north.

The country for the first ten miles was gently

undulating, with cedar in all the ravines, and hills well grassed with grama. We passed close to an antelope "corral" of the Navajoes : these are made of two converging lines of stone and brush. The Navajo warriors, mounting their fleetest ponies, will scour the country for miles, driving before them the luckless game, which after a while reaches the narrowest point of the corral, and there falls a victim to the hunters in ambush. The Indians are careful not to kill all, but to allow a few to escape; this forbearance is partly based upon a desire to allow the game to reproduce, and is partly religious in character.

The type of vegetation was almost the same as that noted on the previous day ; in the valleys, almost exclusively grama ; on the hill-skirts, sage-brush and Spanish bayonet ; on their crests, piñon, and in the shadier ravines cedar, but no pine, the altitude not being sufficiently high.

Grama grass of the finest kind grew luxuriantly everywhere, but there was no flowing water.

Twenty - four miles out on our journey we "nooned" at a little "water-hole" in a box cañon, walled in by whitish sandstone bluffs.

Throughout all this part of Arizona innumerable ravines and small cañons could be walled up and utilised as reservoirs for storing the copious rains of summer, and much land thus gained for pasturage or fruit culture.

An important member of our party, up to this moment ignored, should now be referred to. I allude to our Navajo guide, who had followed us out from the agency.

His name was "George," or "Hidaltchattli," "The Wrestler," the *soubriquet* having been given him for his proficiency in that exercise, of which the Navajoes and Apaches are both extremely fond.   George wore a really beautiful silver belt of seven or eight elliptical placques, not one of which could have weighed less than five ounces.

The greater part of his patrimony must have gone into this superb girdle, and left nothing for the decoration of the rest of his person.   He was cheerful and glad-hearted, and soon worked his way up almost to the command of the expedition.

He knew every foot of the region we were passing over, a knowledge made of use to us at this very moment.   "If you want to give your horses and mules more water," he said to Keam in the Navajo language, "send them along with me ; there is water in the rocks above us."

Through curiosity I followed him to a point in the bluffs, midway between their crests and the vale where we had halted, and there, to my surprise, was shown a reservoir, constructed by the Navajoes for the accommodation of their great herds of sheep which roam over all this section.   A little cleft in the rocks had been walled up by a dam, cleverly constructed of branches of trees, stones, and mud.

Some few yards above this was an outcropping of

coal, mostly all burnt to ashes, and still so hot as to be painful to the hand.

This discovery of an abundance of water induced us to unhitch our mules, turn them out for a roll in the succulent grama, and take for ourselves the luxury of a siesta in the shadow of the cliffs, an indulgence which aided in the digestion of our lunch.

Our travel thus far, since leaving Wingate, had been delightful ; the rainy season had not as yet done much damage to the roads hereabouts, which must be quagmires in bad weather. Most of the soil is clay, with a liberal admixture of sand and " alkali," and so constituted chemically that when heavy rains fall upon the highways, as the ranchmen say, " the bottom *draps* out."

Wreaths of blue smoke curled gracefully from above the pipes of our loungers, who, gradually growing tired of chaffing each other, or of vainly wooing the drowsy god, fell into the ever-pleasant frontier habit of spinning yarns, an art in which the borderer rivals any gallant Jack Tar who ever trod a forecastle.

Webber began to tell what he knew about Indian sorcerers. I pricked up my ears, seized my faithful Faber, and jotted down as follows :—

"Three years ago a lot of Navajoes came to me and said that they had discovered in their band a witch or sorcerer, a bad 'medicine man.' His name was 'Ostin-Bijaca,' or the 'Old Deaf Man.' They had been suspecting him for some months, but now they had the 'dead wood' on him, and were going to kill him that very day. Sure enough, there he was in front of the store, all tied up with lariats, and two or three young men guarding him.

"I tried to reason with them, and told the head-men that there was no such thing as witchcraft, and they had better let the old man go, as he couldn't hurt them any and was bound to die soon anyhow.

"But what was my surprise when the old sorcerer, as they called him, spoke up boldly and said that he *was* a witch; that he had a medicine which would kill the whole tribe, and that it was now ready, and in a few days every last mother's son in the whole outfit would be dead.

"He kept on singing in a loud voice that he was a big medicine man,—a regular bad man from Bitter Creek,—and that he had made this charm of human hair and saliva, human flesh, cow-manure, and pow-dered glass. He had buried the fearful mixture in the ground, and in the maturity of time the whole Navajo nation should be wiped out.

"Well, boys, the Navajoes lost no time with him; they don't discuss questions of emotional insanity. They tied the old buster up for three days and three nights in front of the store, and didn't let him have any food or drink.

"All this time they kept telling the old man, 'You can't do these things; you haven't the power.'

"But the old fellow sturdily held to his first assertion, and, if anything, claimed the possession of still greater influence.

" So they resolved to kill him.   I couldn't do the least thing.   I was all alone, the only white man for thirty miles.   Barney had gone down to Wingate, taking the cook with him, and leaving me to look after the ranch.

" There I was, with 300 Navajoes all crazy with excitement, and I jest dussent say my soul was my own.

" Then they fired an arrow into his body; he plucked it out; they fired another, which stuck in his spine.   Then they began to stone and club him, and, after knocking him down, dropped on his head a big chunk of rock which must have weighed four pounds or more, and which stove in the whole side of his face.

" There he lay in the hot sun for three hours, still alive, but, of course, almost dead.

" I couldn't save his life, and thought the best thing to do would be to have him put out of his misery.   I said to them, ' If he's such a bad man, why don't you kill him at once and stop torturing him ?'

" A young man went up close to him, when the old fellow raised himself up suddenly, and with all his dying strength and hate, threw a club, which came whizzing past that young man's head, and if it had ever struck him would have put his lights out sure.

" The Indians returned this compliment with a couple of bullets which killed him, but they weren't satisfied until they had pounded the body into a gory and shapeless mass with rocks and clubs."

Mr. Keam confirmed this story by telling another of a sorcerer killed near this very nooning-place. His name was Na-klay-dilt-kliltli, or the "Black Butcher," the reasons for his death and the manner of his execution being in strict parallelism with Webber's narrative of the killing of Ostin-Bijaca.

Resuming our travel, we passed in three or four places seams of fine-looking coal occurring between an upper layer of cream-coloured and a lower of hard white sandstone.

The road which had been so good in the early morning suddenly became heavy from mud.

We came upon a band of Navajoes driving a herd of several thousands of sheep. A man, a woman, and two children ran out to speak to Mr. Keam. They had a long story to tell of a recent trouble between some of their people and a party of Mexican bull-whackers.

As the story appeared to have neither beginning nor end, Keam told them to ride down to his ranch in the morning to talk the matter over and get his advice.

The gist of the complaint, as nearly as it could be made out, was that a Mexican had invited a Navajo to wrestle with him. The Indian, finding himself worsted, struck the Mexican in the stomach. The latter demanded payment for the insult, and, failing to get it, flourished a revolver in a threatening manner.

Whether he meant any harm or not did not

appear; but, as the weapon went off, the Navajoes in
their turn demanded recompense, to compel which
they seized the Mexican and held him in duress, only
releasing him upon the request of one of Keam's
waggon-masters.

We drove through broad patches of the wild
potato; the leaves are small, narrow, and lanceolate.
We next reached a field of Navajo corn, defended
by three or four vicious-looking scarecrows: close to
the field were two "hogans" (Navajo houses), with
no occupants visible, but, beyond any reasonable
doubt, still tenanted, because we discovered in front
of them "caches" filled with corn. These "caches"
are holes of various sizes dug in the ground, lined
with the inner bark of the cedar, and roofed with cedar
poles laid in juxtaposition and covered with earth.
In these receptacles grain remains sweet and free
from must for a long period.

When the sun had passed the meridian, the day
became unusually sultry. The last six or seven miles
of our drive lay across a sandy stretch which told
severely upon our animals. The plateau was inter-
sected by many ravines, in whose rocky bottoms
glistened pools of pellucid water, the result of the
summer's rains. The roads from this on were badly
washed out, indicating that a ferocious " cloud-burst "
must have swept across here in the past few days,
and compelling us to make frequent tours through
the cedar woods.

We descended at last into Moqui Cañon, a narrow

" box " ravine, where cooling breezes refreshed us after our long exposure to the burning sun on the plateau.

In this cañon is situated the Moqui Agency and the residence of the missionary teachers.

Here is a small patch of cultivated land, called a garden. There are raised each year a couple of bushels of corn, and perhaps half a dozen melons. The whole area has, at great cost, been enclosed by a substantial stone fence, whole sections of which were, however, carried away bodily by the " cloud-burst " and consequent freshet sweeping down the cañon three or four days previous to our arrival.

The Moqui Indians, as we afterwards had abundant occasion to learn, care but little for the Agency or anybody connected with it. Their nearest villages are fifteen miles away, across a plain of heavy sand, while their most populous community, Oraybe, is between thirty and forty miles by the shortest trail.

The consequence, as might be expected, is that neither agents nor teachers possess the slightest influence over their charge, and might just as well be in Nova Zembla for all the good they effect. Were the Agency to be transferred to Oraybe, a change for the better would soon result.

I mention these facts to emphasise the difference between our slouchy ill-judged methods and the clean-cut, business-like ideas predominating in the Mormon management. The Latter-Day Saints are busy among the Moquis, and have met with considerable success. Their emissaries live *among* the Indians, and not forty miles away, and are constantly improving their opportunities for adding to an influence already considerable and not always friendly to the "Washington Great Father."

At Keam's ranch we met Mr. Alexander Stevens, a bright Scotchman who, during the past twelve years, has had considerable experience as a metallurgist and mining prospector in Nevada and Utah.

He gave me a thrilling account of his journey westward to the country of the Cohoninos, a tribe of Indians living in the cañon of Cataract Creek, near its junction with the Grand Cañon of the Colorado in this territory.

They number only from forty to fifty warriors, live in the cliffs in winter, and build "wickyups" or sapling lodges in summer. They say that the Hualpais, Apache-Mojaoes and themselves are all one people,— Cohoninos,—but that *their* proper designation is the "Ah-Supai."

They raise an abundance of the finest peaches, good corn and melons, and weave unusually fine and beautiful baskets. They are great hunters, and eke out a living by trading off buckskins, and sometimes mountain lion pelts, to the Moquis, Navajoes, and Apaches.

The cañon in which they dwell is 4500 feet deep, and is that of the Cataract Creek, a strong body of clear water tumbling by a series of cascades into the Grand Cañon of the Colorado, 1500 feet still deeper, and separated from their village by a series of blood-curdling precipices and chasms.

The old Navajo chief Ganado Mucho got in after dark, close behind the remainder of our party.

The distance from Fort Defiance (Navajo Agency) is not far from fifty miles, and old Ganado Mucho had passed his seventh decade. For a man of his years, this distance in this hot weather was a wonderful day's ride, and demonstrated the possession of an almost phenomenal vigour.

CHAPTER IX.

WHEN we arose the next morning we had a half-hour before breakfast to employ in looking about the house and its surroundings. Although his mode of life had necessarily many rude features, the fact that Keam still clung to the methods and mode of thought of civilised life was shadowed forth in the interior of his dwelling, which was tastily decorated with fine Navajo blankets, sheepskin rugs, Moqui pottery, and Smithsonian photographs.

A set of shelves in one corner of the living room contained choice specimens of literature—Shakespeare, Thackeray, Dickens, Taine, and other authors, and also an unusually good representation of standard American and English magazines and newspapers.

Chemical re-agents, test-tubes, and blow-pipes covered a table next the solitary window, and added to the tinge of refinement and education suggested by the books and *bric-à-brac*. A Liliputian flower garden claimed much of Keam's attention, and repaid his kindly care with a pleasing tribute of mignonette, candy-tuft, and aster.

Other flowers in pots decked the windows of the bed and living rooms ; the growth of these had lately been blighted either by the gases evolved during the process of assaying, or by the black flies alighting upon them and puncturing them with holes in which to deposit their eggs.

In every other nook and cranny of the long low building bales of wool and sheepskins were packed, awaiting a favourable season for transportation to the eastern market.

The destinies of the kitchen were in the hands of a cook who understood his business, and whose two assistants were " Garryowen," a bright Navajo boy, who waited upon the table, and " Mrs. Pinkham," an old squaw, who faithfully brought the pitcher of goat's milk for our morning coffee.

The water used at this ranch was obtained from three springs directly in front of the door, and was worthy of the highest praise for sweetness, coldness, and purity.

After breakfast, Agent Sullivan, his son, who is employed as the Agency physician, Mr. Taylor, the school teacher, and his brother, visited us.

The Agent was a very kind-hearted, superannu-ated gentleman, about seventy years old, honest and well-meaning, but not able to do much physical or mental labour, and, as goes without saying, entirely without influence over the Indians, whom he was sup-posed to manage.

Mr. Taylor favoured us with the description of a

dance he had witnessed in the Pueblo of Hualpi the previous spring.

One of the tableaux introduced was a cotton cloth, upon which were depicted in high colours seven blazing suns, through these issued seven serpents wriggling over miniature fields of growing corn.

Then came two images of young virgins, bowing to each other and lifting their hands to and from their heads. Finally, a living maiden came out from behind the screen and presented to one of the dignitaries in charge of the ceremony a basket-plate of their sacred corn-meal. The snakes used were made of small hoops covered with skins, and were moved in a life-like way by medicine men stationed in rear of the canvas.

Doctor Sullivan invited our party to go with him on a visit to the ruined Pueblo of Tolli-Hogandi, "The Singing Houses." Keam said that the name here given was a corruption of the Navajo—"Atabi-hogandi, or hoyanni," n and d being interchangeable sounds in the Navajo language.

This ruin lies some ten or twelve miles from the Agency by trail, but nearly double that distance by a road suitable for wheeled vehicles.

For a considerable part of the way we travelled over a high sandy "mesa," thickly covered with cedar.

We saw another antelope corral similar to that already described; this was used by both Navajoes and Moquis, whose territorial possessions overlap in this vicinity.

With Dr. Sullivan I had an interesting conversation about the Moqui clans or " clubs," as the Doctor called them ; among others, he knew of their having those of the " Butterfly," " Eagle," " Snake," Deer, Corn, and Cottonwood. (A complete list will be afterwards given.)

Ostin Bichindi (Old Ghost Man or Spirit Man), an old Navajo, attached himself to our party. We had reached the edge of a box cañon when one of the sudden and violent thunderstorms of this region compelled the Doctor, the Navajo, and myself, who were walking a considerable distance behind the conveyances, to take shelter under a ledge of sandstone which overhung the cañon. Ostin Bichindi said that this was the place where " Chignito," one of his tribe, had committed suicide two or three years ago. Chignito had discovered that his wife was grossly misbehaving herself, and was attacked by her paramour, who drove him away with a pistol.

In chagrin and despair he jumped off the precipice and destroyed himself.

We followed down an old trail leading to a reservoir, still holding many hundreds of gallons of water.

Sand had drifted in and the masonry-retaining walls had been broken away, but with very little labour it might be restored and made as good as ever, with a capacity of from 15,000 to 20,000 gallons.

Trails worn in the face of the sandstone cliff, and a sprinkling of pottery so thick that it almost made a pavement, indicated where the pre-historic " gossips " had gathered at sunset or sunrise to exchange the latest sweet tit-bits of scandal or talk over their simple domestic troubles.

Some of these shards were of primitive patterns, marked as with a knotted buckskin thong or a finger-nail indentation, while other fragments were of newer designs and fresher colours,—a sign that this watering-place had been used for ages past and was still used by the Navajo and Moqui herders.

Below the reservoir the cañon widened into a pleasant little pocket, showing signs of having once been cultivated.

Fourteen miles from the Moqui Agency are the ruins of a Pueblo still standing two and even three feet above the surface. It has so often been mistaken for the ruin of which we were in quest that it has received the name of the False Tolli-Hogandi; but while it does not deserve much mention in the same chapter with the true ruin, it is nevertheless an interesting monument of good area, made of rubble of all sizes of sand-stone and basalt gathered in the immediate vicinity.

The situation of this old Pueblo is peculiar in this, that close at hand is a marked depression of not less than 100 acres in area, which there are reasons for believing was once a reservoir for storing water from melted snow and rain.[1]

Cart-loads of fragments of pottery could be picked

---

[1] Later observations confirmed this surmise ; the Zunis point out on the summit of Toyalani Mountain near their town similar reservoirs constructed by their forefathers.

up all about here, most of them ornamented with a
finger-nail indentation ; one of the specimens found
by Mr. Moran was an almost complete jug, small in
size, but perfect in outline.

The pre-historic race inhabiting this part of America, the ancestors of the present Moquis and Zunis,
must have been farmers of extended acquirements for
savages.   They are to be credited with the construction of reservoirs wherever needed near their building
sites, with the excavation of irrigating ditches, the
utilisation of all springs and tanks and all other provisions against the contingency of drought.

This prudence and circumspection belie the opinion
of those who claim that the rainfall of New Mexico
and Arizona is less to-day than it was 500 years ago.
Those Indians made good, serviceable pottery, bas-
ketry, mats, textile fabrics from the fibre of cotton,
yucca, and agave, and, perhaps, coverlids of rabbit and
cayote skins, such as are so common among the
Moquis to-day.

The baaing of sheep and the bleating of goats
prepared us for encountering a wandering band of
Navajoes, but a sharp bend in the trail brought us in
upon a village of three or four "hogans": two old
squaws, half a dozen children, and a score of snarling,
yellow curs, made up the resident population.   The
squaws were weaving the loveliest of blankets upon
crude looms of cottonwood branches ; the children
and puppies were quarrelling for the possession of the
meat bones scattered over the cayote-fur coverlid

upon which they were reclining; while a young girl, too large to be called a child, and too young to be called a woman, moved with an air of importance about the ground-ovens, where sweet-smelling loaves of bread were baking for the evening meal.

One of our party, Mr. Whitney, lost not a moment in starting a bargain for a sheep and a dozen ears of green corn. The older of the two squaws charged a silver dollar for the whole purchase, and promised to kill the sheep, roast it on a stake-spit, and have it, with the ears of corn, ready for us by the hour of our return from Tolli-Hogandi. We were to have all the mutton we desired to eat, the squaw reserving for herself the blood, entrails, head, and pelt.

This was satisfactory, and the old dame, taking an earthen jar, trudged away to fill it with cold water from one of the many little springs trickling out of the rocks near by.

The great herds of the Navajoes graze in this vicinity, and in spots have eaten the grass to the roots.

A hundred yards or more beyond the Navajo " hogans " we had the satisfaction of discerning the ruins we were seeking, on the point of a promontory, a mile and a half away. It was getting late in the afternoon, yet still early enough to admit of a hasty inspection, as at first arranged.

We followed along the crest of the plateau, and noticed that underneath us on the right hand (to the

south-west) was a valley covered with Navajo corn-
patches.

We had barely reached the ruins before another
one of the boundless series of exasperating showers of
wind, rain, thunder and lightning, deluged the ground
and drenched us to the marrow, driving all to such
protection as could be found inside and under the
conveyance.

In the worst of the storm we heard a triumphant
yell, and in another moment saw emerging through the
down-pouring water our friend Mr. Hubbell, brandish-
ing in his right hand a hindquarter of the mutton,
roasted for us by the old squaw according to promise.

The rest of the meal awaited our orders, and, I
imagine, may be in the "hogan" yet. None of our
party was brave enough or hungry enough to go after
it in the tempest which had now opened the flood-
gates of heaven upon us.

It looked decidedly as if we should have to remain
on the plateau all night, and there was nothing to do
but make the best of it. Our wretched mules had
already been unharnessed and tied to the leeward of
the ambulance, and for ourselves, we sat damp and
dispirited as a lot of hens in the same predicament.
One thing alone was in our favour, we had an abundance of roast mutton and roast corn in the ear.

These, when tested, proved to be delicious. The
mutton was young, tender, and juicy, and the primitive
method of cooking it by roasting on a stake inclined
over the embers preserved all the aroma and flavour.

We ate ravenously, and bestowed unstinted praise upon both meat and cook, conceding that the latter must be one of the few not sent by the devil.

The gratification of our appetites had diverted attention from the tempest. When we looked out again from our moist shelter we greeted with delight the meagre rifts of deep-blue sky visible in the fast-scattering clouds. In another quarter of an hour the declining sun once more beamed upon us in warmth and beauty, and as a brief hour or two of daylight still remained, we could make a hurried examination of the architecture, and then find our way home in the dark as best we might.

These ruins are at least a quarter of a mile square, and walls are still standing 10 feet high and 5 feet thick. These walls are of two kinds: of adobe, *mixed with hay and cut straw*, laid in mud with an intervening stratum of small fragments of pottery between every two courses of adobe; and of natural rubble, averaging 5 inches square by 3 inches thick.

The Moquis tell the story that this town was destroyed by the people of Mu-shang-newy (one of the Moqui villages), who came over in the night, got on the top of the roofs, and tossed bundles of lighted straw down upon the people inside and stifled them.

They explain this attack by saying that the town was full of " singing men," whom the Moquis did not like.[1]

---

[1] *Query.*—Can these have been Spanish missionaries chanting the offices of the Catholic Church ?

The portion of the ruin still standing will represent perhaps as many as forty or fifty rooms, of varying dimensions, 20 feet by 10 being the more usual size.

Mr. Sinclair exhumed a human skull which he gave to me. From its position we were convinced that it was not part of an "intrusive burial" of the Navajoes, who do not inter their dead in this ruin, but, in truth, the cranium of one of those who had perished with the Pueblo itself, and whose bones had afterwards been dragged from their resting-place by cayotes, or washed out by severe storms of rain.

The approach of night and another tempest made us beat a hasty retreat from this most interesting ruin.

The darkness became so dense we could not follow

This surmise is not an untenable one by any means. The material of construction, *i.e.* the adobe made with chopped hay, is a radical divergence from the architectural methods of the Pueblos of to-day ; the fragments of pottery found here bear in numerous cases the impress of the cross—a point in itself of no consequence, but, taken in connection with other facts bearing upon these ruins, entitled to some consideration; and, lastly, we know from history that the Moquis killed the priests who were among them at the time of the expulsion of the Spaniards from this country in 1680, and that no other missionaries ever succeeded in re-establishing themselves among the Moquis after the re-conquest in 1692–94. (See Davis' *Conquest of New Mexico*, pp. 172 and 355.) It is more than possible, it is highly probable, that these "singing men" were missionaries who, at Tolli-Hogandi, had gathered about them a colony of neophytes, whose rapid increase gave alarm and disquietude to the old heathen element, and that the latter, upon the first favourable pretext and opportunity, rallied to wipe out at one fell stroke the hated innovation and its adherents. I am satisfied that this is the ruin of Aquatubi (pronounced Awatúbi) mentioned by Davis on pp. 365 and 366 of his *Conquest of New Mexico*.

the tracks made by our wheels coming on; and at best this would have been no easy task, the downfall of rain having almost washed them out. The foresight of Keam came to our assistance in the worst of our tribulation in the shape of the bright Navajo boy "Garryowen," who walked in front of our mules and guided our driver by the sound of his voice.

We all managed to get back to the ranch before 11 o'clock, and gratefully paid our *devoirs* to a warm and plentiful supper.

"Garryowen" waited upon us at table, smiling complacently at the compliments showered upon his skill as a guide, compliments which his ignorance of our language prevented him from fully comprehending, but which he perceived from our looks and gestures had a personal application.

He was a most graceful, bright, and active boy, with the straight, sinewy figure and square shoulders of his people, and the Oriental appearance commented upon by so many observers.

The almond-shaped eyes and the lustrous, black, coarse hair, bound around by a semi-turban of scarlet or purple cloth, taken with the small moustache, affected by so many of the Navajoes, do much to strengthen the resemblance to the Asiatic races.[1]

[1] See Plate VIII.

CHAPTER X.

The last day's ride—Moqui agriculture—Crow-scarers—A steep ascent
—The Moqui Pueblos—A Barmecide supper—Welcomed in an
Estufa—An impromptu Turkish bath—Jars full of snakes.

AUGUST 11, 1881.—The flies became troublesome at
early dawn, and interrupted our refreshing sleep.

To drive these little pests away from the breakfast
table, the cook had rigged up a " punkah," made of
window-sash frame, covered with newspapers, suspended from the rafters, and operated by a pulley
and a cord, the last ending in the hand of our
esteemed young friend " Garryowen."

" Garryowen," boy-like, looked upon this business
as fun, an opinion which Keam took good care should
not be rudely dissipated.   Much good solid work was
extracted from the youngster by thus humouring his
prejudices, and keeping him out of the mischief in
which he would otherwise have surely been engaged.

Mr. Stevens presented me with an almost perfect
" olla," of very old-fashioned pottery, given to him
by an old Navajo squaw, who explained that her
grandfather had dug it from a ruin in the Cañon de
Chelle (N.W. Arizona).[1]

[1] This valuable specimen is now in the private collection of
Lieutenant-General Sheridan.

Williams, Webber, Moran, and myself strolled down the cañon a short distance, first examining the springs, from each of which the water gushes out in a clear, ice-cold stream, furnishing an abundance for all purposes.

Below the springs, on the bold, vertical face of a flat, sandstone boulder, can be read in plain Roman letters, 3 to 5 inches high, this commemoration of a former visit from Kit Carson :—

> " 1ST REGT. N.M. VOLS.
> August 13, 1863.
> COL. C. CARSON, COMM'D'G."

Mr. Moran and I paid a return visit to Mr. Taylor, the teacher, and his pleasant wife. They received us warmly, and bade us welcome to their comfortable and cosy apartments. Sheep-skins served as rugs ; a respectably large collection of choice books helped to kill monotony, and a cheerful and refined tone was imparted to the walls by the skilful manner in which Mrs. Taylor had arranged the Indian and American *bric-à-brac* gathered during their tour of service.

As we entered they were both hard at work upon their quarterly report of the progress of the mission ; forty copies had to be made for distribution to the various churches contributing to the maintenance fund.

This mass of correspondence, exacted by ignorance or want of reflection, must have been a fearful tax upon the endurance of both Mr. and Mrs. Taylor, even though a copying press was employed.

Mr. Taylor said that if he ever succeeded in learning the Moqui language he should represent that this copying work would seriously impede his labours, but as at that time they had not any scholars, and did not know any thing of the Indian tongue, they had all the leisure necessary for writing the letters demanded by the home body.

Mr. Taylor had developed a creditable skill as an architect, and was building a stone residence, which promised to be neat, commodious, and comfortable— an ornament to the cañon.

At lunch " Garryowen" was immensely elated by the breaking down of our " punkah." What had at first been play had become too serious work for the young imp, who giggled with glee at the sight of the fragments of paper and wood falling upon the table.

Lunch over, we made up the party to go to the Moqui villages, and remain there until after the conclusion of the snake-dance.

Moran, Stevens, Webber, Williams, Sinclair, Hubbell, and Whitney, with the two soldiers, Gordon and Smallwood, and myself, were to go in one batch. Agent Sullivan, his son, and Dr. Elbert went together. Mr. Keam was detained by business, but arranged to drive over early next morning in company with Mr. Taylor, the brother of the teacher, and the old lady, his wife, a well-preserved specimen of the American matron.

A quarter of a mile below Keam's house was a cliff-dwelling, occupied by two Moqui families.

During my first military service in Arizona I was one of the party sent by General Crook to destroy Nanni-Chaddi's, band of Apache-Mojaoes, whom we found living in a cave in the cañon of Salt River. These Apache-Mojaoes are of the same ethnic branch as the Hualpais, Ava-Supais, and Apache-Yumas. When they surrendered in 1873 they told Lieutenant Schuyler, the officer in charge of their agency, that their ancestors had lived in the caves at the heads of Oak and Beaver Creeks and Verde River (Arizona). These facts ought to make us pause before admitting that the "cliff-dwellers," so called, were a race distinct from the Pueblos of our own day.

The distance from Keam's ranch to the nearest Pueblos of the Moquis, those of Suchongnewy, Tegua, and Hualpi, is between fourteen and fifteen miles ; the first seven or eight miles down the Moqui Cañon, and the remainder across a wide sandy plain to the foot of the rocky promontory upon which these villagers are perched.

For the whole fourteen miles one had to bear with patience the intense heat of the sun's rays, reflected back with increased power by the minute crystals of sand. Progress over such a trail is at all times difficult, and with conveyances as heavily laden as ours was vexatiously slow and annoying.

Wherever we looked we saw Moqui corn-fields ; these had been planted in every location promising the most nutriment in soil, protection from floods, or immunity from other dangers. The lives of these savage husbandmen seem to be beset with annoyances. They are constantly in peril on account of water, either from not having enough or from getting too much.

The soil, very thin and sandy, is destitute of moisture at the top ; the constant heat and the dryness of the atmosphere induce evaporation, but the under strata of clay and sandstone retain for a long time much of the rain or surface water which percolates down to them.   Consequently our Moqui farmer buries his seed-grain deep in the ground.   Taking his *planting-stick* in his right hand, he presses with his foot upon the horizontal bar and makes a hole from 12 to 18 inches in depth, into which he drops the kernels of corn.

PLANTING-STICK OF MOQUIS.

The next greatest danger guarded against is that of floods.   The ingenuity of the Moquis is equal to the demands upon it.   They do not plant their corn in rows of a single stalk as we do, but in *bunches*, which effectually resist the sand-blasts of early summer and the full force of the debris-sweeping freshets of the rainy season.

The appearance of a Moqui corn-field is therefore completely at variance with that of our broad acres of the golden cereal.   In the Moqui fields five, six, and even ten stalks will be seen growing close together ; another cluster of same kind 10 feet off, and so on; each

H

cluster almost surrounded at the foot by small branches, wisps of hay, little stones, piles of mud, and other injurious matter swept down by rain-currents.

The wind, the " cut worm," and the crow are other enemies the Moqui farmer has to fight from the moment the corn is dropped in the ground. When the tender leaflets of maize first peep above the surface the fierce winds of May sweep down from the cañons, bearing on their bosoms clouds of sand and dust to overwhelm and destroy. In many of the more exposed situations it becomes necessary to build little ramparts of stone or clay on the windward side of the bunches, to keep them from being torn out by the roots.

The " cut worm" makes its appearance a little later, as the corn is attaining full size; and when the ears have become plump and tempting the dismal chatter of crows calls out the whole available boy strength of the Moqui nation to put to rout the most persistent enemy of all.

Dismal scarecrows, made of the most leprous rags to be seen in this great republic, wave a transient defiance to callow fledglings. The older birds do not heed these phantom terrors, but placidly roost upon them, planning forays upon the luscious harvest, until the stealthy approach of two or three of their dreaded and sleepless foes—the small boys—scares them into a lazy flight.

The life of the Moqui small boy, viewed from the white man's standpoint, is not an enviable one during the weary weeks that the harvest is germinating and maturing ; yet it would be incorrect to assert that it is altogether unhappy.

Every moment of the youngster's time is occupied in play-work, which, after all, is the true happiness of a healthy, vigorous boy. He has enough to do to invest him with the consciousness of important responsibility without the irksome restraint of a set task to be accomplished by a fixed hour.

Whole families move out from the villages during this season, and occupy dug-outs or other temporary shelters in the cañons, or elsewhere, near their fields, to which unremitting care and attention are given.

A brisk rain fell upon us ere we had more than half reached the foot of the mesa. When we finally attained the base of the bold, vertical cliff of sandstone, upon whose crest could be discerned the stone dwellings of the Moquis, our first business was to see that our mules were unhitched, and that water and grass were available for them. Gordon and Smallwood were left in charge, while the rest of the party, Williams and myself in advance, began a toilsome climb for the summit.

At the base of this mesa, and the same may be written of each of the others upon which stands a Moqui Pueblo, is a great hill or dune of sand, piled up by the storms of centuries. This shifted under our feet, and caused the ascent of the little ravine through which ran the trail we were following to be exasperatingly slow and laborious.

This ravine terminated in a small circular field or bench, utilised by the thrifty Moquis as a peach orchard. The trees were bending under the load of well-formed fruit, and, so far as we could judge, gave their owners very little concern.

The site chosen for the little orchard was very happy; sheltered from fierce winds and from the glare of the noonday sun, but benefited by all the water which might drip down from the reservoir close at hand. This we noticed to be well built in a cleft in the rocks, and to be capable of holding a considerable amount of water, probably as much as 20,000 gallons.

Many other receptacles for collecting and storing rain were to be seen in nooks and recesses in different places in the walls, upon the crest or on the flanks of this mesa, some being larger, some smaller, than the one just described. I took no measurements, not being provided with facilities, and, in truth, not thinking that any special benefit would result from so doing.

At the reservoir and peach orchard began the steeper but better part of the trail : from this on we might be said to have had a stone staircase under our feet.

Much hard work had been performed here by the Indians of previous generations, and, excepting that the grade was much too steep to be comfortable, the pathway along the face of the precipice was as well constructed as any engineer could wish.

Fifty feet below the crest the path approached a small altar or shrine, enclosing an idol ; this idol was only a stone " torso," without head, and with only rudimentary suggestions of arms and thighs. Before this the Moquis had laid votive offerings of petrified wood, and of small twigs painted green originally, and tied two and two by little bands of grass.[1]

Our upward progress was so severe a test of our physical powers that, in order not to reach the villages in a condition of exhaustion which might keep us from seeing and enjoying anything that might transpire in the evening, we rested frequently, under the excuse of admiring the beautiful panorama unrolled at our feet.

The Moquis, accustomed all their lives to this toilsome climb, make light of it, and go up and down at as fast a pace as an American moving on level ground.

Parties of them, driving " burros" laden with green corn, or bearing in blankets on their backs five gallon " ollas" to be filled with water at the springs below, passed and repassed going up or down— always greeting us with the friendly salutation " lolamai" (good).

One more steep but brief climb landed us in the outskirts of the first Pueblo,—Hano or Tegua,—inhabited by a portion of the tribe of same name, who fled from the Rio Grande to avoid the Spaniards, some time in the closing years of the seventeenth century.

[1] See Plate XXX.

They still speak their own language, which is
entirely distinct from that of their next door neighbours and every-day associates, the Moquis proper.

We did not tarry long in Tegua, but pushed on
a couple of hundred yards to the middle village—
Suchongnewy—where, in the house of Tochi, one of
the prominent natives, we found the Agent and
Dr. Sullivan, who had started on a couple of hours
ahead of our party.

Learning of our coming, Tochi had set three
squaws at work cleaning out a large room, in which
he gave us permission to take up our quarters—a
courtesy very sincerely appreciated.

Three or four boys were immediately hired, with
as many " burros," and sent down after all our plunder, while the mules were to be allowed to run during
the night with the herds of the Moquis.

Gordon and Smallwood reported their arrival in
less than an hour, and made no delay in preparing
supper.   This we were not to enjoy.   Tochi advanced
and insisted that we should accept of his hospitality.
He became so urgent that to decline would have been
to wound his feelings, so we accepted the situation as
gracefully as possible.

The supper was very meagre in quantity and inferior in quality ; the coffee scarcely strong enough to
conceal the asphaltum taste of the water ; the bread,
the blue " wyavi " or " piki " of this people ; and the
canned pears, a contribution from Mr. Whitney, who,
fortunately as it happened, had put a can in each of

the side pockets of his overcoat before leaving Keam's ranch.

We were not very well pleased,—any of us,—but grumbling was out of the question, and indeed was not thought of. The wholesome nourishing supper we might have had by remaining at our own camp fire obtruded itself upon our imaginations with tantalising persistency.

It would not do to wound the feelings of Tochi, who had acted from a very hospitable impulse, and, as the affair had not a few ludicrous features, we were soon laughing hilariously at the grotesqueness of the situation. For, I should say, that Tochi was not making any endeavour to give us a Moqui collation ; that would have been good enough : but in his ambitious straining after the white man's ways, the idea had seized upon him of giving an American supper, and here it was, in all its grandeur as he understood it, served up in tin cups gathered from all sources, or empty fruit cans received from the Agent for past personal services.

Our thanks to Tochi were, I am compelled to say, more profound than sincere. The old man wanted to know how this would do for an American supper ; we assured him that in every respect it filled the bill, and that very few Americans could get up such a meal as that—a compliment which delighted our host, as well as the squaws who had officiated as cooks and ministering angels during the entertainment.

The sun had long since gone down behind the

distant outlines of San Francisco Mountain when we
arose from our banquet. The proceedings of the
morrow promised to be so replete with interest that I
did not deem it advisable to lose a moment from the
task of accumulating memoranda upon all that was to
be seen and heard in the three villages.

To get the best information obtainable, our party
concluded to split into squads of two and three
each, wandering about at will in every direction in
Suchongnewy, Hualpi, and Hano, and occasionally
re-uniting for comparison of notes.

Each of my comrades was anxious to help me in
my labours, and to each I must concede a grateful
tribute of indebtedness, although to Moran, Williams,
and Webber I am under special obligations for en-
thusiastic and intelligent co-operation in all my plans
from beginning to end.

The first thing that impressed us all was the great
need of an abundant supply of water for the Moquis'
daily consumption. That which they now use on the
mesa has to be carried by squaws on their backs from
the springs 500 and 600 feet below. I saw a few
small reservoirs which were useful as supplying the
wants of the chickens, dogs, and donkeys, but they are
altogether insufficient for the wants of the Pueblo.
The Moquis have not the proper tools to enable them
to construct reservoirs of capacity sufficiently large
for themselves and animals, but were the services of
an intelligent engineer to be called into requisition a
merely nominal sum expended in dynamite and fuse

would blow out from the upper surface of this mesa itself a cubical space large enough to hold hundreds of thousands of gallons of rain. The construction of walls, roofs, and drain-pipes might safely be left to the Moquis themselves.

Going over to Hualpi (which village is at the extreme western end of the mesa and 300 yards from Suchongnewy) I descended into one of the Estufas, and, instead of being repelled, met with urbane treatment from the Indians within.

The apartment was subterranean, rectangular in shape, 25 feet long by 15 wide, and 10 feet high, built of stones and mud, the roof of heavy pine timbers covered with twigs, earth, and stone.

There was a party of nineteen Indians within— men and boys, all naked save the breech-clout, with spots of white paint scattered over limbs and body.

I shook hands with three or four of the older members, and was invited to share their feast of blue corn bread ("piki" or "wyavi"), mutton stew, and chile colorado, of which all were eating voraciously.

The walls of the Estufa I knew were of rubble masonry, but so completely hidden by dance trappings, rattles, coyote and fox pelts, red buckskins, etc. etc., that an observer could not learn in what manner they were ornamented, or whether or not they were plastered.

On the far or west side of the room, on the floor, was an altar, if I may so call it, portrayed in fine sands and clays of different neutral tints.

A gray rectangular field, 25 inches square, contained a rude representation in yellow of a Rocky Mountain lion bleeding at the nose. This field was bordered by narrow, black, yellow, and reddish bands, all of clay, and surrounding the whole was a railing of vertical willow saplings, 12 inches high, painted black, their lower extremities resting in balls of mud and their upper terminating in eagle feathers and corn-shucks.

The Indians motioned that these saplings or twigs were to be used as drum-sticks, but I heard later from one of them who spoke a little Spanish that they commemorated the dead of their people—the " old men," or spirits of the nation.

Around the altar, under and outside of the willow railing, was a band of gray, either fine ashes or sand, but probably the former.[1]

The ladder leading up from the Estufa was crowned with a bow, decorated with yellow horse-hair, eagle feathers, and rabbit skins, while from the topmost rung of the ladder itself floated a skein of bright red yarn.

Agricultural implements, principally hoes and "planting-sticks," were piled behind the ladder and very close to it; on the opposite side of the hatchway a half-dozen eagle feathers were tied in a vertical position to a bunch of grease-wood.

The bright light of the moon streaming down from a serene sky made the vicinity of this Estufa almost as

[1] See Plate XVIII.

clear as day, and enabled me to discern and jot down everything worthy of note near the entrance. Having done this, I re-descended into the Estufa, and mingled again with the Indians. They had, most of them at least, finished their meal and were in pleasant humour. I was suffered to inspect everything about the Estufa, not excepting the "altar," in front of which I discovered, in the feeble, flickering light, an earthen platter piled up in globular shape with finely pulverised corn-meal.

I repeat I experienced no molestation whatever; on the contrary, I was the recipient of marked courtesy, and should have been delighted to remain all night had it not been for the stench and heat, which were simply overpowering.

After enduring it as well as I could for an hour or more, I sallied out, reeking with perspiration.

I did not regret having to leave, as much of importance could be learned in other parts of the Pueblo. There did not appear to be anything doing in the Estufa that night, and if I could do nothing better, I could go quietly to sleep and awaken refreshed for work by the dawn of day.

Mr. Whitney, who had carefully watched a sacred dance going on in the Pueblo of Tegua (or Hano) as we entered this afternoon, gave the following account of it :—

"The dance was held in front of a house distinguished by a cottonwood sapling stuck in the ground. The dancers were in two lines, facing each other;

one line dressed in white cotton kilts, the other in red, and all shaking rattles.   Corn-meal was profusely sprinkled upon the ground, and garlands made of leaves of the new corn were displayed.   An old man with an eagle feather sprinkled water from an earthen basin.   The decorations worn by this old man were the red feathers either of the red-headed wood-pecker or of the parrot, but, in all likelihood, of the former."[1]

Doctor Sullivan had learned that the snakes to be used in the dance were caught eight days before, or rather that eight days before the dance the young men begin to catch them.   The young men assemble in the house of one of the " caciques " or priests, where they receive good advice and recite certain prayers, using "medicine water " or " holy water " and holy corn-meal.   In separating, the catchers go to the north, the west, the south, and east in turn, devoting one day to each point of the compass, and at end of that time, if not enough be caught, they roam all over the country to obtain all that can possibly be procured.

" All the snakes captured are kept concealed in one of the Estufas, no person being permitted to see them or even to know where they are."

Not putting much confidence in the accuracy of the

---

[1] This dance was not noted more carefully at the proper moment because several of the Indians gave us to understand that it was in the nature of a rehearsal for the events of the morrow, which proved afterwards to be the case.

last statement, and remembering certain large earthen jars, covered with sheep-skin, which I had dimly discerned in the gloom of the Estufa during my last visit, I made up my mind to go back there a third time and ascertain for myself something upon this head.

I found three large four or five gallon ollas, and my suspicions as to their contents were confirmed by one of the boys who answered my question in Spanish, with all of that language at his command,—the single word, " culebra " (snake). The ollas were covered very tightly and carefully, and so placed as not to be unnecessarily disturbed.

In the Estufa I met an old man, answering to the English name of Molasses, the head Governor or Mungwee of these three towns. He said that in this dance the Moquis use all kinds of snakes.

He also said that the people of the present Moqui towns had destroyed the Pueblo of " Tolli-Hogandi," killing the men, and carrying the women and children away captive.

Our party assembled on the flat roof of our house, and made the witching air of night musical with the stirring words of old army songs and choruses. It was almost dawn before Sherman got through " Marching through Georgia," and we had thrown ourselves down upon our blankets to catch a short nap before morning.

Our first sleep was rudely broken by a fierce dog-fight in front of our door, and so close to my own blankets that the final round was fought on top of the bloodthirsty bed-bugs which had been slowly eating me alive.

A chair-rung did effective work upon both victor and vanquished in the last act, the epilogue being a series of marrow-freezing howls, which brought women and children out of their beds and houses.

CHAPTER XI.

The morning of the festival—An exhausting struggle—House architecture—The tribal divisions—The interior of an Estufa—The
snakes again—A native prayer—Ancient implements—A weak
guardian.

AUGUST 12, 1881. Roused out of bed at 4 A.M.,
before daylight, at which early hour the Moquis were
already astir, most of them dressed for the festivities
of the day. Squaws were busy as bees getting out
from underground ovens earthen pots of fragrant
mush, covered with grass and corn-husks to exclude
dust.[1]

The Moqui children, or those belonging to the
three villages on this mesa, were congregated at the
foot of the precipice and near its N.W. corner, and
were manifestly preparing for some unusual occurrence.

They first sang a song, whose shrill notes reached
with perfect distinctness our exalted position 700 feet
above them. Then, at a shout from an old Indian, the
youngsters started on a foot-race, bounding along the
ground like so many jack-rabbits. They could hardly
be made out as children, they looked so small in the

[1] See Plate XXVII.

dim twilight of early dawn. Umpires and station-
keepers had been selected from among their elders,
who stationed themselves at various pre-arranged
places along the line of the race, but who won, or
what the object of the contest was, no one could
advise us.

For all that we could see, there might as well have
been no race at all; the figures of the contestants
were hard to distinguish, they were so far below us;
and, speaking for myself at least, their positions could
be detected more certainly by the jingling of the little
bells they all wore than by actual vision.

Attention did not long converge upon the children;
there was another race of greater importance between
the young men. This was not a spurt to show which
had the most speed for a short distance; it was a test
of endurance, bottom and wind as well as of speed. The
race had commenced at a clump of rocks six or seven
miles from the foot of the mesa,—our estimates all
varied greatly—and from that distant point the young
men could be seen running like deer straight towards
the Pueblo.

About the moment that the little boys had finished
their struggle, the advance-guard of the adult runners
appeared above a small knoll a mile off, and rushed
rapidly forward in the direction of the cluster of bushes
where the children had drawn up in line to receive
them. When the two parties came together a regular
war-whoop rent the air, and every bell's jangling
was redoubled, the combined mob of boys and men

running as hard as possible to the base of the precipice.

Here a delegation of young women was expecting
them, and ran with them, still at full speed, up the
steep trail, crossing sand-dunes and climbing the steep
precipice, which was, as I have before said, not less than
600 feet above the plain beneath.

The trail ascended by the runners was, if anything, steeper and more arduous than the usually
travelled one which we had climbed; yet none of
them paused a moment in their upward and onward
career. Had an American, unused to ascending
and descending these rugged paths, attempted the
same feat he would have died of palpitation of the
heart.

Before I had finished my notes upon this part of
the race the runners were abreast of our position, one
of them leading his comrades by 200 yards.

It did not take more than a glance to show that
this was no joke ; every one of the men was streaming with perspiration, and the thumping of hearts
and wheezing of lungs could be plainly heard.

A small loin-cloth constituted the sole raiment of
the men, but the squaws all wore mantles of white
cotton. The children, who streamed in by dozens,
were absolutely naked, and all greatly exhilarated by
the excitement of the morning. I am not prepared
to say that they took off any clothing in honour of
the festival, since the Moqui youngsters, of both
sexes, until seven, eight, and even nine years old,

I

roam about in the classic costume of the Garden of Eden.[1]

The elderly Moquis this morning carried all their ornaments on their persons, a great help to me in my investigations. I saw the olivette, abalone, and other sea-shells, chalchihuitl and coral, worn as bead-necklaces, as earrings, or as pendants upon the breast.

The young maidens of the villages were out in full force, decked in the most gorgeous finery of native manufacture : their freshly-cleaned tresses of raven-black were done up in flat, circular coils, one over each ear, the general effect being to make them resemble Chinese.

Our mules were brought up from the plain very soon after daybreak ; nobody in the Pueblos could be hired for love or money to take care of them during the dance, and, as a measure of prudence, they should not be exposed to the risk of bites from the venomous reptiles which the Moquis might release after the ceremony and allow to wander unchecked over the country. The chances were largely in favour of their being bitten, and I was not willing to incur any such responsibility.

The Moqui houses are of rubble sandstone masonry,

---

[1] "Races were held at the chief temples of Mexico under the auspices of the priests, at which prizes were awarded to the four competitors who succeed in first gaining *the topmost of the* 120 *steps.*' — Bancroft, H. H., vol. ii. pp. 296, 297.

The Aztecs claimed a northern origin. May it not be possible that the forms of their " teocallis " or temples commemorated a period when their ancestors dwelt upon precipices ascended by stone steps ?

laid in mud; the materials obtained from the mesa itself. The stones are of all sizes, from 2 inches cube to 10 inches cube; the foundations rest upon the solid rock surface of the mesa. Some of the houses are plastered with mud on the outside and all on the inside. The rooms vary greatly in capacity; our bedroom, which was the common or living room of the house to which it belonged, was 30 feet long, 18 feet wide, and 6 feet 6 inches high. The average room in the Moqui villages—at least in the three on this mesa—may be put down as 10 feet by 12 feet, by 7 feet high.

Many of the rooms are used for storage purposes, in which case it is not seldom a matter of doubt as to whether they should be classified as small rooms or large closets. The houses are arranged compactly alongside one another, or in terraces one above the other, as fancy and convenience may have suggested.

The angles are finished with little care, and are all "slouchy." The lintels and jambs are both of sandstone and of saplings or split timber, very rarely of American make. The windows are glazed with American panes in the few instances where any at all are used, but neither mica nor selenite are to be seen. Our bedroom had two windows, one of a foot square, the other of 12 inches by 8 inches; the lintels of split wood (cedar or cottonwood); the sills and jambs of sandstone. An air-hole a foot square in the ceiling could in emergency be used as a mode of exit to the roof and houses above.

The round joists were 8 inches in diameter, of peeled pine, supporting small cedar branches placed in juxtaposition ; over these were laid yucca fibre, and above all a coating of earth.   The walls were plastered with mud, washed with lime or kaolin, and in some places tinted with a yellowish-red earth, probably ochre.

A fireplace, in the middle of one side, was built in the American style, 18 inches high by 15 inches wide.   This house was evidently quite modern.

An old Indian kindly gave me the names of the snakes to be used in the dance as far as he knew them. There were, he said, generally fourteen different kinds to be collected in this vicinity (he counted the number on his hands); this year, for some reason, the crop was light, but still he thought that the full number would be represented.

The principal ones to be seen this time would be (1), Chú-a (Rattler) ; (2), Le-lu-can-ga (this has yellow and black spots, and may be the Bull snake) ; (3), Tá-ho (runs very fast—may be the Racer); (4), Pa-chu-a (a water-snake) ; and (5), Tegua-chigui.   Of all these the Rattler would be most numerous.

The head medicine men alone know the secrets of this ceremony, the means to be taken to keep the reptiles from biting, and the remedies to be applied in case bites should be received.

The clans or gentes of the Moquis, according to my informant, who expressed himself with great intelligence, although he spoke but little Spanish, are as follows :—

1. Bôli,	Mariposa,	Butterfly.
2. Kuâja,	Aguila,	Eagle.
3. Ká-ah,	Maiz,	Corn.
4. Chia,	Vibora,	Rattlesnake.
5. Sui,	Conejos,	Rabbit.[1]
6. Honan,	Oso,	Bear.
7. Piba,	Bunchi,	Tobacco (native).[2]
8. Honáni,	Tejou,	Badger.
9. Pá-jeh,	Agua,	Water.
10. Pá-kua,	Sapo,	Toad or Frog.[3]
11. Ta-jua,	Sol,	Sun.
12. A-tó-co,	Grulla,	Crane (now extinct).
13. Shu-húi-ma,	Venado,	Deer.
14. Ku-ga,	Leña,	Firewood (almost extinct).[4]
15. I-sha-hue,	Coyote,	Coyote.
16. Huspoa,	Paisano,	Road-runner (Chapparal cock).
17. Quingoi,	Eucina,	Oak.
18. Omá-a,	Nube,	Cloud. (See also pp. 335-336.)

The Moquis call themselves Hopii or Opii, a term

[1] The Spanish word "Conejos" was given, but I am too well acquainted with the employment by the Indians of this word for "liebre" (a hare or jackass rabbit, and *vice versâ*), not to feel it my duty to point out the uncertainty of the translation.

[2] No. 7 is named from the Bunchi or native tobacco, cultivated by all the Pueblos of New Mexico and Arizona.

[3] In like manner, the Spanish "Sapo" (toad) is used so generally by the Indians instead of "rana" (frog), and I am so well satisfied that Pá-kua in the Moqui language means "frog," that I have felt constrained to give that as the name of the tenth gens.

[4] The Indian could not explain what this meant; he repeated "leña, leña" (firewood), but whether "alamo" (cottonwood), or some other tree like the cedar or pine, I could not make out.

My informant, I must take care to say, was old Tochi or "Moccasin," our host of last night. He said that he himself belonged to the Bôli or Butterfly gens, that his wife and children were of the Aguila or Eagle, his father was Venado or Deer, and his son had married a Quingoi or Oak, and his brother a Leña or Kú-ga.

not now in the language of every-day life, but referring in some way to the Pueblo custom of banging the hair at the level of the eyebrows.   This mode of wearing the hair distinguishes them from Apaches, Utes, and Navajoes, and, as Tochi wished me to bear in mind, showed that they were once "todos los mis mos" (all the same) with the Mojaoes, Yumas, Maricopas, and other bands of Arizona, whose practice of "banging" the hair used to strike me as being in such curious contrast with the loose, unkempt manner of wearing it peculiar to the Apaches.

The Moquis call the Apaches Yúte-shay; the Navajoes, Ta-shá-va-ma; the Utes, Yutama; and the Comanches, Comanshima.

In this interview I was much assisted by a bright youngster, answering to the name of Sam, and, towards the close, by Dr. Sullivan, who, to the extent of his knowledge, confirmed all that had been extracted from Tochi.

The Doctor then walked over with me to Hualpi; on the mesa, midway between this village and Suchongnewy, in a sheltered niche, was another altar with its stone torso idol and its votive offerings— the whole a complete duplicate of the one observed by the road last evening.

In Hualpi itself was a sacred rock, with a depression in one side, in which was still another idol, with the usual devotional pledges of petrified wood and green-painted twigs, bound with yucca fibre or filaments of grass.

We descended into an Estufa, of which there were no less than nine on this mesa, viz.—five in the village of Hualpi and two each in Tegua and Suchongnewy. These Estufas combine the triple uses of chapels, council - chambers, and workshops, and in the last-named service are often occupied by the women while weaving blankets or sashes.

In the Estufa now spoken of we found five young men painting the cotton kilts to be worn in the coming dance.

These kilts were made of cloth of cotton, of *native growth*, and were painted with a ground colour of reddish-yellow, upon which, at top and bottom, were two narrow bands of yellow and green, each one inch wide, and bordered by a very narrow black stripe. At the bottom was a fringe of small bells, or jinglers, of lead and tin, precisely the same as are placed by the Apaches upon their moccasins. A black snake was painted in folds upon the kilt ; the snake was bordered by very narrow white lines, and covered with white spots which, upon closer examination, resolved themselves into white arrow heads and polka-dots, the latter arranged longitudinally, two and two.[1]

The emptiness of this Estufa gave us full opportunity to examine and measure it. It was rectangular, almost entirely underground, 35 feet long by 25 feet wide and 7 feet high, made of stone, in same general style as the houses, and plastered on the inside.

[1] See Plate XXII.

A banquette of stone and earth, 10 inches high and 10 inches wide, ran around on three sides, and on the fourth or north side widened into a dais of same height, but some 5 feet broad.

The entrance was by ladder, the rectangular aperture in the roof being left uncovered to admit the fullest amount of sunlight and air.

In time of storm the hatchway could be closed by a mat made of yucca fibre and grass with string, tied in a Malay hitch.

Three small windows in the east wall gave additional ventilation.

On the east wall was painted a symbolical design or " prayer," representing three rows of clouds in red and blue, from which depended long, narrow, black and white stripes typical of rain, while from right and left issued long red and blue snakes emblematic of lightning. The accompanying sketch will afford a clearer conception of the painting.[1]

It was explained to me that this was a prayer to Omá-a, the God of the Clouds, to send refreshing rains upon the Moqui crops. Yellow, so Dr. Sullivan said, was used in all prayers for pumpkins, green for corn, and red for peaches.

These colours are obtained as follows :—

The green from a mixture of carbonate of copper and piñon pitch. The carbonate of copper is extracted from out-croppings said to exist on the north flank of San Francisco Mountain, which looms up

[1] See Plate XXIII.

grandly seventy-five miles to the west and south of the villages.

Black is from coal and charcoal; yellow is from yellow ochre, found in this region; and the white was, I am satisfied, impure kaolin.

The oil is extracted from pumpkin seeds.

The young men, who were working in the Estufa at the moment of our arrival, maintained an almost perfect silence, addressing each other only through necessity, and then in low whispers.

I next went down into the Estufa where I had observed the ollas full of snakes last night.

There were nine naked men and boys (wearing only the breech-clout), getting themselves ready for the dance. The ollas had disappeared, and I was on the point of asking in a whisper where the snakes could be found, when one of those present tapped me on the shin and pointed to the west side of the chamber, back of the altar.

There they were! No doubt at all about that; emitting, unless my imagination deceived me, a very pungent, foul, and loathsome smell.

They were in a knotted, fœtid mass, close up against the wall, "herded," as may be truly said, by the older men of the party.

As I took fuller notes of these snakes and the manner of caring for them at a later moment, I make no special comment at this point, to avoid needless repetition.

The altar next engaged my attention. I made a

very careful sketch, noting the colours as exactly as possible, and believe that the picture[1] is a faithful reproduction of a remarkable example of aboriginal taste and skill, and of the religious symbolism of the Moquis.

There were hanging on the walls, or lying on the floor, sacred wands with round wooden handles painted red, and having incised upon them a long green snake. Eagle feathers tipped the upper extremity. My expression of a desire to purchase one of these was met with a polite but decided refusal.

Tortoise-shell and sheep-toe rattles were present by the dozen. The number of these rewarding a careful search through any of the New Mexican or Arizonan Pueblos would cause astonishment to any one not personally acquainted with the constant use made of them in all festivals and religious ceremonies of the South-Western Indians.

Besides these snake-wands, used only in this dance, there were many others to be borne by participants in this and other processions, which were made in much the same way of a wooden handle and almost any kind of feathers, except those of the owl. It may be remarked that at this point my memoranda are a trifle incoherent and disjointed,—a fact which will need no explanation or apology after I have stated that, while writing them, I happened to look up and saw a young Indian slowly and sedately descending the ladder, bearing in his hand a wriggling, writhing

[1] Plate XVIII.

rattlesnake, at the least five feet long, and a regular
" buster " in every sense.

At one corner of this snake altar was a sacred
earthen basket of corn-meal,[1] and another of medicine
water. The centre of one of the bounding lines was
occupied by an abalone [2] shell, and in the centre of
another were several oddly-shaped stones which might
once have been used as hammers, but impressed me
rather as having been arbitrarily sanctified, and as the
crude idols or fetishes of a long-forgotten era.

One of the old men held up a gourd-rattle, shook
it, lifted his hands in an attitude of prayer towards
the sun, bent down his head, moved his lips, threw
his hands with fingers opened downward towards the
earth, grumbled to represent thunder and hissed in
imitation of lightning, at same time making a sinuous
line in the air with the right index finger, and then,
seeing that my attention was fixed upon him, made a
sign as if something was coming up out of the ground,
and said, in Spanish, " mucho maiz " (plenty of corn),
and in his own tongue " lolamai " (good).

The young men with him in this Estufa were
making moccasins; these had soles of raw hide, covering the " plant " of the freely-extended foot, and
coming well up on the sides. The uppers were of red
buckskin, made very closely after the pattern of our
low quarter shoes, with a wide tongue reaching above
the ankle.[3]

[1] See Plate XXI.   [2] The Haliotis.
[3] See Plate XXII.

The Moquis understand how to colour buckskin, feathers, and cloth, or the yarn of which this last is to be woven.

I left this Estufa and descended into another, where there was but one person—an old man—making moccasins. He evinced a disposition to be conversational, and told me that this was the Estufa or Kiba (in the Moqui language) of the Bôli or Butterfly gens. Here also was a ground altar of about the same dimensions (about a yard square) as the one sketched and described previously. The design was, however, different, and represented a bank of four layers of yellow, green, red, and white clouds, from which darted four snakes or streaks of lightning, coloured white, red, green, and yellow respectively.[1] There was the same railing of blackened twigs stuck in clay balls, the upper extremities of the twigs decorated with eagle feathers, corn-shucks, and the down of eagles and turkeys stained a bright red. The old man said that these commemorated the Moqui dead.[2]

He then pointed to each snake and called out its colour, or rather the colour of the lightning which it symbolised :—

1. Cuécha, White.   3. Shiscuámpa, Green.
2. Bálampi, Red.   4. Ko-té-a-ta, Yellow.

Flat plate-like baskets, woven of willow twigs, and bearing designs of deer and other animals, in red, blue, black, and yellow, were heaped high with corn-meal, and placed in a row around this altar; there

[1] See Plate XIX.   [2] See Plate XXI.

were also small ollas filled with water, but whether medicated or not, I couldn't learn.

The baskets, in all cases but one, were the flat ware of the Moquis above described; the exception was an excellent specimen of the exquisite work of the Cohonino Indians of the Grand Cañon of the Colorado.

The ollas, as they are here called, merely for the sake of distinction, were the pottery baskets, decorated with the water emblems of the frog and the tadpole.[1]

Behind this altar and close to the wall was a bundle of freshly-cut stalks and ears of corn; near these were five pipes of clay, of various shapes. These are to be seen in sacred ceremonies only; neither among Zunis nor Moquis are pipes any longer in common use.

A long pile of stone implements, regularly arranged, were placed at the back of the altar, and almost upon the green corn-stalks. These were all of green stone and slate, and, unless I am greatly mistaken, were all agricultural implements, such as hoes, trowels, etc. I hoped to come across some specimens of work in obsidian or chalcedony, but did not, much to my disappointment. However, it does not follow that there were none there, as the implements were piled two, three, four and five high in a single row running almost around the altar. I was not permitted to touch them, and there may, for all

[1] See Plate XXI.

I know, have been obsidian knives, lances, and arrow heads which escaped my notice [1]

Finally, there were three water-worn fragments of sandstone, rudely fashioned by rubbing into something of an approach to the outlines of tójo-bûcu, the mountain lion.

The idols described up to this time have all been fragments of reniform, concretionary sandstone, or of water-worn rocks roughly shaped to some sacred configuration.

The Moquis possess other idols showing a greater amount of artistic skill in conception and execution, but it may be said that the ruder, uglier, more misshapen, more archaic, an idol is, the more reverence does it command from these deluded heathens.[2]

The old man in the Estufa understood Spanish to a limited extent; Sam, who had followed me down, spoke a good deal of English, and so, in one way or another, vastly more information was obtained than might at first be thought possible.

There were no snakes in this Estufa, but from the old man's words and motions it was inferred that they were to be brought here before the dance and procession began, and from here would be carried in the mouths of the "medicine men" and others around the sacred rock.

This Kiba, or Estufa, was evidently a sanctuary high in repute; but, disregarding the sanctity of the den, I made a bold attempt to secure some of

<hr>

[1] See Plate XX.   [2] See Plate XXX.

these valuable specimens, and tried to ask the aged
custodian to name a lump sum for the whole outfit,
excluding the snakes, which had not yet been brought
here, and for which I had no particular use.

He appeared to grasp my meaning very readily,
and speculation blazed in his eyes as he looked
cautiously about the Estufa, to satisfy himself that
nobody but Moran and I were near him—Sam
having just left, and Moran having entered in search
of me.

The scale of prices was arranged without a great
deal of trouble. Three of the pipes were handed over
for a silver dime each, and a stone hoe, as it appeared
to be, for a silver dollar.[1] These were the old man's
own terms. The money was laid before him, and he
picked out the amount he was willing to accept for
each article. He declined to part with the largest
pipe[2] at any price, saying very firmly, "Ka-lola-
mai" (bad) every time I offered to even touch it.
Neither would he let me have any other stone implements from the lot under his care ; he said, " basta,
basta " (you have enough), and made signs for me
to conceal the purchase from the notice of the other
Indians. I acted upon the old fellow's suggestions,
and fearing lest some revulsion of feeling might make
him repent of his conduct and recall the bargain, I
determined to preserve these treasures by flight, and
to conceal them in my blankets or hand-valise, where
they should be secure.

[1] See Plate XX.   [2] See Plate XX.

CHAPTER XII.

Farther wanderings through the Pueblo—More Estufas—Moqui idols
—Native baptism—Domestic arrangements.

HAVING placed them beyond reach of recovery, I
went again to the Estufa where the snakes were, and
remained for some time. There was noticeable the
same acrid effluvia already mentioned, emanating from
the coils of the snakes as I supposed and believed;
when the dank vapours of this reptile dungeon became
insupportable I ran up the ladder into the pure air:
how delicious it was to inhale, after breathing the
fœtid, musky atmosphere of the snake den!

Dante's Hell struck me as a weak, wishy-washy,
gruelly conception alongside of this horrible, grim
reality.

I stuck a pin in my leg. Could this be the nineteenth
century? Could this be the Christian land of America?

"Lootinint!" interposed Gordon, the intensely
practical-minded cook, who didn't take no stock in
Injuns nohow—— "Lootinint, shall we fry some
bacon or open that can of mackerel for supper?"

Yes, I was in the nineteenth century.

For a few moments I remained standing upon the
roof of the Estufa drinking in the pure air of heaven.

In front of me the warm, bright sun, and directly above my head, attached to the topmost part of the ladder, a "medicine-bow," gaily trimmed with bright red horse-hair and other trappings.

All of our party hurried to the house, where we were to partake of lunch—Gordon, the cook, called every meal except breakfast "supper"—and ate heartily and hastily, not knowing whether or not we should find time to take any further refreshment during the day.

After lunch I went down into the Estufa of the Conejos or Rabbit gens; there was nothing in it but stone seats or stools, which were blocks of flat rock used by squaws while weaving blankets. I left this and entered a fourth Estufa, where also there was no furniture other than the stone seats above mentioned. Next to the wall was a blanket-frame, upon which stretched, half woven, a pretty blanket, such as the young women wear, with the diamond and diagonal ribbing peculiar to the work of the Zunis and Moquis.

In this Estufa was a small earthen jug, unpainted, without cover or handle, and an old stone axe.

One of the Moquis explained as well as he could that in the Estufas they frequently offer up invocations to Omá-a, the Cloud Chief or Rain God. From him is received water to refresh the parched crops.

In each Estufa may be seen a small niche, sometimes in one of the walls, sometimes in the floor, in which offerings of corn, tobacco, pumpkin seeds, and sacrificial plumes are deposited for this deity upon occasions of ceremony.

K

Dr. Sullivan learned that in the dance of this day over fifty persons were to participate. He classified them as eight chiefs or medicine men, twelve watchers, sixteen dancers, and eighteen neophyte cochinos or singing men.

Our party united and strolled over to Tegua or Hano, a quarter of a mile from our house. We descended into one of the two Estufas of that village. There were the usual cubical stone stools and a blanket, nearly finished, on a frame. The Moquis evidently did a great deal of their weaving in these underground apartments.

There was an unpainted drum, of a cottonwood log, hollowed out and faced with sheepskin, and a stone mortar and pestle for grinding the paints needed for the decoration of dancers in the various festivals.

In this Estufa the niche or " door of Omá-a " was not in the floor as is generally the case in the Moqui villages proper. The difference is hardly worthy of note, but it should not be forgotten that the Teguas are not of the same blood as the Moquis, but belong to the same tribe as the people of San Juan and San Ildefonso on the Rio Grande.

A niche in the wall of this Estufa answered the necessary purpose, and was well filled with poorly-made images of unburnt clay and other pledges of the devotion of the Tegua worshippers.[1]

---

[1] Unburnt images, identical with these, have been dug up from ruins in the neighbourhood of Prescott, Arizona, 175 miles south-west of the Moqui villages.

On the west wall was a well-executed symbol of
the sun, occupying a space not less than two feet
each way.[1]

The second Estufa of the Pueblo of Tegua is a
counterpart of the first, and provided like it with stone
seats and a half-woven blanket. Here we found three
cylindrical masks of buckskin, painted green. Around
the eyeholes were heavy circles in yellow; the noses in
two cases were made of black wooden pegs, and in the
third was shaped thus, T.

Each mask was provided with a necklace of corn-
shucks and cedar leaves, perfectly concealing the
identity of the wearer.

In Tegua I bought several flat wooden gods or
doll-babies. They are both. After doing duty as a
god, the wooden image, upon giving signs of wear and
tear, is handed over to the children to complete the
work of destruction. These gods are nothing but
coarse monstrosities, painted in high colours, generally
green.

All of our party obtained an assortment of native
pottery at low rates. Mr. Williams bought and gave
me a small wooden image, which I recognised as
Phallic in character.[2]

Returning to Suchongnewy, we were told that the
champion runner in the race of the morning was
named Honáni, the Badger, a member of the Nube or

[1] See Plate XXVI.

[2] It was a rude carving, representing one of the participants in the
Phallic dance, which I have since seen four times among the Zunis.

Cloud gens, and the son of a member of the Tejon or Badger (Honani).

Dr. Sullivan called this gens the Gopher, but the Spanish word used by the Moquis was Tejon or Badger.

We went down into the Estufa of the Quingoi or Oak gens. On its west wall were delineated two pictures of the antelope, one two feet square, and the other nearly twice that size. The artist had essayed his task with freedom and boldness, and in the execution of the larger had departed somewhat from the conventional outline tracing of the native races, and had made a representation of the animal's hindquarters.

On this wall was also another one of the rain or cloud prayers.[1]

Under these figures were a number of English letters and one or two numerals, which, with scores of small and apparently meaningless scratchings, were beyond question the idle work of some boy, who had been taught to make or half make our letters and numbers.

One of these scratchings would indicate that the Moqui children possessed the game of "Fox and Geese." Not only in the Estufa now visited, but in various places in the three Pueblos on this mesa, could be seen on suitable slabs of sandstone the game of our school-days.

[1] See Plates XXV. and XXVI.

The last Estufa, that of the Maiz or Corn gens, was in very bad condition, and not deserving of note.

Tochi, whom I had hired as guide to make the rounds, told me, in his broken Spanish, that when the water (rain) did not come from the sky, the Moquis came into this Estufa and " danced for it "; that here also came the young men to be "bautista por cochinos " (baptized for medicine men).

The idea that the ceremony of baptism, or any mode of illustration to which that designation could be applied, was in existence among the Moquis, surprised me much.

I made Tochi repeat all he had said, and then asked for an explanation. He said that after all the big dances, as, for example, after that of to-day, the young men who were to learn all the secrets would come to one of the Estufas and there have their " cabezas lionpiados con agua " (heads washed with water) by the old men. As he said this he made the motion of pouring a few drops of water upon the head of some one kneeling beneath him.

The whole description was so graphic and earnest that it at last satisfied me of the existence in some of the ceremonies of this people of a lustration by water ; but to what extent this lustration partakes of the nature of the sacrament of baptism it was impossible for me to conjecture, and impossible for Tochi, with his attenuated stock of Spanish, to make known.

Granting that such a thing is practised, it is quite likely to be a reminiscence of the teachings of the early

missionaries.   Indians are as imitative as monkeys, and
could hardly neglect to adopt a parody upon a rite
of whose mysterious significance they must have
heard so much from the first European invaders.[1]

Any notes or memoranda made upon the Pueblo
of Zuni will apply in almost every respect to these
three villages of the Moquis, with the limitation that
the Moqui Pueblos are much more primitive and
much more filthy than the Zuni.

The Moquis make great numbers of coverlets of
mixed wool and fur,—loosely stranded woollen framework with long strips of coyote and rabbit fur fastened
in,—which are made to serve as mattresses, blankets,
and curtains for the doors in cold, windy weather.

Their houses have very few doors, and very few
windows.

Feathers, paints, beads, necklaces, and other precious
articles are kept in the odd-looking, cylindrical home-
made wooden boxes to be seen in all the other Pueblos.

Moqui men show great skill in the art of *knitting*.
While the women do all or most of the weaving of
blankets, petticoats, girdles, and sashes, the men, as
do those of the Navajoes likewise, reserve to themselves the task of knitting the blue woollen leggings
worn by both sexes.

In one of the houses we saw a cast in buckskin of
Rocky Mountain sheep-horns, called Pángawa.   Tochi

---

[1] Bancroft, H. H., speaks of " Holy Water " as used by the Aztecs
(vol. ii. p. 611) ; and of "Baptism," as understood by them (vol. ii.
p. 670).   Other allusions to such a ceremony are to be found on pp.
272 and 274 of same volume.

claims that this animal was formerly very abundant close by the Pueblos ; now it has become very scarce. In the same room with this cast was a false head of black sheep-skin, untanned, and with wool still on; the face was of buckskin, painted red, with round holes for eyes and mouth,—altogether a very good piece of work.

There were also large wooden tablets, painted with a green ground, ornamented with the rain prayer, and some one of the countless Moqui gods.

The little bird in the clouds suggests the Thunder Bird of the Plains Indians.

The Moquis build stone houses for their dogs and chickens ; and each family also has within its rooms bins made of sandstone slabs, in which corn is stored in quantities. Besides these bins, large rooms are used as granaries, in which are stored enough of the cereals to last the family for two years.

This precaution proves that in former days famine was the dreaded enemy of this people.

Before being stored, the corn in the ear is thoroughly dried by long exposure to sun and wind, and is then either piled up like cord-wood with us, or hung in strings to the rafters, as our farmers suspend onions.

The Moqui women own the houses, crops, sheep, and orchards—all that pertains to the comfort of the family. The men own the horses and donkeys.

When a man marries (the Moquis are monogamists), he goes to the house owned by his wife ; the act of marriage does not sever his connection with his own clan, but his children follow their mother's clan.   It may, perhaps, interest ladies to know that the women possess and exercise the right of choosing their own husbands, and seem also—although this was a point I did not care to determine—to have the reciprocal privilege of divorcing themselves if the husband does not suit.   Property owned by the wife descends, upon her death, to her daughters.

Marriage must be exogamous, as concerns the gens; that is, a man and woman belonging to the same gens or clan cannot enter into the marital relation. A Badger man cannot marry a Badger woman, but must mate with one from a different gens.

The reason of this is that as all the members of each gens descend from a common maternal ancestor; in the Moqui construction of the term, they are brothers and sisters.

When both parents die, the children, if any, are cared for by the *mother's* gens.

All construction and repair of dwellings is the business of the women; when anything of that kind is to be done, the woman most concerned will summon half a dozen of her gossips, who are nearly always of her own clan, and with their assistance will do the work of puddling mud and laying the courses of masonry and adobes; but the husband must bring the timbers for the support of the earth roof, and in Oraybe-Sumopowy, Mushangnewy, Supowolewy, and Acoma, I have seen them bring the necessary rock for the walls.

CHAPTER XIII.

Snake herding—A dangerous occupation—Devout demeanour of the natives—Marine shells as sacred ornaments—Small-pox and the Moquis—An unpleasant neighbour.

TOCHI came up while I was making these inquiries, and told me excitedly that I must hurry over to the Estufa of the Eagle gens. I lost no time in following his advice, and descending into the Estufa.

Here I saw that the " altar " had been dismantled, the railing thrown down, and the snakes set at greater liberty. They were still on one side of the chamber, but no longer confined with much strictness.

They sinuously writhed along the foot of the wall, slimily crawling along the floor, and climbing up along the rough surface of the adobes and rocks until their tails alone seemed to rest upon the ground, and then falling down again upon the fœtid, stinking mass of their comrades. The lazier coiled and knotted themselves in venomous clusters, suggesting the head of Medusa ; those that were more ambitious, or more energetic, would languidly thrust out their flattened heads and peer at us with leaden, lack-lustre eyes, in which scintillated a faint glitter that a moment's excitement would fan into flame.

The air was heavy with a stench like that of a rotten cesspool: only a stern sense of responsibility kept me at my post. Moran remained with me for some time, sketching as fast as time, bad light, and foul air would permit; the other members of our party came down and departed at once; some of them could not stand it at all.

Before the altar the Indians had now placed an earthenware bowl or basin, covered with a white cotton cloth. I lifted the cloth, and found the basin or platter to be one of the ordinary red ware; it was filled with water, and contained three large sea-shells. The water had a slightly saline taste, and evidently contained " medicine."

The shells, which I call marine, were such as I have seen on the seashore, but not knowing anything whatever of conchology, I dare not be positive in the assertion.

The hurried drawings of two of them[1] may serve to indicate the type to which they belong.

How many men and boys were in the Estufa at the time of this visit I do not remember. I think there were twenty or twenty-one, all naked, with the exception of the breech-clout. The younger members were hard at work painting their bodies and preparing their paraphernalia. There were two very old men, one on each side of the Estufa, who reclined at full length upon the floor, and, to all intents and purposes, were *herding* the reptiles. They lay in the

[1] See Plate XXI.

postures of men drunk, or under the influence of narcotics, indifferent to all that transpired about them, but not by any means asleep, as would be shown every now and then when some venturesome serpent would start to wriggle itself on a voyage of discovery across to the other wall. Then the old men were alert enough, and would quickly raise themselves to upright positions, and gently brush the fugitives with the eagle wands. [1]

This mode of assault had a discouraging influence upon all the snakes ; generally they turned tail at once, and made their way back to the slimy, sickening mass of their less energetic associates.

As nearly as I could make out the drift of Tochi's remarks upon this subject, the Moquis believe that snakes have an instinctive dread of their powerful and unrelenting foe the eagle, whose mode of attack is to tap the serpent gently with one of his wings, and exasperate it into making a spring. When the snake has lunged out with all its force and struck nothing but feathers, its strength is gone, and it lies uncoiled upon the ground. From this position it cannot recover before the king of the air has seized it in his talons, and soared away with it to his eyrie upon some distant mountain peak.

Tochi thought, and perhaps rightly, that the snakes recognised the eagle feathers, and showed their fear by their attempts to avoid them. With a very few exceptions, they turned and fled the instant the wand was rubbed against them.

[1] See Plate XXII.

Only once or twice did the old men have to resort
to extreme measures. There were several very stubborn reptiles, which persisted in gliding beyond the
limits assigned them, and, paying no attention to the
raps of the wand, advanced almost to the centre of
the floor.

These refractory individuals were seized just
behind the head, and redeposited firmly but very
gently in the middle of the pile, the old men always
behaving much like a devoted but determined mother
managing a rebellious child.

Let it not be imagined that these snakes were
harmless, that their fangs had been extracted, or that
they themselves were under the influence of some
drug ; we were all convinced that they had been
subject to no treatment whatever. The bulk of the
pile seemed to be composed of rattlesnakes, and while
they made no assault upon any one near them, their
noxious character was made visible by the care exer-
cised by their guardians to prevent them from getting
beyond their control.

The most rigorous silence was imposed, no one
being allowed to speak except upon affairs of urgency,
and then only in subdued monosyllables.

Whenever one of the occupants of the Estufa
happened to want anything he would point to it, and
the person nearest would hand it to him.

Although the people there at my arrival, or who
came in afterwards, were industriously arranging such
clothing and decorations as they were to use in the

procession, or were actively painting their own bodies
or those of their friends, there was none of the uproar
inseparable from a group of the same size among us;
no whistling, no coughing, no hawking, no spitting
with loud noise, no shuffling of feet, no giggling, and
no sibilant whispering.   Gravity and sedateness
marked every countenance, and communicated themselves even to the two white visitors.   Moran showed
himself to be impressed with the idea that we were
in presence of one of the most curious religious phases
of the Moqui character; as long as he could manage
to endure the noisome hole his pencil flew over the
paper, obtaining material which will one day be serviceable in placing upon canvas the scenes of this
wonderful drama.

The young men manifested no fears of the reptiles;
at least, not so long as they remained *uncoiled*.
Several youths came down the ladder during the hours
of my stay; one with a bag slung across his shoulders
containing a select half-dozen; and two others, one of
whom has already been noticed, carrying in their
hands fat, burly, wriggling monsters, the very sight
of which sent a chill through me.   I have always had
an antipathy to snakes, and cannot say that my repug-
nance was in the least overcome by an enforced proximity to such numbers of them this day.   As a nerve-
training this closeness may have had its advantages,
but it has not in my own case brought about a change
of feeling towards them.

The mode of carrying the snakes was uniform.

They were held firmly with the left hand, just behind the head, with the thumb extended forward and
upward to prevent the snake from turning its head ;
the right hand, meanwhile, was kept travelling with
an easy, caressing, downward stroke from near the
head to near the tail. This served the double purpose
of soothing the reptile and of hindering it from coiling.
Once coiled round the arm or neck of its holder the
snake would be in a position to do mischief, and might
become unmanageable.

It has been said that the young men were not
afraid of the uncoiled reptiles. The expression is
hardly strong enough, as they took every occasion to
show their power over mankind's first enemy in the
brute creation so long as the snakes were uncoiled ;
but the very instant that one of the stubborn reptiles
began to make ready for battle and to rapidly involve
itself in folds, the old men were appealed to to take
the rebel in hand.

These old men, from the respect they inspired,
must have been of great consequence among their
people. Each wore upon his wrist a string of the little
olivette shells, which are never to be seen upon the
person of an ordinary warrior ; indeed, I have never
detected them upon the wrist of any Moqui or Zuni
who was not invested with some trust or dignity of
great importance in the eyes of his tribe.

Presuming upon a little service just rendered me
—a little service which I appreciated highly, since it
was no less a one than picking up a snake which,

while I was standing absorbed in the writing of my notes, had stealthily shot out from a dim recess in the wall, and had projected its flat, arrow-shaped head to a point midway between my No. 11 brogans, whose exquisite symmetry it was admiring—presuming upon this service, I sat down by one of the old men and tapped the string of olivette shells on his wrist. He whispered quietly in Spanish, first touching the shells and then indicating a great distance in the west by pointing his right index finger and waving his hand in that direction, "muy lejos, muncha agua" (very far, heap water), an explanation which I took to signify that these shells had been brought from a great distance, *from the sea.*

In this interpretation I may not be sustained by the facts. The olivette may not be a marine shell; it may be a fluvial, or it may be both; but be that as it may, I cannot dispel from my mind a conviction that the Moquis betray, in the shells, salt-water, sand, abalones, and other features of this dance, a derivation from a people who once knew, and perhaps worshipped, the ocean.

The point may not be well taken; nothing is claimed for it beyond the humble merit of being no more absurd or stupid than the great percentage of the hypotheses advanced in North American ethnology, and the further claim that, until refuted, it is entitled to consideration, however slight, in future investigations into the history of this people and their congeners, the other Pueblos.

It can be seen that by rising so early we had secured the inestimable benefit of a very long day. We had gulped down a hasty breakfast at four in the morning, and had begun our pilgrimage about the town before the sun had peeped above the eastern hills. The compact situation of the three towns, our own familiarity with much that was to be seen (nearly every one of our party had been here on previous occasions, and my own acquaintance with the Moquis dated back to 1874, when I had first come among them with General George Crook), and, finally, our numbers, which gave me so many more eyes with which to see and hands with which to take notes.

Not an instant of the whole day had yet been lost; every moment had told its own story, and by eight o'clock, when Gordon had summoned us to a second breakfast, much valuable information had been gathered.

I had been not less than three hours in the Estufa, and was glad of an excuse for breathing fresh air, and anxious to fill my stomach with warm food, hoping that this course might avert the deleterious effects of exposure.

We enjoyed our meal hugely, although each was anxious to get back to the particular point which interested him most.

In company with Moran, Webber, and Williams, I made an examination of ten or twelve houses, buying pottery, doll-babies, toys, baskets, beautiful girdles, mortars, mullers, and pestles of stone. Few of the buildings on this mesa are more than two stories high; and in most cases the ground-floors are untenanted.

We entered a number of apartments whose occupants were eating a noonday meal. We were always invited to share their hospitalities, and should have done so had we not just arisen from our own lunch. A favourite dish to be seen in all families was boiled green peaches.

A considerable number of the older men and women bore traces of the smallpox. The story was given me that the name Moqui now borne by this tribe is a contraction for a whole phrase meaning the "dead people," and bestowed upon them by adjacent tribes in allusion to a former epidemic of this loathsome disease which almost extirpated the seven Pueblos.

Such a story, if true, must refer to some date beyond our history of the Moquis, who were, I am certain, styled by this name in the earliest Spanish chronicles.

The whole morning had been extremely sultry ; the burning rays of the sun beat down upon the unprotected surface of the mesa with not a breath of air stirring to temper their ferocity. A cooling shower broke upon us shortly after noon, settling the dust, taking the furnace-like heat out of the air, and gently reviving our exhausted strength. Moran and I took refuge in a little arcade between the sacred rock and the Estufa of the Eagle gens, and there he rapidly worked in the details of sketches taken since sunrise,

L

while I jotted down the notes and memoranda which could not be left to a later moment.

Our actions attracted the notice of two or three dozens of little brats, who congregated about us, naked, dirty, and curious, but perfectly respectful. The notes finished, I returned to the Estufa of the Eagle gens.

Both old and young men were now there in crowds, making haste to complete their toilets, carefully rubbing their long black locks with brushes of hay, and chewing a "medicine," a piece of which I quietly picked up and slipped into my pocket.[1]

Each man while in the Estufa wore a breech-clout and nothing else, not even moccasins.

Their bodies and legs were first coated with a mixture of red and white paints (ochre and kaolin respectively) moistened with saliva, and laid on with the palms of the hands. After this had dried a second coat was daubed on of a greenish-black substance, which, after a time, I ascertained was green corn buried in a damp place and allowed to rot. This was mixed with a small quantity of the salty liquid contained in the large flat bowl in front of the altar holding the sea-shells,[2] of which liquid all present seemed to be drinking freely.

---

[1] To the best of my knowledge it was an almost pure clay, creamy-white in colour and even in texture. If I may be permitted to anticipate a little, it was not chewed as an antidote for snake-poisoning, but rather to fill the mouth and the angles of the teeth, so that when snakes were to be grasped between them the danger of hurting and irritating the reptiles would be reduced to a minimum.

[2] See Plate XXI.

While I was writing the above, one of the young men was leaning against me looking over my shoulder at the, to him, mysterious characters so rapidly taking their places on the pages. Turning round, I saw to my horror and amazement that he was holding in his hand the biggest snake in the whole collection, a rattler not less than five feet long.

The assurance that no harm would come to me down among those Indians so long as I remained perfectly quiet and did just as they did was strongly fixed in my mind, but hardly strong enough to keep me from running up the ladder in a panic. However, I managed to hold my ground ; and if the Indian had counted upon scaring me, my countenance did not betray how completely he had succeeded.

The old custodians were still in their supine postures, and here may be mentioned Moran's remark that he was almost certain that they were under the influence of narcotics. An examination of the pupils of their eyes was not of course practicable, and though they sometimes looked at me when I was near, the general dimness of the place kept me from scrutinising their features very carefully. 1 will record my impression that they behaved very much like drunken men, without having any fetor of breath or other peculiarity which might trace the stimulant employed.

They now began to put the snakes in cotton and buckskin bags, handling the reptiles with perfect impunity.

I was reminded of the little I had read of East

Indian and African snake-charming. All the men present (there were no women and no children) were very rash in their behaviour, that is, judging it from my standpoint. They lifted the reptiles singly and in pairs, stepped among, around, and even *upon* them with their naked feet.

My astonishment must have made itself manifest in my countenance, and had the effect of inciting the old men to show me what *they* could do. They gathered the snakes up in double handfuls, and, after a while, even carried them suspended from between their teeth, a ghastly thing to look upon!

CHAPTER XIV.

The ceremonies begin—Taking up good places—Stone worship—
The views from the house-top—A legend of a famine.

THE treatment accorded me during the whole of my
visits to the Estufa had been most courteous, much
more so than I had any right to expect under the
circumstances. Early in the morning, and late the
night before, when I first entered, it is true that some
of the Indians then there evinced a desire to have
me leave, and made signs that my room would be
more agreeable than my company ; but, feeling how
important it was that a series of notes should be prepared on the spot, I quietly ignored all hints, and
when addressed by the more aggressive, fell into the
error of supposing that they wanted to shake hands,
and bestowed upon them a " pump-handling " vigorous
enough to have secured my election had I been running for Congress.

Tochi, early in the forenoon, had asked if I was
from Washington, and had the great father sent me;
questions which I thought prudent to answer boldly in
the affirmative. The dissemination of this answer among
the men in the Estufa may have helped me a little, but
our numbers, and the deference paid by the soldiers,

impressed them with the belief that I was a personage of considerable consequence in my own country.

Gordon and Smallwood took in the situation; they not only approached me at all times with an air of the most profound respect, and saluted me with a punctiliousness which would have made a martinet's heart leap for joy, but they made it their business to explain to everybody that I was a "mungwee" of the highest rank, and a "soldier-captain," and "heap big chief," whom it would be well for the Moquis to propitiate.

The way had been further prepared for me by Mr. Frank Cushing of the Smithsonian Institution, who had come here in the spring to obtain a guide to take him to the country of the Cohoninos, in the Grand Cañon of the Colorado.

Mr. Cushing, knowing that I purposed making this trip, and feeling sensible of the importance of removing all obstacles from my path, had alluded to my coming, and recommended me in the strongest terms as one of the great father's officers.

The stench had now become positively loathsome; the pungent effluvia emanating from the reptiles, and now probably more completely diffused throughout the Estufa by handling and carrying them about, were added to somewhat by the rotten smell of the paint, compounded, as we remember, of fermented corn in the milk, mixed with saliva! I felt sick to death, and great drops of perspiration were rolling down forehead and cheeks, but I had come to stay, and was resolved that nothing should drive me away.

Mr. Tom Keam arrived from his ranch in the afternoon. He had not started with our party, being detained by business engagements.

However, he got in just in the nick of time, and descended for a brief moment into the Estufa of the Eagle gens after the final preparations had been completed and all were ready to sally out.

Mr. Taylor, brother of the missionary, and the cheery-looking old lady, his wife, also reached the mesa a short time before the procession moved.

One of the old men laid his hands upon my shoulder, and by a combination of gestures and words, the latter in broken Spanish, broken English, Moqui, and Navajo, informed Keam, Moran, and myself, that the paint the dancers were applying to their bodies would ruin our clothes; that everything was now ready for the dance to begin in the open air; that the snakes (which they had begun to carry out shortly before Keam's arrival) had been taken to the Estufa of the Rabbit gens, there to remain for a brief space; and that if we wanted to get good seats, we ought to take them at once, on the first roofs beyond the sacred rock, whence we could command a view of the procession from the instant it began to emerge from the arcade.

The streets were lively with the tramp of feet and the hum of voices; men, women, and young girls were dressed in their best, and the children were putting in practice the principle that beauty un-adorned is adorned the most.

The men had arranged their hair with scrupulous

neatness, cutting it off square at the level of the eye-brows in front, and of mouth at the sides, and gathering it up in rear in a queue which, was tightly wound with red yarn.

The mode followed by the unmarried women can best be understood by consulting Plate XVI.

Matrons banged their hair about the level of the eyebrows and parted it on top, at right or left hand, according to individual fancy; it was cut square at level of chin, and clubbed at back of neck much after the manner of the men.

A prolonged barking of dogs, and the cries of children, gave warning of the approach of a bold coyote, which had crept up to the very foot of the mesa, hoping to lay in a supply of good, fat Moqui lamb chops before being discovered.

A brisk fusilade of bullets, no less than the howls and yells of the Moquis, admonished the daring marauder that he had been a trifle rash, and that the best thing to do would be to scamper away across the plain, which he did, making an excellent record for speed.

Our party took up our station on the second story of a house near the sacred rock, about ten yards from a lodge erected of cottonwood saplings and a buffalo robe (the only buffalo robe, by the way, to be seen in the three villages), and about same distance in another direction from the brink of the precipice.[1]

The space below us and between the houses and

1 See Plates I. and II.

the vertical face of the sandstone cliff upon which
they were built was an irregular rectangle fifty yards
in length and twenty yards in breadth, although at the
lower or eastern end some buildings intruded upon
the space and broke the width down to ten yards.

In this rectangle or " plaza" was the "sacred
rock," and near this a cottonwood sapling thrust in
the ground ; between the two was a lodge, shaped like
the tépis of the Plains tribes (but not more than one-
half so large as those used by them in our day), and
made of a buffalo robe, wrapped with the hairy side
in, around a framework of cottonwood saplings in full
foliage.[1]

Whether this sacred rock, with its niche and idol
and attendant offerings, may be looked upon as a survival of " stone-worship,"[2] this cottonwood sapling,
placed in a position of honour, as a corresponding reminiscence of tree adoration, and the buffalo lodge,
upon its sapling framework, as a reminder of a period

[1] See Plate XVII.

[2] Stone-worship in a perfectly well-defined form prevails among
all the Indians of the south-west. Perhaps the best emphasised instance is that of the Hualpais of Northern Arizona, who live just west
of the Moquis. The " medicine men " of this tribe are in the habit of
going out to pray and sing close to certain sacred rocks, against which
they rub themselves with the happy effect of reinvigorating exhausted
necromantic powers.

The Apaches, upon approaching certain localities, will pause by
the heaps of small stones, known in the language of the frontiersman
as " Apache Post-Offices," and add a pebble and a handful of grass to
the accumulation. So, too, will the Zunis, who have such heaps, stop
and pray by them. Curiously enough, these stone-heaps, associated
with the worship of ancestors, as is best to be understood from the

in the dim past when the Moquis were tent-dwellers
and nomads, are questions for ethnologists to discuss.

Six or seven hundred feet below us, at the foot of
the mesa (Hualpi has an altitude of 6730 feet),
stretched a broad plain, bounded on the distant
horizon of the south-east and east by a long, low
broken line of bluish buttes, in all the fantastic forms
of towers, buttresses, and pinnacles which Nature
loves to carve out of the hills of this strange country.

This plain, which to the eye is apparently a broad
expanse of barren sand and rock, is in dozens of sheltered nooks dotted with the tiny fields of the Moquis,
vividly green with ripening corn and wheat, or decked
in darker hues with the foliage of peach orchards.

From half a dozen ravines springs discharge petty
streams of water, and the clayey subsoil retaining a
large percentage of this and of all other moisture fall-

Apaches, survive among the Mexicans of the Rio Grande, as the Des-
cansos or Rests, alongside which funeral processions halt on the way
to the grave.

Dozens of these little mounds of stone, each surmounted by a
plain wooden cross, line the roads leading out from Santa Fé.

" In Guatemala small chapels were placed at short intervals on all
the lines of travel, where each passer halted for a few moments at
least, gathered a handful of herbs, spat reverently upon them, placed
them prayerfully upon the altar with a small stone and some trifling
offering of pepper, salt, or cacao."—Bancroft, H. H., vol. ii. p. 738.
And Squiers (*Nicaragua*, ii. p. 358) notes that by the Indians of that
country sticks or grass were thrown upon certain stones at the road-
side, by which they thought they would be less subjected to hunger
and fatigue.

Tree-worship survives among the Dacotahs, in whose Sun-Dance it
plays an important part.

ing during the winter or in the rainy season, gives life
to the growing crops without irrigation.

Wherever it is possible to build a dam of stone and
clay, there is a reservoir of water, and close to it a
corral for sheep and goats.

On the flat rocks, closer to the foot of the mesa,
are often spread traps for luring and killing doves, or
small cleared spaces upon which bushels of luscious
peaches are drying in the sun.

Not a sign of animation breaks the placidity of the
scene, since yonder sedate donkey, trudging solemnly
down to the springs for a drink, that great herd of
goats and sheep browsing in the middle distance, or
this half-dozen old women toiling so slowly up the
almost vertical face of the precipice with five gallon
ollas of water wrapped in their old and faded blue
blankets, can scarcely be called animate.

They have rather the appearance of vague, dim,
hazy recollections, dreams of things which have been
alive, than of things which are.

Immediately under my feet, at the eastern line of
the rectangle, is Moran sketching, his every movement watched by a coterie of four naked boys, three
mongrel pups, two full-grown Navajoes, and six
Moquis, who form his admiring clientelage.

Here you have the projecting beams of the ladder
leading down into one of the Estufas; close to this
the sacred rock, with its niche containing the sandstone torso idol and the largess of petrified wood,
eagle-down, and corn-shucks.

On this side of the sacred rock the cottonwood lodge and the sacred tree, and right back of these you can place a medieval jumble of masonry, for all the world like the half-ruined castle of a Rhine robber-baron of six centuries ago.

Fill every nook and cranny of this mass of buildings with a congregation of Moqui women, maids and matrons, dressed in their graceful garb of dark-blue cloth with lemon stitching; tie up the young girls' hair in big Chinese Puffs at the sides; throw in a liberal allowance of children, naked and half-naked; give colour and tone by using blankets of scarlet and blue and black, girdles of red and green, and necklaces of silver and coral, abalone, and chalchi-huitl.

For variety's sake add a half-dozen tall, lithe, square-shouldered Navajoes, and as many keen, dyspeptic-looking Americans, one of these a lady; localise the scene by the introduction of ladders, earthenware chimneys, piles of cedar-fuel and sheep manure, scores of mangy pups, and other scores of old squaws carrying on their backs little babies or great ollas of water, and with a hazy atmosphere and a partially-clouded sky as accessories, you have a faithful picture of the square in the Pueblo of Hualpi, Arizona, as it appeared on this eventful 12th day of August 1881.

The aggregate of spectators could not have been 1000; 750, in all likelihood, would be closer to the true figure, and in this must be included the small number of Navajoes and Americans and representatives of other Pueblos.

Oraybe, the largest of the Moqui Pueblos, sent only two delegates, a paucity of numbers to be attributed either to the bad feeling existing between that village and those on the easternmost mesa, or, more probably, to lack of interest in the celebration.

The Oraybes, as I have since learned, have a very elaborate snake drama or dance of their own, and do not feel the same curiosity as do the Navajoes, among whom this rite is not known to exist.

Tochi, who sat by my side while we patiently awaited the coming of the procession, remarked that the Teguas came to this mesa from the Rio Grande at the time the Mejicanos came to the country. They came "so that all could be friends and fight together."

"Once there was a big famine in this region and much suffering ensued. The Moquis were the only Indians who had anything to eat : their reserve supplies were not exhausted. The Pi-Utes came down here because they were all nearly dead, their women and children starving. The Moquis helped them, gave them meat and corn, and they lived here for two winters, over near those springs (on the north side of the mesa)."

When this happened was more than Tochi could say ; "it was a long while ago."

CHAPTER XV.

A WHIRRING sound resembling that of rain, driven by summer gusts, issued from the arcade ; with this came the clanking of rattles and gourds filled with corn. The dancers were moving down towards us.

First came a barefooted old man, crowned with a garland of cottonwood leaves, holding in his hands in front of him a flat earthen bowl, from which he sprinkled water upon the ground, very much as a Catholic priest would asperse his congregation.[1]

The second old man carried a flat basket of fine corn-meal.

The third held his left hand up to a necklace of bears' claws, while with his right he gently rattled an instrument shaped thus, T, painted white.[2]

The next five men were armed with the same odd-looking rattles, but as they marched close behind one another in single file they were not considered as holding the same rank or as discharging functions of an

[1] See Plate XII. [2] See Plate XXII.

importance equal to those of the old men who advanced alone.

Numbers 9 to 17 inclusive were little boys, from four to seven years old, marching in single file, each bearing one of the T shaped rattles.

An interval of five paces separated them from the grown men who had preceded them, and a like distance intervened between them and an old man who bore aloft in his left hand a bow (one of those so gayly ornamented with feathers and horse-hair which had been noticed upon the upper end of the Estufa ladders).

With his right hand this old man rapidly twirled a wooden sling, which emitted the shrill rumble of falling rain so plainly heard as the head of the procession was emerging from the arcade.[1]

This was the first division of the dance.

The second and last was composed of forty-eight persons, two of them children, and all males ; each bore wands of eagle feathers in both hands. The last man of this division bore a bow, the counterpart of that carried by the sling-twirler of the first division.

All the dancers wore, tied to the right knee, rattles made of tortoise-shells and sheep or goat toes, which clanked dismally whenever the leg or body moved. Small bunches of red feathers were attached to the crown of the head, their long black hair hung loose down their backs, their faces were blackened from brow to upper lip, while mouth, lower lip, and chin

[1] See Plate II.

looked ghastly by contrast with the kaolin daubed over them. Collars of the white sea-shell beads of their own manufacture hung round their necks, and nearly all wore abalone shells glistening on their breasts. Sashes of sea-shell beads covered their bodies from the right shoulder to the left hip.

Their bodies, legs, and arms were naked and greenish-black, without mark or design. Kilts of painted cotton cloth[1] hung from waist to knee, and dangling down to the heels in rear were skins of the fox and coyote.[2] Red buckskin fringe hung from the waist in most cases; and in others, again, cotton-ball pendants ornamented the girdles. The feet were covered with red buckskin moccasins, fringed at ankles, and broad white armlets encircled the elbows.

Each division marched solemnly around the sacred stone and between it and the sacred lodge and tree, the first division completing this formula shortly before the second.

The first division aligned itself with back to houses, but quite close to them, and with its right abutting against the lodge and tree.

The old "medicine man," or priest, whom for the sake of convenience we have called No. 1, stood in front of and facing the lodge, holding well before him the platter of water and eagle-feather wand.

When the second division had finished its tour it formed in two ranks facing the first division, and not more than four paces from it. When this alignment

[1] See Plate XXII.   [2] See p. 37 note.

was perfected the men and boys of the first division shook their rattles gently, making the music of pattering showers. This movement was accompanied by the men of the second division who waved their eagle-feathers from right to left in accord with the shaking of the rattles.

This was repeated eight or ten times, all singing a refrain, keeping time by stamping vigorously with the right foot : " Oh-ye-haw, oh-ye-haw, ha-yee-ha-ha-yee-ha-ha-yi-ha-a-a-a," chanted a dozen times or more with a slow measure and graceful cadence.

This part of the ceremony over, the old man in front of the cottonwood tree and lodge began to pray in a well-modulated and perfectly distinct voice, and sprinkled the ground in front of him with more water, while the second medicine man scattered corn-meal from the platter he was bearing.

Excepting the water-sprinkler[1] (No. 1) and the sling-twirler (No 8), all the first party wore red plumes in hair, red moccasins, and white cotton kilts ; and their bodies, as already stated, were naked and greenish-black.

The first division remained in place, while the second, two by two, arm in arm, slowly *pranced* around the sacred rock, going through the motions of planting corn to the music of a monotonous dirge chanted by the first division.

A detachment of twenty squaws, maids and matrons, clad in rich white and scarlet mantles[2] of

[1] See Plate XII.　　　　[2] See Plate XVI.

M

cotton and wool, now appeared, provided with flat baskets and platters, from which they scattered corn-meal in every direction.

This ended the first act.[1]

The first division remained aligned upon the sacred rock, the head priest (No. 1) intoning a long and fervent prayer, while the second division quietly filed off, going through the arcade. The interlude was very brief. The second division re-emerged from under the arcade, marching two and two as before; but in this section of the programme the left hand files carried snakes in their hands and mouths. The first five or six held them in their hands with the heads of the reptiles to the right. As the procession pranced closer and closer to where we were seated we saw that the dancers farther to the rear of the column were holding the slimy, wriggling serpents *between their teeth !* The head of the animal in this case also was held towards the right, the object of this being very manifest. The Indians in the right file of the column still retained the eagle wands which their comrades had discarded. With these wands they tickled the heads, necks, and jaws of the snakes, thus distracting their attention from the dancers in whose teeth they were grasped so firmly.

The spectacle was an astonishing one, and one felt at once bewildered and horrified at this long column of weird figures, naked in all excepting the snake-painted cotton kilts and red buckskin moccasins;

[1] See Plates X. and XI.

bodies a dark greenish-brown, relieved only by the broad white armlets and the bright yellowish-gray of the fox skins dangling behind them; long elfin locks brushed straight back from the head, tufted with scarlet parrot or woodpecker feathers; faces painted black, as with a mask of charcoal, from brow to upper lip, where the ghastly white of kaolin began, and continued down over chin and neck; the crowning point being the deadly reptiles borne in mouth and hand, which imparted to the drama the lurid tinge of a nightmare.

With rattles clanking at knees, hands clinched, and elbows bent, the procession pranced slowly around the rectangle, the dancers lifting each knee slowly to the height of the waist, and then planting the foot firmly upon the ground before lifting the other, the snakes all the while writhing and squirming to free themselves from restraint.

When the snake-carriers reached the eastern end of the rectangle they spat the snakes out upon the ground and moved on to the front of the sacred lodge, tree, and rock, where they stamped strongly with the left foot twice, at same time emitting a strange cry, half grunt and half wail.

The women scattering the corn-meal now developed their line more fully, a portion occupying the terrace directly above the arcade, two or three standing on ladders near the archway, the main body massing in the space between the sacred rock and the sacred lodge, and two or three, reinforced by a

squad of devout old crones, doing effective work at
the eastern line of the rectangle.   Nearly all carried
the beautiful, closely-woven, flat baskets, in red,
yellow, and black, ornamented with the butterfly,
thunder bird, or deer.   These baskets were heaped
high with finely-ground corn-flour, which from this
on was scattered with reckless profusion, not, as
previously, upon the ground, but in the air and upon
the reptiles as fast as thrown down.

This corn-meal had a sacred significance, which it
might be well to bear in mind in order to thoroughly
appreciate the religious import of this drama.   Every
time the squaws scattered it their lips could be
detected moving in prayer.

In the religious exercises of the neighbouring
Indians, the Zunis, the air is fairly whitened with the
handfuls of the " Cunque," as they call it, flung upon
the idols, priests, and sacred flute-players.   In all the
Pueblos along the Rio Grande, or near it, the same
farinaceous mixture (since it is generally a mixture of
corn-meal, pounded chalchihuitl, and other ingredients)
is offered as a morning sacrifice to the god of day.
Go into any house in Jemez, Zia, Santana, San Felipe,
Acoma, or Zuni, and you will find in a convenient
niche a small bowl or basket filled with it to allow
each person in the family to throw a small pinch to
the east upon rising in the morning.   The Zunis and
Moquis are never without it, and carry it in little bags
of buckskin tied to their waist-belts.

The use of this sacred meal closely resembles the

crithomancy of the ancient Greeks, but is not identical
with it.   Crithomancy was a divination, by throwing
flour or meal upon sacred animals, or upon their
viscera after they had been sacrificed; the forms or
letters assumed by the meal gave to the soothsayer
the clue to the future of which he was in quest.
While the Greek priest scattered meal upon the sacred
victims, it goes without argument that he prayed,
and up to this point the resemblance is perfect; beyond this it would be rash to say that any parallelism
exists.   The Moquis do not attempt to foretell the
future by this means, or at least if they do, my
researches have been misleading.[1]

After a snake had been properly sprinkled it was
picked up, generally by one of the eagle-wand bearers,
but never by a woman, and carried up to the Indians
of the first division, which, as was remarked, had
preserved its alignment near the sacred lodge.   Most
of the snakes were transferred to the infant grasp of
the little boys who had come in with the first
division.   One five-year old youngster, in the fear-
lessness of infancy, stoutly and bravely upheld the
five-foot monster which, earlier in the day, had so
nearly scared me out of my senses.

This part of the ceremony lasted scarcely a
moment; the serpents were at once taken away from
the boys and handed to the first old man, whom we

---

[1] The Moquis cast corn-meal under the feet of the horses of the
Spaniards who visited them in 1692.   See Davis' *Conquest of New
Mexico*, p. 256.

have learned to regard and designate as the head priest; and by him, with half-audible ejaculations, consigned to the sanctuary of the sacred lodge.

From this the reptiles made no attempt to escape, the hairy coating of the buffalo skin which lined it keeping them from crawling upward or outward. As fast as the members of the second division had dropped the first invoice of snakes they returned with more, repeating precisely the same ceremony following their first entrance, the only discrepancy being that in their subsequent appearances *every* man carried a sinuous, clammy reptile between his teeth; one of the performers, ambitious to excel his fellows, carried two; while another struggled with a huge serpent too large to be pressed between his teeth, which could seize and retain a small fragment of the skin only, the reptile meanwhile flopping lazily, but not more than half-contentedly, in the air.

The devotion of the bystanders was roused to the highest pitch; maidens and matrons redoubled their energy, sprinkling meal not only upon the serpents wriggling at their feet, but throwing handfuls into the faces of the men carrying them. The air was misty with flour, and the space in front of the squaws white as with driven snow.

Again and again the weird procession circled around the sacred rock. Other dancers, determined to surpass the ambitious young men whose achievements have just been chronicled, inserted two snakes in their mouths instead of one, the reptiles in these

cases being, of course, of small size. I must repeat
that no steps had been taken to render these snakes
innocuous either by the extraction of their fangs or by
drugs, and that if they are quiescent while between
the teeth of the dancers, it was as much because their
attention was distracted by the feather-wands plied so
skilfully by the attendants, as from any " medicine "
with which they had been bathed or fed ; that as soon
as they struck the ground, most of them began to
wriggle actively and coil up, to the great consterna-
tion of the spectators in closest proximity, and that
when so moving, the attendants first sprinkled them
with corn-meal and then began to tickle them with
the eagle-wands to make them squirm out at full
length, when they would pounce upon them behind
the head, and carry them, held in this secure manner,
to the little boys who, grasping them in the same
way, seemed to have no apprehensions of danger.

Once or twice snakes of unusual activity had
coiled themselves up in attitudes of hostility, from
which they were driven, not by the ordinary eagle-
wand-bearing attendants, but by older and more dexterous manipulators, whom it is fair to assume were
expert charmers. This impression, or assumption,
will be strengthened by instances to be recorded later
on in the drama.

Two or three serpents struck viciously at all who
approached them ; one quickly wriggled his way in
among the men packed on the outer line of the rectangle, at the crest of the precipice, and another one

darted like lightning into the midst of a group of
women corn-throwers, raising, especially in the
latter case, a fearful hubbub, and creating a stampede,
checked only by the prompt action of the charmers,
who, without delay, secured the rebellious fugitives
and bore them off in triumph, to be deposited in the
buffalo skin sanctuary.   After the snakes had all been
carried in the mouths of dancers, dropped on the
ground, sprinkled with sacred corn-meal, picked up,
held by the small boys, passed to the chief priest, and
by him been prayed over and deposited in the buffalo
lodge or sanctuary, a circle was formed on the ground
in front of the sacred rock by tracing with corn-meal
a periphery of 20 feet diameter.

The snakes were rapidly passed out from the
sanctuary and placed within this circle, where they
were completely covered up with sacred meal, and
allowed to remain, while the chief priest recited in a
low voice a brief prayer.

The Indians of the second division then grasped
them convulsively in great handfuls, and ran with
might and main to the eastern crest of the precipice,
and then darted like frightened hares down the trails
leading to the foot, where they released the reptiles
to the four quarters of the globe.

While they were running away with the snakes,
the first division moved twice around the sacred rock
and buffalo lodge, the old man armed with the sling,
twirling it vigorously, causing it to emit the same
peculiar sound of rain driven by the wind which had

been heard on their approach. In passing in front of the sacred rock the second time each stamped the ground with his right foot.

The whole dance did not occupy more than one-half or three-quarters of an hour. The number of snakes used was more than one hundred ; the dancers ran backwards and forwards so confusedly that it was not possible to determine certainly how many times the whole division had changed snakes, but it must have been not less than four, and more probably as many as five times.

The opinions of the American bystanders varied as to whether or not any of the dancers were bitten. None were so reported by the Indians, and the proper view to take of this matter must be that while all, or nearly all, the snakes used were venomous, the knowledge and prudence of those handling them averted all danger.

Williams and Webber said that while the dancers were gathering up the snakes to convey them from the sanctuary or buffalo lodge to the circle of corn-meal in the last act one man held *ten* and another *seven*.

After freeing the reptiles at the foot of the mesa the men of the second division ran back, breathless and agitated, to their homes.

This was the Snake-Dance of the Moquis, a tribe of people living within our own boundaries, less than seventy miles from the Atlantic and Pacific Railroad in the year of our Lord 1881.

And in this same year, as a clipping from the Omaha *Nebraska Herald* states, the women of the United States subscribed for the diffusion of the Gospel in *foreign* lands, the munificent sum of six hundred thousand dollars.

The snake-dance over, our party rode back to Keam's, in order to obtain needed repairs for our ambulance, and new shoes for our mules; at that point also had been left the bulk of our traps and provisions which we should need in further travel. For a couple of silver dollars we hired three donkeys and three Moqui packers to carry all our bedding and the mule harness from the village of Suchongnewy down to the spring at foot of precipice, near which the ambulance had been allowed to remain. To encourage the Indians, they were promised double pay if they carried our baggage without damage, and led down our mules without injury.

Night was approaching, the sun, a burnished copper ball, was sinking slowly behind the golden outlines of San Francisco Mountain. To save time, we asked to be conducted, if possible, by a shorter route than the comparatively easy ramp by which we had ascended. The Moquis smilingly nodded assent, and bade us follow them down what, to all intents and purposes, was the vertical face of the sandstone bluff. The sure-footed " burros " trotted unconcernedly down paths which were nothing less than steep stone staircases. The ruggedness of this trail would put the bridle-paths of the Andes in the shade.

Breathless, we got to the bottom, with everybody and everything safe and sound; we paid off our packers, and complimented their skill as highly as our limited knowledge of their language would admit.

Our baggage was soon loaded into the vehicle, our mules hitched up, and as the last rays of the sun illumined the western hills we started at a brisk pace for Keam's ranch and the Agency.

Hardly had we gone three miles ere a tempest assailed us, and—after an hour and a half's buffeting with rain, cold, darkness, and mud—we were very fortunately obliged to halt on the crest of the knoll looking down upon the little creek which, in the wet season, flows out of Moqui Cañon.

Far above the roar of the storm and the growls of the thunder could be heard a more sullen growl, a more fearful roar: the dry sandbed—which yesterday, in derision merely, we had called a creek—had gathered to itself the powers of a giant, burst its bounds, and now poured a volume of water, the size of a great river, down the cañon.

We examined our immediate neighbourhood as well as could be done in the dense darkness, and counselled among ourselves upon what should be done. To go forward was simply to rush into the torrent; to go back was perhaps equally hazardous; to remain would do us no harm, as the position occupied seemed to be a hammock a good distance above the rushing water. Our frightened mules were unhitched and tied to the wheels, while the human members of the party

cuddled as best they might inside the shelter of
the ambulance.

The storm increased in vehemence ; the wind blew
in great gusts, and the rain fell in solid sheets ; a few
feet below us the torrent surged and bellowed in impotent fury.   We were beyond its power, and were
sheltered also from the full force of the hurricane by
a promontory directly in front of our position, but on
the other side of the narrow stream-bed.

We were seven in number, packed like sardines,
soaked to the marrow, each man wet, cross, and dispirited, adding to the gloom of his neighbours.   The
storm lulled shortly after midnight, and almost immediately followed a subsidence of the torrent.   Stevens
and Williams, who knew the country well, determined
to try to make their way up the cañon and reach
Keam's, so as to exchange their wet clothes for dry.
The rest of us protested against the folly of this course
as strongly as our intense drowsiness permitted, but
all fell asleep while arguing the question, Moran
drowsily grumbling that if the Moquis had celebrated
the snake-dance in order to bring rain, they had most
certainly accomplished their object.

As soon as the light of a damp cloudy morning
would allow, we resumed our march up the cañon, the
road being very badly "washed," sandy, and heavy.
As nearly as the signs along the banks would enable
us to estimate, the flood rushing down during the
night must have been at least ten feet deep.   Everything from this on seemed to be plain sailing, but

appearances are often deceitful. In crossing the creek, by this time wonderfully shrunken and placid, we got into a quicksand, broke one of our lead-bars, and had one of our wheel mules badly mired. As it so happened, Agent Sullivan, Mr. Whitney, and Mr. Hubbell, who had left the villages a few minutes before our own departure, had been caught by the tempest, and had been benighted only a few yards from where we now were. Seeing our predicament, Whitney and Hubbell—who were on horseback, came over, pointed out the best ford, and helped us out of our trouble.

Webber carried Moran across on his back, and Hubbell gave me a "lift" upon his pony. Agent Sullivan took Webber in his carriage, and although the sogginess of the roads made slow marching necessary, we had not many miles to go, and reached Keam's at nine in the morning pretty well fagged out.

Stevens had had a warm breakfast prepared for us, and with the first swallow of steaming hot coffee our weariness and sense of discomfort disappeared.

CHAPTER XVI.

The Moqui people—Secrecy of the natives—A Moqui legend—Ancestor worship—The origin of the dance—Further explanations —Primitive secret societies.

I MAY be pardoned for arranging in this chapter all that I have been able to learn at any time, without regard to date, concerning the drama just described, whether among the Moquis or adjacent tribes, and such remarks upon the subject of Ophiolatry in general as the meagre facilities at my command have enabled me to gather from various sources of authority.

The Moquis themselves say that everything relating to the dance is kept secret from those not initiated; that those who handle the snakes eat nothing for a day before the dance begins; that they have medicine for the bites; and that after the dance is over, all the performers swallow a potion which induces prompt and effective vomiting.

Certain it is they will not sell, barter, or give away the trappings of this ceremony. None of our party succeeded in obtaining any of the eagle-wands or kilts. The stone implements and pipes obtained were the result of a successful attempt to corrupt the fidelity of an avaricious old man left in charge of the

Estufa of the Butterfly ; but a second proposition to buy a few specimens was received with scorn.   No price would tempt them to dispose of an eagle-wand. " Why !" said one of the old men in the Navajo language to Keam, who had come in just as the Moquis began to take the snakes away from the Estufa, " why ! if I sold them, I'd be sure to have bad luck, my body would swell up and burst, and I'd die !"

At a later visit to the Moquis Pueblos, in September and October 1881, almost the same opinion was expressed by one of the young boys, who affirmed in very fair English and Spanish that all kilts and wands used in the snake - dance were buried in a secret spot.   He declined to tell whether he knew of the place or not ; would accept no money as a bribe ; said that it was not proper that any one outside of the tribe should know of these things, and were he to make disclosures he would expect to become blind, and to have his limbs paralysed.

The members of our party conferred in regard to the dance, and as each had been in the Estufas, and had had the best of opportunities for viewing the procession and all the attendant ceremonies, their conclusions, as men of intelligence, are entitled to respectful consideration.

Without a dissenting voice, it was agreed that the snakes, or the greater percentage of them, were venomous, and that nothing had been done to render them innocuous, saving such charming as they had been subjected to, or such " medicine " as the dancers might have carried to stupefy the reptiles while in their mouths. All concurred likewise in the opinion that the two old men lying listlessly on their backs in the Estufa of the Eagle, and who have been spoken of as custodians of the snakes, were really such, and that they were "herding the snakes," as Webber tersely expressed it.

The next point discussed was whether or not these old men were under the influence of narcotics. Moran was strongly in favour of the affirmative upon this question, and was strongly supported by Stevens. The latter had given a little attention to the study of medicine, and claimed that the two old men manifested all the symptoms of narcotisation, with the exception of dilatation of the pupils, which could not be definitely determined on account of the feeble light in the Estufa.

"Ate" (Louse), a Moqui of the Coyote gens, said that he did not know anything about the "medicine" used in this dance. "Medicine" was used, but only the head men knew what it was, and kept it an inviolable secret. Nahi-vehma (the Peacemaker), an Indian of some intelligence, of mixed Navajo and Moqui parentage, gave the following account of himself, and the following legend regarding the snake-dance :—

He said that he belonged to two gentes or clans ; that of the "Hushpoa" or chapparal cock, and that of the "Quingoi" or Oak. Pressed for an explanation upon this incongruity, he said that his mother being a Navajo, and both father and mother dying when he was very young, his training and maintenance were looked after by the clans or gentes of his grandparents.

As to the sea-shells seen before the altars, he remarked as follows :—" Many years ago the Moquis used to live upon the other side of a high mountain, beyond the San Juan River" (in the extreme S.W. corner of Colorado. This is the same mountain which the Navajoes call Notizan). "The chief of those who lived there thought he would take a trip down the big river to see where it went to. He made himself a boat of a hollow cottonwood log, took some provisions, and started down. The stream carried him to the seashore, where he found those shells. When he arrived on the beach he saw on top of a cliff a number of houses, in which lived many men and women. They had white under their eyes, and below that a white mark." (*Query*—Is this a reference to prehistoric painting and tattooing ?) "That night he took unto himself one of the women as his wife. Shortly after his return to his home the woman gave birth to snakes, and this was the origin of the snake family (gens or clan) which manages this dance. When she gave birth to these snakes they bit a number of the children of the Moquis. The Moquis then moved in a body to their present villages, and they have this dance to conciliate the snakes, so they won't bite their children."

Nahi-vehma spoke in Navajo, and Mr. Keam made the translation.

N

My own suspicion is that one of the minor objects
of the snake-dance has been the perpetuation in
dramatic form of the legend of the origin and growth
of the Moqui family. For example, the salt-water,
sand, and sea-shells seen in the Estufas may have
symbolised their emergence from the ocean (their
landing upon our western coast), while their huddling
together and smoking in company with the crawling
reptiles in all probability conserved the tradition of a
prehistoric life in caves which snakes infested. To
this primitive condition succeeded one slightly improved in some of its features, when they may have
dwelt in lodges made of cottonwood branches, like
those used to this day by their immediate neighbours
the Apaches, or covered with the skins of animals
slain in the chase, as are the tépis of Sioux, Utes,
Paunees, Arapuhoes, Cheyennes, Kiowas, and Comanches of the plains.

Posterior to this came the time when they began
to acquire additional comforts and to enjoy improved
food from their fields of cotton, corn, and vegetables
respectively. These ideas seemed also to be exemplified in the dresses; these surely indicated an archaic
state of life, and the same governing principle of
symbolism attached to the old stone and clay pipes
and implements, none of which are to be found in
common use at the present day. Mortars, mullers,
pestles, "metales" for grinding corn, and flint-pointed
bow-drills, can still be found with frequency among the
various Pueblo tribes; but stone knives, lances, fire-

sticks, axes, hammers, hatchets, and picks have passed from common use, and reappear only in religious ceremonies.

Religion is at all times conservative ; it is never more so than among the savage races, where the functions of the hierophant have not been differentiated from those of the doctor, the sorcerer, the dramatist, and the historian ; and, therefore, in the religious dances of such peoples as the Zunis, Moquis, and Querez, suggestions of their history and previous environment will crop out in features which from any other point of view would be without import.

The fact that the snake-dance reflects in some manner the worship of ancestors has already been indicated, but beyond learning that the willow wands standing around the altars commemorated their dead, nothing was elicited at Hualpi. Investigation may show that instead of devotion to ancestors it is a spirit worship, pure and simple, well pronounced traces of which have been discovered among almost all tribes of American Indians. The Okis of the Canadian Indians, described by the early French missionaries (see the works of Francis Parkman), and the Chidin or Ghosts of the Apache cult, are one and the same thing.

Should it be shown positively, as I think can be done, that snake worship and ancestor or spirit worship are combined in the same rite, we may go a step farther, and with a little more patient work determine whether or not the Moquis have ever believed in the transmigration of souls. The Zunis certainly have so believed, unless some of the stories jotted down while among them were egregious falsehoods.

Finally, the admixture of tree and stone worship has also been indicated.

In November 1881 Nanahe, a Moqui Indian, adopted among the Zunis, gave me the following account of the snake - dance, through Mr. Frank Cushing.

It is necessary to state in advance that Nanahe was an unusually bright Indian, very quiet and well-behaved, and one whose evidence carried more weight than did that of Nahi-vehma, whom we had met at Keam's. He said that he was a member of the Maiz or Corn gens of the Moquis, but also a member of the snake order, to which is entrusted the preparation and care of the dance. By a rule of the Moquis no one not a member of the snake gens can belong to this order, unless it happen that a member of the snake gens dies, in which case his son will be allowed to participate in the drama.

Nanahe said first :—" I know all about you. I was over at the dance, and saw you there (*i.e.* at Hualpi), both during the dance and down in the Estufa before the dance began. You must not ask me to give you any information about that order. I am a member of it. It is a secret order, and under no circumstances can any of its secrets be made known. Very few people, even among the Moquis, know any-

thing about it, and its members would be more careful to keep its affairs from the knowledge of the
Moquis, not members, than they would from you.

" This order was first organised in the Grand Cañon
of the Rattlesnakes, the Grand Cañon of the Cohoninos, the Cañon of the Ava-Supais, and our people
in their migration from that point eastward brought
the secret with them. At first all members of the
order were members of the Rattlesnake gens, but as
time passed the descendants of that clan became too
numerous, and were mixed up with all the other
gentes of our people. To keep the order from getting
too big, no members were taken in unless they were
members of the Rattlesnake gens, or sons of the
members of that gens, as in my case. But if a man
had no other claim than by inheritance, and did not
possess the qualifications demanded of aspirants, he
would surely be rejected ; while I think that a man of
brave heart and good character, willing to comply
with all the rules imposed would be likely to be
admitted without consideration of his father's or his
mother's want of connection with the Rattlesnake gens.
From the Moqui villages the order spread to other
villages ; the headquarters, however, always remained
among the Moquis. If a man was bold and courageous,
and had a stout heart, and led just such a life as the
order told him, and obeyed its orders, he could carry
snakes in his mouth and they couldn't hurt him ; but if
he did not conform his conduct to such requirements, a
bite from one of those snakes would be as fatal to him

as to any one else.   We tell all sorts of stories to outsiders, even in Moqui.

"Of course that is lying, but if we adopted any
other course our secrets wouldn't be kept very long.
You must not get angry at me for speaking thus to
you, but I cannot tell you what you want to know,
and I don't want to deceive you.   I saw you in the
Estufa at the dance; you had no business there;
when you first came down we wished to put you out.
No other man, American or Mexican, has ever seen
that dance as you have.

"We saw you writing down everything as you sat
in the Estufa, and we knew that you had all that
man could learn from his eyes.   We didn't like to have
you down there.   No other man has ever shown so
little regard for what we thought, but we knew that
you had come there under orders, and that you were
only doing what you thought you ought to do to learn
all about our ceremonies.   So we concluded to let
you stay.

"No man—no man"—(with much emphasis) "has
ever seen what you have seen—what you have seen
—and I don't think that any stranger will ever see it
again.   One of our strictest rules is never to shake
hands with a stranger while this business is going on,
but you shook hands with nearly all of us, and you
shook them very hard too.[1]   There never was a man
who took notes of the dance while it was going on
until you did; any one who says he did tells a lie.   I

---

[1] This was true enough.

don't know how many snakes we had in that dance ; it
was more than a hundred.   We get all we can ; all the
venomous ones in that country.   In some dances we
have had as many as five hundred.   There are only
four kinds that we care to use.   These moccasins I now
have on were made at the time of that dance.   All the
clothing a man then wears is new.   The reason you
were allowed to see so much of the dance was because
Cushing had been in there a short time before and
told the Moquis you were coming to write this all
down for the great father, and that he (Cushing)
was coming back with you.   I knew all about you,
and they told me all they had heard from Cushing
about you.   Therefore I knew beforehand."

To show that my disappointment had not made
me angry, I invited Nanahe and the Indian with him,
old Nayuchi, to join Cushing and myself in a cup of
tea : they accepted.   Nayuchi said aside to Cushing
that Nanahe represented a "medicine order ; " that
its secrets were sacred, but that if I laid before him
"a little bundle," not in the way of a bribe, but as a
sort of *honorarium,* or token of friendship, according
to the rules of his order, he might give me some
information about it.

"Yes," said Nanahe, after a moment's reflection,
"that is so ; you being a foreigner, and ignorant of our
language, can do us no harm, and cannot divulge our
secrets to the mean and vicious in our own tribe, or
in other Pueblo tribes, who would scatter them to the
four winds, and destroy our order.   A secret order is

for the benefit of the whole world, that it may call
the whole world its children, and that the whole
world may call it father, and not for the exclusive
benefit of the few men who belong to it. But its
privileges are the property of its members, and should
be preserved with jealous vigilance; since, if they
became known to the whole world, they would cease
to be secrets, and the order would be destroyed, and
its benefit to the world would pass away."

The remarks of these two uneducated Indians
certainly contained much food for reflection.

Neither Cushing nor myself was a Mason, or
member of any secret society; and, speaking for
myself, I must admit that I had accepted as final
the conclusions of Thomas de Quincey that Masonry,
the oldest of the secret orders of our day, was
nothing but an offshoot from the society of the
Illuminati which sprang up shortly after the Refor-
mation in Germany, from which country it was
brought by Roger Ashmole in the early years of the
seventeenth century.

My faith in this belief, in the comparative youth
of secret societies in general, was staggered by the
earnestness of the Indians, and I became more than
half convinced that secret societies were not an
evolution from the refined and æsthetic conditions of
modern civilisation, but that possibly they might
have originated in the necessities of primitive man.
This is not so remarkable after all. The first object of
these associations is the advancement of the interests

of their members, and afterwards, perhaps, the general interests of the community in which those members move.   Law and order may owe their first establishment among rude and savage men to the potent and dreaded, because ubiquitous and mysterious, influences of secret societies.   Not alone would such confraternities be overwhelming from an exaggeration of their strength due to the mystery and secrecy of their combinations, but in all probability they mustered other agencies for increasing their ascendency over the human mind by appeals to its sense of fear, of veneration, or of curiosity.

As among the Zunis and Moquis to-day, secret societies in primitive ages enlisted religion, medicine, and the drama under their banners; each of these auxiliaries adding an increment of influence, and each in its turn receiving great benefit by being more thoroughly developed and systematised.

As a further exemplification of the principle here suggested as the genetic basis of secret societies, let us cite our own young settlements of Durango, Tombstone, Leadville, and other mining districts, where we find civilised man but primitive society, with elements of lawlessness against which the machinery of modern justice is powerless.   The organisation of Vigilantes — secret societies emphatically — causes crime and scoundrelism to "flee like pole-cats before a prairie fire."

One word more.   Nayuchi had spoken about the tender of a "little bundle" to Nanahe.   This "little

bundle" has been alluded to in italics as an "honorarium," the name given by physicians several generations ago to the reward for their services, which is
now called a fee.

This "honorarium," as we read, was not given to
the physician direct, but usually consisted of a guinea,
which was wrapped in paper and left upon the draw-
ing-room mantel for him to take away at the end of
each visit.

The matter may not be of sufficient consequence
to repay investigation, but it does look as if we had
in Nanahe's "little bundle" a connecting link between
the skilled practitioner of this generation and his
humble brother, the "medicine man" of the untutored
races from whom he has been evolved after centuries
of study and progress.

CHAPTER XVII.

The secrets of the order—The account of the rites—Initiation—
Relics of prehistoric times—Snake and ancestor worship.

CUSHING arranged with Nanahe to return with his friend the next evening, and promised by that time to have the " present of ceremony" (the " little bundle ") ready, and to have us waiting for them in my room, apart from all idle or unnecessary spectators.

The next evening, with the coming of darkness, Nanahe and Nayuchi tapped at the door, which opened quickly, and they glided in like shadows.

All was ready for them, including the present mentioned yesterday, which comprised old clothes, canned fruits, three or four gaudy handkerchiefs from Mr. Graham's store, and an attenuated pile of small silver coin, so displayed as to make it appear as imposing as possible.

Nayuchi had with him a calendar-stick or tally, cut somewhat after the fashion of the Ogham of the ancient Irish. The months began with the full moon, were composed of thirty days, divided into three Zuni weeks of ten days each. A nick indicated each day; a

larger and somewhat longer nick the first day of the
week; and one half across the tally, the commencement of the month.

Beginning at the right, days, weeks, and months
were nicked upon the sharp upper edge of the tally,
until the end was reached with the termination of
the seventh month, whereupon the stick was turned,
and the remainder of the year marked upon the other
side.

Certain minute conventional dots and signs indicated various festivals, and strengthened the resemblance to an Ogham. This mode of checking dates
may have been introduced by Spanish missionaries,
who remained for years among the Zunis, building
a monastery, school, and great church, now half
ruined.

Cushing told me, in speaking upon this matter,
that the Zunis have a tradition of the former employment by their ancestors of a calendar of knotted
cords, which would recall the Quippu of the Peruvians.

The calendar-stick was laid to one side, and
Nanahe began his story. His agitation nearly mas-
tered him; he trembled violently, and showed all the
outward signs of a powerful inward emotion. He
said: " We have four kinds of medicines in that
dance, four kinds of roots—the red root, the yellow
root, the blue root, and the root which I now give
you to taste." (These are the names by which the
medicines are known to the members of the order of

the snake.) "I have none of the others with me, as I brought none of them away."[1]

Nanahe continued : "The members of the order always carry these medicines with them, and when they meet with a rattlesnake they first pray to their father, the sun, and then say : 'Father, make him to be tame ; make him that nothing shall happen that he bring evil unto me. Verily, make him to be tame.' Then they address the rattlesnake and say : 'Father, be good' (*i.e.* kind or tame) 'unto me, for here I make my prayers.' This being done, the rattlesnake is captured, but not in a bold or careless manner, and taken home. I want to tell you that the *red* root is ground up fine and scattered in sacrifice like cunque' (sacred corn-meal) 'to secure abundant and hasty' (rapid) 'harvests, and to make the melons grow large. The rattlesnake, being at home, is thoroughly washed in good cold water, in which the *yellow* root medicine has been mixed, and then the Moqui himself, throwing away every particle of clothing he has been accustomed to wearing, even his wrist-guard'

---

[1] Being ignorant of botany, I did not ask him to describe the plants, fearing that a confused notion of them might arise. The piece of root given me as the principal medicine was about 2 inches long, $\frac{1}{4}$-inch in thickness, and perfectly smooth. A fragment was submitted to Surgeon Forwood, U.S. Army, for microscopic examination, but he failed to classify it. One of the four medicines, I have some reasons for believing, was the "golondrina"—a specific among Mexicans and Indians for all venomous bites. It is a small-leaved, lactaceous vine, growing close to the ground. To botanists it is known as *Euphorbia prostrata*. Surgeon B. J. D. Irwin, U.S.A., has treated exhaustively of its merits in a monograph already published.

(bow-guard), 'washes himself thoroughly in the same water.

"Everything about him is washed thoroughly, and then he fasts for one day, and dances through the night.

"In the evening of the day of fast they first go and feed the rattlesnakes, and then they themselves are permitted to go and eat.[1]

"After this meal they enter the Estufa and place their sacred wands of office around the altar; in the midst of these wands stands the large sacred stone pipe, and the leaves of all plants known to them,— pine, *hemlock*, corn,—everything, all mixed up, and the bowl filled with them.

"The pipe is lit, and the clouds from it rise and form rain clouds, and the rain falls upon the altar and sacred things.

"It is grand! it is magnificent! And thus the altar is sanctified with ourselves.

"Then the sacred song is sung by the members.[2]

---

[1] Subsequent questions brought out the fact that this feeding was largely a matter of courtesy, or merely a ceremonial observance.

[2] This would have taken too much time to translate, and would have wearied him, and kept him from telling us things of probably greater value, so I deferred asking for the song until a more fitting occasion, contenting myself with learning that much of it was in the "ancient language." What this language is, I don't know. Both Zunis and Moquis, and, I think, all the other Pueblos, have a hieratic language, known only to the priests and members of these curious secret societies or secret orders;—a language entirely different from the demotic, and not understood by any of the common people. This "ancient language" may be the badge of religious subserviency to another people now extinct, just as the Latin ritual of the Catholic Church proclaims the fact that missionaries in the early Christian ages moved out from Rome as a

"Then the time comes for the *Name Chorus*, and everything is complete.[1]

"At this point those who were taken in to be initiated are considered as initiated, and are conducted by the older members to their homes, where they are at liberty to don their sacred dresses, moccasins, breech-clouts of deer or antelope skin, and their sacred plumes of red feathers.

"These are the medicines I have told you of; the uses of them and the attributes by which we are distinguished from other people.

"This is all of a strictly sacred nature that we possess, but it is precious.   It is valuable, and we prize it very much.   I might tell you a lie, and tell you a

centre; or it may be that the changes undergone by the Zuni language of some centuries ago have been resisted only in the liturgy of the "medicine men," in which obsolete forms have been tenaciously preserved. Nanahe's imaginative description of the effects induced by the smoking of the sacred pipe would suggest an exhilaration due, perhaps, to the *Hemlock*.[2]

[1] This is the repetition of a sacred or magic word like our Presto ! It may be, in the hieratic language spoken of, the recapitulation of the different attributes of the sun or the rattlesnake, just as in the litanies of the Christian churches we meet with such ejaculations as Alleluia ! Kyrie Eleison ! or expressions like Almighty One, Eternal in the Heavens, etc.   The same idea kept presenting itself during the Tablet Dance at Santo Domingo, where each verse ended with the line—

"Wi-ka-tolli-na-mashe,"

several times repeated.

[2] "Acosta mentions that 'Oliliuhqui' was taken by persons who desired to see *visions*. This latter was a seed which was also an ingredient of the 'teopalli' or *divine medicine*, composed besides of India-rubber, gum, *ocotl*, resin, tobacco, and sacred water."—Bancroft, H. H., vol. ii. p. 601.   On the preceding page he says that "*ocotl*" was *a kind of pine*. (*Query*—Was it or was it not *hemlock* ?)

great deal more, and deceive you about the matter, but I do not wish to tell you a lie."

Hereupon he took off his hat-band and moccasins, bent his head and his shoulders over the bundle we had given him, and which rested on his lap, and prayed fervently in a reverent and distinctly audible tone. Then, rising, he took Cushing by both wrists, pressed his arms back upon his (Cushing's) breast, blew upon his hands and down his throat, and said, " May the light of our medicines and gods be shed upon you and meet you, my child."

He repeated this formula to old Nayuchi and myself, and told us that this made us honorary members of the order of the Rattlesnake. What privilege this distinction confers I know not, unless it be the proud one of dancing and prancing about with a rattlesnake in one's mouth, once every two years.

Nanahe continued : " Nobody *outside* of our order has told you these things, because he couldn't ; and no one inside the order has done it, because he *wouldn't ;* it's against our rules.

" Before they go out to hunt the snakes the young men meet in the house of the head man of the order, and there have prayer and a bowl of sacred corn-meal. They make their sacrificial wands of the feathers of the eagle and the blue jay before going out to catch the snakes, for which they begin to search eight days before the dance, going north, south, east, and west. When they catch a snake they seize it back of the head, hold it up towards the sun in their left hand, and stroke it lengthwise with the right, repeating the prayer I gave you.

" The sea-shells you saw in the Estufa were brought by our forefathers to the country of Moqui.   They are very old.   They were not obtained in trade with other tribes.   They came from the *country of the new*.[1]

Nanahe resumed : " The Cohoninos, the Hualpais, the Mojaoes beyond the Hualpais (*i.e.* to the west), and all the tribes which have their hair cut across the eyebrows, are one and the same people with us,—the Opii, but the Apaches are different.   The people west of Zuni who cut (bang) their hair are all one people.

" The buffalo robe was obtained from some eastern tribe in trade.   Our sacred songs are repeated from four to six times."

Nayuchi : " The Moquis and Zunis have an identical religion, and depend upon each other for help in their sacred ceremonies."

Nanahe : " The stone axes, hammers, pipes, etc., you saw in the Estufa are very very old relics of our order, and we have had them for years and years and years.   No one knows when we got them. The squaws throw meal to have it blessed by the snakes ; after the snakes have crawled through it the squaws gather it up and keep it as sacred.   You didn't see any snakes leave that corn-meal circle ; they *couldn't*.   If the snakes *could not bite*, why

---

[1] This expression, or its companion—"The country where the Zunis or Moquis came up out of the ground "—is employed when speaking of the cradle of their race, wherever that may have been.

O

should we be so careful to pray, etc., and if they *could* bite, who would be brave enough to pull their teeth ? I shouldn't try that with an ordinary rattlesnake.

" At this last dance there were some of the young people,—I don't know why they should be so foolish, and make such fools of themselves ;—they were standing around grumbling, and they said, 'Humph ! those snakes have no teeth !' And the next day they found two of the snakes that had been used in the dance, and they killed them (*our fathers*), and sure enough they had teeth and fangs like any other snakes.

" The kilts we wear, as you saw, are coloured red, green, yellow, and black.[1]

" One of the objects of our order is this : Whenever anybody gets bitten by a snake, he sends for one of our order, presents an offering, as you have done ; then a prayer is made over the offering, as we have done this evening, the medicine is administered, and the patient immediately gets well."

Nayuchi (in answer to a question) : " Yes, you know that human sacrifice was the custom of our grandfathers. If the tribes to the south in Mexico did that, they were one people with us."

Nanahe : " Yes. We are one people. We have one religion ; that human sacrifice was the practice of our grandfathers " (ancestors).

" The Padres (Catholic missionaries) used to come to the Moqui towns, but they never stayed among our

---

[1] *i.e.* The same colours as the four kinds of lightning depicted in the Estufas.

people, and the Moquis never became their converts.
For a short time they established themselves at Ah-
wat-tenna,[1] which is the same place the Navajoes call
Tolli-Hogandi. I have never heard the story you
tell about the Moquis having murdered them, but I
don't doubt it at all.[2]

"All the villages of the Moquis have the snake-
dance."[3]

The interpretation of the above was carefully
made by Mr. Cushing, and written down verbatim, the
notes being my own. To these notes nothing is to be
added beyond calling attention to the persistency with
which Nanahe spoke of the snakes as his "fathers,"
a reverential expression which of itself would go far
towards establishing a connection between the rattlesnake-dance and ancestor worship.

After the long conversation had ended Nanahe
and Nayuchi were offered a little collation, of which
they partook with great relish.

[1] Aquatubi. See Davis, p. 355.

[2] Nanahe had come over among the Zunis when only ten years
old, and never returned to the Moquis except every second year or
so for the snake-dance. It is not at all remarkable that he should be
ignorant of this tradition.

[3] This confirmed my own impressions, formed during visits to the
Estufas of Mushangnewy, Sumopowy, Supowolewy, and Oraybe. In
each were seen portions of attire and decorations, not yet finished, for
use in the dance.

CHAPTER XVIII.

IN my journal of November 1881, made at Zuni, are the following jottings of a conversation with the old chief, Pedro Pino, who possesses a very competent knowledge of Spanish:—"In the days of long ago (eu el tiempo de cuanto hay) all the Pueblos, Moquis, Zunis, Acoma, Laguna, Jemez, and others, had the religion of human sacrifice (el oficio de matar los hombres) at the time of the Feast of Fire, when the days are shortest. The victim had his throat cut and his breast opened, and his heart taken out by one of the Cochinos (priests); that was their 'oficio' (religion), their method of asking good fortune (pedir la suerte). The Mexicans came, and they had another method: *they* used to go to the 'iglesia, para pedir á Dios' (go to church to pray to God)." They would not allow the Pueblos to keep up the good old costumbre (custom), but for a long time a modified ceremony (or symbolical imitation, as I should call it) was adhered to in secret. The victim, generally a young man, had his throat cut, and blood was allowed to flow freely; then he was carried to a house and laid upon his back; much singing and shouting were kept up by the procession of men and women, but there was "no llorando" (no crying). The wounded man was covered with a white blanket, while the three head "medicine men" with eagle feathers, sprinkled "medicine" upon the gash, and "muy pronto" (very soon), as Pedro assured me, the wound healed up (se sana), and the wounded man recovered (se cura).

On account of the fact that some people were very talkative (muy hablador), the Mexicans (*i.e.* the Spaniards), got wind of the ceremony, which they denounced as "muy hechicera" (full of witchcraft), and abolished without delay.

"Pero, todos los Pueblos hiciéron asina" (but all the Pueblos did the same thing).

In former times, too,—the "good old times,"—all the Pueblos had the rattlesnake-dance, and carried snakes in their mouths as the Moquis do to-day. He had heard of the "way" of the people of Péco. When Juan Setimo's father was alive he used to live in the front of this very house, and spoke Mexican very well. When people came from the Péco Pueblo to buy anything, they would get talking about the "goings-on" in their Pueblo. They said that whenever one of their children was bitten by a rattlesnake they had a "remedio" (remedy) for effecting a prompt cure. The people of Jemez used to have the same ceremony as the Moquis, dancing about with rattlesnakes in their mouths, and their tails around their

necks ; and also a rattlesnake in each hand. But of
the report still whispered about among the other
Pueblos that the people of the now abandoned village
of Peco or Pecos used to give the blood of their own
children to snakes, he either knew nothing or would
say nothing.

He contended that the people of Zuni had not forgotten how to carry snakes in their mouths just as
well as the Moquis do, but "we don't keep up the
custom any more,"—"tenemos vergüenza y tenemos
miedo de la gente tambien" (we are ashamed, and are
also afraid of the people outside).

He insisted that on one occasion, while on the
Rio Grande, below Albuquerque, he had heard the
roar of the sea-serpent (culebra del mar)! in the existence of which mythical animals all the Pueblos have
an abiding faith, exemplified in traditions, decorations upon the walls of their Estufas, and upon their
pottery.

In another conversation with Pedro Pino he made
the following remarks:—"The time to go to the
Moqui villages from here (Zuni) is about four days,
going at a pretty good gait (making an 'amble' or
'lope' with his hands). The buffalo robe you say
you saw at the snake-dance must have been bought
of the Utes.   I have seen the snake-dance a long time
ago. *Then* the Moquis used to gather up *all* kinds of
animals,—all kinds that moved on the ground,—
snakes, rattlesnakes, toads, jack-rabbits, etc.,—and
take them to an Estufa where there was an old man

who knew a great deal about medicine.   He had to stay down there for four days, and couldn't go near his wife all that time, and when the animals were brought in he spat (escupio) upon them and they became subdued (silencio).

" And those snakes they take in their mouths *have* teeth (anuelas), and they *can* bite (picar), but they don't bite on account of that medicine.   What it is I don't know, but I think that there is some of the weed (yerba) ' golondrina.' [1]   Golondrina is good for snakes. There is a ' remedio ' (cure) for everything, and the ' remedio ' grows near the animal always.   The medicine of the snake-dance is known to only a few Moquis ; they are nearly all of them snake ' gente.' [2]

" The shells you saw came from the sea.   The Moquis came from the west, just as the Zunis did. [3]

" The Moquis plant cotton, and have always done so ; at least that is what our old men say.   We buy cotton dresses from them.   The Zunis never have planted cotton, or not for a long long time."

Bearing upon the question of the diffusion of this snake cult among the tribes of Arizona and New Mexico, it is pertinent to this monograph to say that in 1870 I saw a small piece of pottery picked up from a ruin near old Camp Grant on the San Pedro River, Arizona.   This piece of pottery represented a snake

---

[1] This golondrina or swallow weed is the *Euphorbia prostrata* of botanists, as shown in preceding pages.

[2] The Spanish " gente " means gens or clan.

[3] Efforts to induce the old man to talk more upon this point were unavailing.

biting its own tail. The head, mouth, and corruga-
tions along the serpent's back were represented, the
whole fragment being about two inches in diameter.

Again, in digging in one of the old cliff-dwellings
near the Rio Verde, in 1882, I uncovered two small
fragments of wood ; one shaped exactly like the snake
sling of the Moquis, but unpainted, and the other
fashioned like the "fire-sticks" still in common use
among the Apaches, and brought into requisition in
the religious ceremonies of Zunis and Moquis.

Major C. S. Roberts, U.S.A., states that not far
from the military post of Fort Yates, Dakota, is a
ravine which some few years since was infested with
venomous snakes. The Sioux Indians seemed to
stand in great awe of this place, in which they left propitiatory offerings of small eagle feathers tied to twigs.
These sacrificial feathers or plumes correspond closely
to those which the Zunis, Moquis, Acoma, Jemez, and
other Pueblos bury in their fields to secure good crops.

That very intelligent Indian lady, Mrs. "Bright
Eyes" Tibbles, assured me not long since that she was
satisfied that the same religion once prevailed among
Indian tribes living along the Missouri.

Chateaubriand (*Génie du Christianisme*, p. 191)
adverts to the influence the American aborigines possessed over snakes, citing in a vivid and graphic
manner an instance coming under his own observation
of a vicious rattlesnake which a Canadian Indian
soothed into submission with the music of a flute.
This occurred in 1792.

The following citations from approved authorities may be of assistance to those who have enough curiosity to learn more about Ophiolatry or snake worship in general :—

"As an object of worship, the serpent is pre-eminent among animals. Not only is it malevolent and mysterious, but its bite—so trifling in appearance and yet so deadly—producing fatal effects, rapidly and, apparently, by no adequate means, suggests to the savage almost irresistibly the notion of something divine, according to his notion of divinity. . . . The animal is long lived, and easily kept in captivity; hence the same individual might be preserved for a long time and easily exhibited at intervals to the multitude. In other respects the serpent is a convenient god. Thus in Guinea, where the sea and the serpent were the principal deities, the priests, as Bosman especially tells us, encouraged offerings to the serpent rather than to the sea, because in the latter case there happens to be no remainder left for them. . . . I cannot agree with my friend (Mr. Fergusson) in supposing that the beauty of the serpent or the brilliancy of its eyes had any part among the causes of its original deification. Nor do I believe that serpent worship is to be traced up to any common local origin, but, on the contrary, that it sprang up spontaneously in many places and at very different times. In considering the wide distribution of serpent worship we must remember that, in the case of the serpent, we apply one name to a whole order of animals ; and that serpents occur all over the world except in very cold regions. On the contrary, the lion, the bear, the bull, have less extensive areas, and consequently their worship could never be so general.

"If, however, we compare, as we ought, serpent worship with quadruped worship, or bird worship, or sun worship, we shall find that it has no exceptionally wide area.

"Mr. Fergusson is surprised to find that the serpent god is frequently regarded as a beneficent being. Muller, in his *Scientific Mythology*, has endeavoured to account for this by the statement that the serpent typified not only barren, impure nature,

but also youth and health.   This is not, I think, the true explanation.   It may be that the serpent god commenced as a malevolent being who was flattered, as cruel rulers always are, and
that in process of time this flattery, which was at first a mere
expression of fear, came to be an article of faith.

"If, moreover, the totemic origin of serpent worship, as above
suggested, be the true one, the serpent, like other totemic deities,
would, from its origin, have a benevolent character.

"The serpent was worshipped anciently in Egypt, in India,
Phœnicia, Babylonia, Greece, as well as Italy, where, however,
it seems not to have prevailed much. . . . .

"Among the Lithuanians every family entertained a real
serpent as a household gold.   In Asia evidence of serpent worship has been found in Persia, Cashmere, Cambodia, Thibet,
India, China (traces), Ceylon, and among the Kalmucks.   In
Africa the serpent was worshipped in some parts of Upper Egypt
and in Abyssinia.

"Among the negroes on the Guinea Coast it used to be the
principal deity.   Smith, in his *Voyage to Guinea*, says 'that
the natives are all pagans, and worship three sorts of deities.   The
first is a large, beautiful kind of snake, which is inoffensive in its
nature.   These are kept in fetish houses, or churches, built for
that purpose in a grove, to whom they sacrifice great store of
hogs, fowl, sheep, and goats, etc., and if not devoured by the
snake are sure to be taken care of by the fetish men or pagan
priests.'   From Liberia to Beneguela, if not farther, the serpent
was the principal deity, and, as elsewhere, was regarded as being
on the whole beneficent.   No negro would intentionally injure a
serpent, and any one doing so by accident would assuredly be
put to death.   Some English sailors having once killed one which
they found in their house were furiously attacked by the natives,
who killed them all and burned the house.

"All over the country are small huts, built on purpose for
the snakes, which are attended and fed by old women.   These
snakes are frequently consulted as oracles.

"In addition to these huts were temples, which, judged by a
negro standard, were of considerable magnificence, with large
courts, spacious apartments, and numerous attendants.   Each of

these temples had a special snake. The snake of Whydah was reverenced beyond all others, and 'an annual pilgrimage was made to its temple with much ceremony. It is rather suspicious that any young women who may be ill are taken off to the snake's house to be cured. For this questionable service the attendants charge a high price to the parents. It is observable that the harmless snakes only are thus worshipped.' The Kaffirs of South Africa have a general belief that the spirits of their ancestors appear to them in the form of serpents. . . . So in Madagascar and Feejee the serpent was worshipped and consulted as an oracle. In the Friendly Islands the water snake was much respected. In America serpents were worshipped by the Aztecs, Peruvians, Natchez, Caribs, Minatarris, Mandans, etc.

"Alvarez, during his attempt to reach Peru from Paraguay, is reported to have seen ' the temple and residence of a monstrous serpent, whom the inhabitants had chosen for their divinity, and fed with human flesh. He was as thick as an ox and seven-and-twenty feet long, with a very large head and very fierce though small eyes. His jaws, when extended, displayed two ranks of crooked fangs. The whole body, except the tail, which was smooth, was covered with round scales of a great thickness. The Spaniards, though they could not be persuaded by the Indians that this monster delivered oracles,. were exceedingly terrified at first sight of him, and their terror was greatly increased when on one of them having fired a blunderbuss at him he gave a roar like that of a lion, and with a stroke of his tail shook the whole tower.' "—Quoted by Lubbock from Charlevoix, *History of Paraguay*, vol. i. p. 110.

"The worship of serpents being so widely distributed and presenting so many similar features, we cannot wonder that it has been regarded as something special, that attempts have been made to trace it up to one source, and that it has been regarded by some as the primitive religion of man."—Lubbock, *Origin of Civilisation*, p. 174-180.

In an article published in *Harper's Weekly*, March 25, 1882, entitled " Snake-Charmers of Central America," occurs the following :—

" The Indians of Central America celebrate the 21st of March with the singular rites depicted in our engraving. Three or four months before the ceremony the younger men of the village begin the work of capturing snakes by means of ingeniously-contrived snares.

" The more daring make choice of the most venomous and dangerous species, and tame them in various ways, using a rude reed pipe, a fan, and a strip of blanket for the purpose. The snake-tamers are often bitten by their strange pets in the course of the training, but their knowledge of efficacious antidotes almost always protects them from serious consequences. On the day of the ceremony the inhabitants of the village assemble in an enclosure built of poles and reeds. The chiefs and other notables seat themselves before a kind of lodge, the entrance to which is closed with a curtain. Within is a stone idol on a rude altar, or perhaps the wooden image of a saint.

" There the snake-charmers are also concealed, stripped nearly nude, and awaiting a signal from the head chief. After an interval of solemn silence he begins a low and monotonous chant to the accompaniment of a drum and rattle.

" Gradually the assembly joins in, and then the charmers issue forth, each with a snake in his hand or coiled around his body. They make the round of the enclosure, and then take their places on the ground. Each one as he is called up begins his performances with the snake he has tamed and trained. Great mastery over the creatures is exhibited by these Indians, and the tricks are often astonishing.

" After all in turn have presented themselves, the chant becomes more lively, and the charmers assemble in a cluster, and suddenly fling the snakes into a heap, where they lie wriggling and twisting themselves into knots. Then each charmer tries to pick out his own particular reptile.

" This is dangerous work, and they constantly partake of a certain liquid which is supposed to contain a powerful antidote to snake poison. At the conclusion of the games the charmers retire into the lodge, and the audience rises.

" A priest sprinkles the ground with water, facing alternately the four cardinal points of the compass, and the ceremony is over."

In this description numerous points of resemblance to the Moqui snake-dance present themselves. In catching the snakes the Central American Indians are represented as using *fans*. Are not these of *feathers?* They are reported to possess "a knowledge of efficacious antidotes."

"The enclosure built of poles and reeds" corresponds to the stone enclosure called an Éstufa. The "lodge" of the Central American dance has its prototype in what was designated in the preceding chapter the "sacred lodge." There may have been an idol in the Moqui lodge; idols are plentiful enough among the Moquis, and it is not at all improbable that one was to be found within this sanctuary. This point, however, was not determined.

In both cases those engaged in the ceremony constantly partake of a certain liquid which is supposed to contain a powerful antidote to snake-poison.

In both the snake-charmers are "nearly naked."

In both, after an interval of solemn silence, the head chief begins "a low and monotonous chant to the accompaniment of . . . a rattle."

"Afterwards the charmers issue forth each with a snake in his hand." "They suddenly fling the snakes into heaps."

"In each case a priest sprinkles the ground with water, facing alternately the four cardinal points."

Taken together, the points of contact between these two ceremonies are too many, the contact itself is too intimate, not to carry convictions that they belong to the same religion. Discrepancies will always exist in the narratives of two observers, even where they are writing of one and the same ceremony. How much greater must be the divergence when they attempt to describe at different times and in different countries ?

Squiers (*Nicaragua*, p. 406), figures a plumed serpent from the cave-dwellings near Lake Nihapa, and again (Part II. p. 36), one appears, sculptured, open-mouthed on the head of an idol dug up on the Island of Peusacola (Nicaragua).

This author expresses the opinion that the snake worship suggested, by the carvings upon the Nicaraguan idols afterwards yielded, to some extent, to the worship of *alligators*.

A snake is represented on the pottery bowl engraved upon p. 101 of Di Cesnola's *Cyprus*. In speaking of the set to which this bowl belonged, Di Cesnola observes (p. 102)—

"Some of these vases are identical in character with those found by Dr. Schliemann in his excavations at Hissarlik. These tombs are, in my opinion, among the oldest found in Ilium."

On p. 145 of same work is figured a snake carved on stone, with a dolphin. Of this the author says—

"On the right of the reptile had been carved an inscription of several lines in Cypriote characters. . . . It (the stone) originally stood outside the temple and close to the entrance."

Snakes represented in rings, ornaments, intaglii,

etc., are figured in various places throughout the same work; for example on pp. 373, 374 (*bis*), 375, 377 (*bis*), 380, and 384. Di Cesnola, however, takes occasion to remark in substance that he does not consider that these amulets are necessarily religious, and he ventures the surmise that the ornaments so engraved were worn to avert danger from snakes. This argument, if I apprehend it correctly, is far from being conclusive.

In heathen religions there has always been as much of an effort to appease malign deities as there has been to propitiate benevolent ones. Granting that, at the period when these rings were in use, the serpent cult had long since fallen into desuetude, perhaps even into oblivion, the efficacy superstitiously ascribed to these rings, etc., would be as much a "survival," as much an indication of the *former* existence of snake worship, as is our boyish game of "snapdragon" of the days when Druids worshipped the sun god and fire in groves of mistletoe-laden Celtic oaks.

CHAPTER XIX.

M. LE PLONGEON, in a letter to the American Antiquarian Society (published in *Proceedings* of April 1881), refers to the fact that Cocorn, one of the rulers of Mayapan, is represented as holding a rattlesnake in his left hand. This is the same manner of holding the reptile as can be witnessed at the Moqui snake-dance to-day.

Mr. W. E. Gladstone, in his Introduction to Schliemann's *Mycenæ*, p. 13, speaks of a three-headed snake carved on the band of the shield presented to Agamemnon by Cynisas of Cyprus.

" Another vase has the most curious ornamentation of all. It shows what appears to be intended for the head of a serpent."—Schliemann, " Description of the Pottery found in the second Tomb or Sepulchre at Mycenae," p. 161. Mention is made again of the same symbol of the serpent on p. 318, and still again on pp. 323, 324.

The serpent appears on the shield of the left-hand figure in the picture called " Last Night of Troy," upon a vase exhumed at Naples, and reproduced upon p. 79 of Prince's *Pottery and Porcelain*.

" In some cases departed relatives are regarded as reappearing in the form of snakes, which may be known from ordinary snakes by certain signs, such as their frequenting huts, not eating mice, and showing no fear of man. Sometimes a snake is recognised as the representative of a given man by some peculiar mark or scar, the absence of an eye, or some similar point of resemblance. In such cases sacrifices are sometimes offered to the snake, and when a bullock is killed part is put away for the Amatongo or dead, who are especially invited to the feast, whose assistance is requested, and whose wrath is deprecated."— Lubbock, *Origin of Civilisation*, pp. 163-164.

" In Peru, even at the time of the Conquest, many species of animals were still much reverenced, including the fox, dog, llama, condor, eagle, and puma, besides the serpent."—Lubbock's *Origin of Civilisation*, pp. 180-188.

The Feast of All Saints (November 1) at the Pueblo of Isleta embodies the worship of ancestors. During the religious exercises at that place in 1881 I saw the floor of the church covered with corn, grapes, bread, bottles of native wine, and pies or cakes, several of which bore upon their upper crust the *figure of a snake*. Upon this subject (of ancestor worship) Mr. Tylor remarks (*Anthropology*, 351, 352) :—

" One has only to cross the channel to see how the ancient feast of the dead still keeps its primitive character in the festival of All Souls, which is its modern representative ; even at the cemetery of the Père la Chaise they still put cakes and sweetmeats on the graves ; and in Brittany the peasants that night do not forget to make up the fire and leave the fragments of the supper on the table for the souls of the dead of the family who will come to visit their home."

P

In the monograph upon *Serpent and Siva Worship*, by Hyde Clarke, M.A.I., and C. Staniland Wake, M.A.I., with the prefaces thereto by Alexander Wilder, M.D., will be found in a very condensed form about all that the ordinary reader will care to learn upon this topic. A few extracts from this valuable little work will be inserted in this chapter for the benefit of those who may not be able to obtain the original.

Dr. Wilder says in the Preface :—

" The researches and explorations of travellers, scientists, and learned investigators are every day adding to our knowledge of the serpent cultus. It is rising above the old conception of an obscure and ill-defined superstition to the dimensions of a religion, distinctly outlined in its characteristic features, and by no means without a recondite metaphysical basis. Not only did the children of Israel burn incense to the symbolical animal, from Moses till Hezekiah, but the Hamitic races, 'from Memphis to Babylon,' and all indeed at the far east and remote west, who accepted as sacred what Mr. Brown denominates 'the great Dyonisiak Myth.' . . .

" In the beech and birch forests of Scandinavia and the Frozen Ocean, and the remotest nooks of Polynesia and the American continent, the serpent, in all his forms, with hood, horns, or rattles, has been venerated by the various tribes of men as a god ! If he conducted to the tree of prohibited knowledge in the Garden of Eden, he was also an Esculapius, the healer of men in the wilderness of Sinai, the good spirit of many a world-religion, the source of diviner inspiration, and the imparter of the highest, holiest, most essential life. Indeed, serpent love is the literature of the earlier periods of ancient history."

Again, in the Introduction, he remarks :—

" The remains of serpent worship are to be found in all quarters of the earth, among nations geographically remote from each other and supposed to be distinct in characteristics of race, habitude, intellectual constitution, and religious belief. Some faiths, like that of the Buddhists,—perhaps the oldest of all,—still maintain a qualified veneration for the sacred animal as a part of their worship; while others, even among the more modern, do not hesitate to display the serpent symbol conspicuously among their ecclesiastical decorations. We see it in the architecture of churches, and even find its reliques in the garb of priests. Moses is recorded as having erected the symbol of the Phœnician Esculapius, the sun god of autumn, as ' a sign of salvation.' The like device was borne upon the respective standards of the Assyrians, the Persians, the Romans, and even the British. It was thus honoured by Christians as well as ' heathen.' Whole sects, we are assured by the early fathers, used to partake of the Eucharistical supper after it had been consecrated by a living snake coming from a coffer and entwining its coils about the loaves of bread."[1]

Quoting from the Rev. John Bathurst Deane's *Worship of the Serpent*, and from Henry O'Brien's *Round Towers of Ireland*, Dr. Wilder continues:—

" No nations were so geographically remote or so religiously discordant but that ONE—and only one—superstitious characteristic was common to all; and the most civilised and the most barbarous bowed down with the same devotion to the same

---

[1] Allusion is here made to the Gnostic sect of the Ophites, who flourished in the East from about 161-250 A.D. Their theological tenets are not well understood, as they had among them no intellectual celebrities, and have left behind nothing in the way of accurate treatises. With them the serpent was a sacred symbol, and they are believed to have reverenced Judas above the other apostles on the ground that he betrayed his Master with good intent and from a desire to precipitate the coming of His kingdom. They maintained that the real Christ was not crucified, but that at the moment of ascending the cross a phantasm was substituted for Him. (See also p. 221.)

engrossing deity ; and that this deity either was, or was represented by, the same sacred serpent. . . . Its antiquity must be
accredited to a period far antedating all history. . . . The sacred
serpent of America is generally, especially among the wandering
tribes, the rattlesnake. . . .

"The fact is, that the serpent was only a symbol, or at most
an embodiment, of the spirit which it represented, as we see from
the belief of certain African and American tribes, which probably
preserves the primitive form of this superstition.

"Serpents are looked upon by these people as embodiments
of their departed ancestors, and an analogous belief is entertained
by various Hindu tribes. No doubt the noiseless movement and
the activity of the serpent, combined with its peculiar gaze and
marvellous power of fascination, led to its being viewed as a
spirit embodiment, and hence also as a possessor of wisdom.

"In the spirit character ascribed to the serpent we have the
explanation of the association of its worship with human sacrifice
noted by Mr. Fergusson, this sacrifice being really connected with
the worship of ancestors."

Mr. Baldwin (*Ancient America*, vii. pp. 185, 186)
remarks that—

"The serpent worship is full of significance. This was a
great feature of the religion of the Cushites ; but the 'serpent'
will convey a very poor notion of its meaning to those who do
not understand what it was. The serpent was regarded as a
symbol of intelligence, of immortality, of protection against the
power of evil spirits, and of a renewal of life or of the healing
powers of nature. . . . Religious symbols are found in the
American rivers which remind us of those of the Phœnicians,
such as figures of the serpent, which appear constantly. . . .
There was sun worship in America, and the phallic ceremonies
existed in some places in the time of Cortez. In Asia these
ceremonies and figures of the serpent were usually associated with
sun worship."

Clarke (*Serpent and Siva Worship*, p. 28), speak-

ing of the religious ceremonies in honour of Saba, a
god of Phrygia, says :—

"Serpents figured largely in the initiations, midnight mysteries, and processions. A golden serpent was dropped into the
bosom of the initiate, falling out of the bottom of the frock."

In another place he says :—

"Many of the Hindu gods are decorated with snakes, for
such is the inheritance of serpent worship; but Siva is more
particularly so provided. There are two Hindu legends of the
Creation, but that most popularly depicted represents Vishnu
sleeping on a serpent."

Commenting upon Professor W. M. Gabb's elaborate paper upon the *Indian Tribes and Languages of
Costa Rica*, Mr. Clarke says :—

"The staff of the priests is gathered with care and devotion
from a mystic timber, because it is guarded by a venomous
snake. A circumstance particularly noticed by Mr. Gabb is that
the songs of the priests are in a peculiar language, and although
most anxious to obtain information on this head, he was most
unfortunately prevented."

Mr. Staniland Wake (*Origin of Serpent Worship*,
p. 1, *et seq.*) says :—

"The subject proposed to be discussed in the present paper
is one of the most fascinating that can engage the attention of
anthropologists. It is remarkable, however, that although so
much has been written in relation to it, we are still almost in
the dark as to the origin of the superstition in question.

"The student of mythology knows that certain ideas were
associated by the peoples of antiquity with the serpent, and that
it was the favourite symbol of particular deities ; but why that
animal, rather than any other, was chosen for the purpose is yet
uncertain."

After citing whole pages of incidents tending to
show the former existence of this cult in all parts of
the world, and among all, or nearly all, races of men,
—the brazen serpent of the Hebrew Exodus; the
important position occupied by the serpent in the
mythologies of the Chaldeans, Assyrians, Phœnicians,
Egyptians, Grecians, Scythians, Latins, British Celts,
Goths, Scandinavians, Esthonians, Finns, Persians,
Hindus, Africans; the people of the Indian Islands,
Polynesia, and China,—Mr. Wake continues :—

"The evidences of serpent worship on the American continent have long engaged the attention of archæologists, who have
found it to be almost universal under one form or another among
the aboriginal tribes.   That animal was sculptured on the temples
of Mexico and Peru, and its form is said by Mr. Squier to be of
frequent occurrence among the mounds of Wisconsin.   The most
remarkable of the symbolic earth-works of North America is the
great serpent mound of Adam's County, Ohio, the convolutions
of which extend to a length of 1000 feet. . . . Let us now see
what ideas have been associated with the serpent by various
peoples.   Mr. Fergusson mentions the curious fact, that 'the
chief characteristic of the serpents throughout the East in all
ages seems to have been their power over the wind and rain.'

"According to Colonel Meadows Taylor, in the Indian
Deccan at the present day offerings are made to the village
divinities (of whom the nâg, or snake, is always one) at spring-
time and harvest for rain or fine weather, and also in time of
cholera or other diseases or pestilence.   So, among the Chinese,
the dragon is regarded as the giver of rain, and in time of
drouth offerings are made to it. . . . One of the leading ideas
connected with the serpent was, as we have seen, its power over
the rain; but another equally influential was its connection with
health.   Mr. Fergusson remarks that, 'when we first met with
serpent worship, either in the wilderness of Sinai, the groves of
Epidaurus, or in the Sarmatian huts, the serpent is always the

agathodaemon,—the bringer of health and good fortune.' . . .
Ramahavaly, one of the four national idols of the Madacasses,
bears a curious analogy to the serpent gods of wisdom and healing;
. . . he can cause rain in abundance when wanted, or can with-
hold it so as to ruin the crops of rice. . . . Among various
African tribes this animal is viewed with great veneration, under
the belief that it is often the real embodiment of a deceased
ancestor. This notion appears to be prevalent also among the
Hindus, who, like the Kafirs, will never kill a serpent, although
it is usually regarded with more dislike than veneration. Mr.
Squier remarks that 'many of the North American tribes
entertain a superstitious regard for serpents, and particularly for
the rattlesnake.' Though always avoiding, they never destroy it,
lest, says Barham, 'the spirit of the reptile should excite its
kindred to revenge.' Mr. Squier adds that, 'according to Adair,
this fear was not unmingled with veneration.' Charlevoix states
that the Natchez had the figure of a rattlesnake, carved from
wood, placed among other objects upon the altar of their temple,
to which they paid great honour. Heckwelder relates that the
Linni-Linape call the rattlesnake 'grandfather,' and would on no
account allow it to be destroyed. Henry states that the Indians
around Lake Huron had a similar superstition, and also designated the rattlesnake as their 'grandfather.' He also mentions
instances in which offerings of tobacco were made to it, and its
parental care solicited for the party performing the sacrifice.
Corver also mentions an instance of similar regard on the part
of a Menominee Indian, who carried a rattlesnake constantly
with him, treating it as a deity, and calling it his great father.
. . . The facts cited prove that the serpent superstition is
intimately connected with ancestor worship, probably originating
among uncultured tribes who, struck by the noiseless movement
and the activity of the serpent, combined with its peculiar gaze
and marvellous power of fascination, viewed it as a spirit embodiment. As such, it would be supposed to have the superior
wisdom and power ascribed to the denizens of the invisible
world, and from this would originate also the ascription to it of
the power over life and health, and over the moisture on which
those benefits are dependent.

" The serpent spirit may, however, have made its appearance for a good or a bad purpose, to confer a benefit or to inflict punishment for the misdeeds of the living.   The notion of there being good and evil serpent spirits would thus naturally arise. Among ancestor - worshipping peoples, however, the serpent would be viewed as a good being who busied himself about the interests of the tribe to which he had once belonged.   When the simple idea of a spirit ancestor was transformed into that of the great spirit, the father of the race, the attributes of the serpent would be enlarged.

" The common ancestor would be relegated to the heavens, and that which was necessary to the life and well-being of his people would be supposed to be under his care.

" Hence, the great serpent was thought to have power over the rain and the hurricane, with the latter of which he was probably often identified.   When the serpent was thus transferred to the atmosphere, and the superstition lost its simple character as a phase of ancestor worship, its most natural association would be with the solar cult."

Mr. Wake next quotes from Professor Ch. Gubernatis to the effect that

" Serpents are revered in India as embodied souls of the dead. . . . To kill one of these serpents is to kill the head of the family.   Under this aspect, as a protector of children, as a giver of husbands to girls, and identified with the head or progenitor of the family, the serpent is again a phallical form.   Æneas, it will be remembered, when about to celebrate at the tomb of Anchises the anniversary of his death, was surprised at the appearing of a huge snake that glided among the altars and tasted the banquet, after which it retired to the bottom of the tomb. He did not know whether it was the *genius loci*, or his father's attendant demon."—Quoting from Virgil, *Æneid*, line 84.

The following are among Mr. Wake's conclusions :—

" First.   The serpent has been viewed with awe or veneration from primeval times, and almost universally as a re-embodiment of a deceased human being, and as such there were ascribed to it the attributes of life and wisdom and the power of healing.

" Secondly. The idea of a simple spirit reincarnation of a deceased ancestor gave rise to the notion that mankind originally sprang from a serpent, and ultimately to a legend embodying that idea.

" Thirdly. This legend was connected with nature, or rather sun worship, and the sun was therefore looked upon as the divine serpent father of man and nature."

CHAPTER XX.

FERGUSSON, in his excellent work, *Tree and Serpent
Worship* (London : Indian Museum, 1868), expresses
himself as of opinion

"That there are few things which appear to us at the present day so strange, or less easy to account for, than that worship which was once so generally offered to the serpent god.
If not the oldest, it ranks at least among the earliest forms
through which the human intellect sought to propitiate unknown
powers. Traces of its existence are found not only in every
country of the old world, but before the new was discovered by
us, the same strange idolatry had long prevailed there, and even
now the worship of the serpent is found lurking in out-of-the-way
corners of the globe, and startles us at times with the unhallowed
rites which seem generally to have been associated with its pre-
valence."—Introduction, page 1.

"When it comes to be more closely examined, the worship
of the serpent is not so strange as it might at first sight appear.
As was well remarked by an ancient author (Sanchoniathon) :
'The serpent alone, of all animals without legs or arms, or any
of the usual appliances for locomotion, still moves with singular
celerity ;' and he might have added grace, for no one who has
watched a serpent slowly progressing over the ground with his
head erect, and his body following apparently without exertion,
can fail to be struck with the peculiar beauty of the motion.
There is no jerk, no reflex motion, as in all other animals, even

fishes, but a continual progression in the most graceful curves. Their general form, too, is full of elegance, and their colours varied and sometimes very beautiful, and their eyes bright and piercing.   Then, too, a serpent can exist for an indefinite time without food or apparent hunger.   He periodically casts his skin, and, as the ancients fabled, by that process renewed his youth.   Add to this his longevity, which, though not so great as was often supposed, is still sufficient to make the superstitious forget how long an individual may have been reverenced in order that they may ascribe to him immortality.

"Though these qualities, and others that will be noted in the sequel, may have sufficed to excite curiosity and obtain respect, it is probable that the serpent would never have become a god but for his exceptional power.   The destructive powers of tigers or crocodiles are merely looked upon as ordinary exaggerations of a general law, but the poisoned fang of the serpent is something so exceptional, and so deadly in its action, as to excite dread, and when we find to how few of the serpent tribe it is given, its presence is only more mysterious.   Even more terrible, however, than the poison of the cobra is the flash-like spring of the boa, the instantaneous embrace, and the crushed-out life, all accomplished faster almost than the eye can follow.

"It is hardly to be wondered at that such power should impress people in the early stage of civilisation with feelings of awe, and with savages it is probably true that most religions spring from a desire to propitiate by worship those powers from whom they fear that injury may be done to themselves or their property."—P. 2.

". . . The essence of serpent worship is as diametrically opposed to the spirit of the Veda, or of the Bible, as it is possible to conceive two faiths to be ; and with varying degrees of dilution the spirit of these two works pervades, in a greater or less extent, all the forms of the religions of the Aryan or Semitic races.

"On the other hand, any form of animal worship is perfectly consistent with the lower intellectual status of the Quranian races, and all history tells us that it is among them, and essentially among them only, that serpent worship is really found to prevail.

". . . It is nearly correct to say that wherever human sacrifice prevailed, there serpent worship is found also, though the converse does not appear so capable of proof.

" Serpent worship did continue to exist when, at last, human sacrifices had ceased to be performed, though even then it is not quite clear whether it was not only from the disuse of one part of what had once been associated. . . .

" In Judea, so long as any traces of serpent worship prevailed, the idea of human sacrifices seems to have been familiar, but after Hezekiah's time we simultaneously lose all traces of either. . . .

" In Mexico and Dahomey, where in modern times human sacrifices have been practised to an extent not known elsewhere, there too serpent worship was and is the typical and most important form of propitiation : while in India there can be little doubt but that the two existed together from the earliest time. . . . Notwithstanding all these coincidences, and they might, easily be extended, it must not be overlooked that nowhere can we trace any direct connection between the two forms of faith. No human sacrifice was anywhere made to propitiate the serpent, nor was it ever pretended that any human victim was ever devoured by the snake god.

. . . " Of the Ophites Tertullian tells us ' They even prefer the serpent to Christ, because the former brought the knowledge of good and evil into the world.   They point also to his majesty and power, inasmuch as when Moses raised the brazen serpent in the wilderness whoever looked at it was healed ; and they even quote the Gospels to prove that Christ was an imitation of the serpent, because it is said, " As Moses lifted up the serpent in the wilderness, so must the Son of Man be lifted up."   Epiphanius describes these ceremonies in the following terms : " They keep a living serpent in a chest, and at the time of the mysteries entice him out by placing bread before him. The door being opened, he issues forth, and having ascended the table folds himself above the bread.   This they call a perfect sacrifice.   They not only break and distribute these among their votaries, but whosoever wishes it may kiss the serpent.   This the wretched people call the Eucharist.   They conclude the cere-

monies by singing a hymn through him to the Supreme Father.'"
. . . (See also p. 211.)

"In Africa not only does serpent worship flourish at the
present day, but it exists in conjunction with all those peculiarities of which only traces can be found elsewhere.   Ancestor
worship, accompanied by human sacrifices on the most lavish
scale, is the leading characteristic of the Dahoman religion. . . .

"The principal deity of the Aztec pantheon seems to have
been Tezcatlipoca, or Tonacatlicoatl, literally the sun serpent.
According to Sahagun, in his character of God of Hosts he was
addressed by the Mexican high priest : 'We entreat that those
who die in war may be received by thee, our Father, the Sun,
and our Brother, the Earth, for thou alone reignest.' The name
of the primitive goddess, the wife of Tezcatlipoca, was Cihuaco-
huatl, or Tonacacihua, the female serpent, or the female sun.
She, according to the Mexicans, gave to the light, at a single birth,
two children, one male, the other female, to whom they refer the
origin of mankind.   A still more remarkable myth is that of
Quetzal-Coatl, literally the feathered serpent.

"He is by some represented as born of a pure virgin in the
province of Tullan ; by others, as a stranger coming from a far
country, sometime between the sixth and ninth century of our
era.   Be this as it may, he was the great lawgiver and civiliser
of the inhabitants of Anahuac.   He taught them religion, gave
them laws, instructed them in agriculture and the use of metals,
and the various arts of life.

"He is generally represented as an old man, with a white
flowing beard and venerable aspect.   He was, in fact, the
Lycurgus and the Bacchus of Central America, and having
finished his mission he withdrew, like the former, it is said, by
sea, promising to return.   So implicitly was this believed by
his subjects that when the Spaniards appeared on the coast
they were joyfully hailed as the returning god and his com-
panions.

"Alas ! they came only to destroy them and their institu-
tions ! . . . It should be mentioned, however, that in America
the snake that is worshipped is always the indigenous rattlesnake.   Whether as separate images or as adorning the walls of

the temples of Yucatan, this characteristic seems invariable, and in so far would favour the local origin of the faith. The greatest difficulty of the investigation arises from almost absolute destruction of all the monuments of the capital by its barbarous conquerors, and the consequent paucity of real reliable data on which to found our conclusions. . . .

"If, however, we may trust Bernal Diaz, he tells us that living rattlesnakes were kept in the great temple at Mexico as sacred and petted objects. They were kept in a cabin of diversified form, in which a quantity of feathers had been strewed, and there they laid their eggs and nursed their snakelings. They were fed with the bodies of the sacrificed, and with dog's meat. The same author tells us that when Cortes marched to Mexico they arrived at a place called Terraguea, which the Spaniards called the town of serpents on account of the enormous figures of these reptiles which they found in the temples, and which the natives worshipped as gods. But though it is impossible to read any of the narratives of the conquerers without being struck with the frequency with which sacred serpents and serpent worship are spoken of, it is always as a thing accursed and to be avoided, never as an object worthy of attention or to be inquired into, and their narratives, consequently, throw very little light on the subject. . . . It need hardly be remarked that human sacrifices were found accompanying serpent worship in America almost to as great an extent as in Dahomey."—Fergusson, pp. 1-39.

Solis (*Conquista de Mejico*, p. 210) expresses his incredulity concerning the collections of venomous snakes reported in Mexico itself, but Wallace, whose romance, *The Fair God*, seems to be a well-digested exposition of the manners and customs of the Aztecs at the date of the Conquest, follows Diaz and the early chroniclers.

That curious compound of erudition and nonsense, *Isis Unveiled*, by the Countess Blavatsky, has no less

than thirty references to serpent worship and serpent
charming ; it is not worth while to repeat any of them
here, since all that is there to be found is condensed
in this chapter, which has drawn upon the same, or
almost the same, authorities.

Bancroft tells us (*Native Races of the Pacific
Slope*, vol. ii. p. 164) that in Montezuma's " Menagerie" were to be seen " serpents in long cages or
vessels large enough to allow them to move' about
freely.   These reptiles were also fed on human blood
and intestines."   Speaking of this " Menagerie,"
Prescott says that it was " placed under the charge
of numerous keepers, who acquainted themselves with
the habits of their prisoners, and provided for their
comfort and cleanliness."

But Bancroft (vol. ii. p. 165) quotes Thomas
Gage to the effect that alongside of this " Menagerie"
was the oratory, in which " Montezuma prayed in the
night season, and in that chapel the devil did appear
unto him and gave him answer according to his
prayers."   We learn, too, from Bancroft (vol. ii. p. 576)
that the fourth month in the Aztec Calendar was
called the " Feast of the Snake," while the fifteenth
in the series (they had eighteen of twenty days each)
was the " Moon of the Serpent of Clouds."

On p. 578 of the same volume he tells us that
the wall surrounding the great temple in Mexico was
carved with stone serpents.   On p. 584 we are
informed that the drum used in the ceremonies of this
temple was covered with snake skins ; and on the next

page it is stated that the portals of the Quetzal-Coatl
temple were a snake's jaws with fangs exposed.   So
much for the serpent cult among the Aztecs.   The
above will show that they had the serpent as a religious symbol beyond question.

Concerning snake-charming the following is also
from Bancroft, vol. ii. p. 797 :—

> " Cogolludo, for instance, speaking of the performances of a
> snake-charmer, says that the magician took up the reptile in his
> bare hands, as he did so using certain mystic words, which he
> (Cogolludo) wrote down at the time, but finding afterwards that
> they invoked the devil, he did not see fit to reproduce them in
> his work."

Baldwin (*Ancient America,* p. 28) asserts that no
" symbolic device is more common among the antiquities of Mexico and Central America than the form
of the serpent, and it was sometimes reproduced in
part in architectural constructions."

The fourth volume of Bancroft's work contains in
numerous places examples of serpent symbolism as
found among Aztecs, Mayas, and Quichés ; this
volume, however, does not enter quite so deeply into
the subject of American archæological remains as could
have been done had its publication been deferred a few
years.

The south-western part of our own country has
been penetrated by the railroad and the telegraph since
the years when Mr. Bancroft completed his then monu-
mental collection of data.   Not a day now passes
that some new discovery is not made by the ubiquitous

newspaper correspondents, untiring mining prospectors, tourists, or government scouts, who are poking
about in all the bends and angles of what less than a
decade ago was more of a *terra incognita* than Central
Africa.

In quoting these authorities I desire to make one
comment only. Not one of them has alluded to the
resemblance between the undulatory motion of the
serpent and the sinuous meandering of lightning, a
resemblance patent to every one, and portrayed by the
Moquis in the altar figured on Plate VI. This may help
to explain why the serpent was transferred to the
heavens and began to appear in the ceremonies of sun
worship.

To persons familiar with the difficulties of obtaining at remote army posts treatises upon special studies,
I am sure that no apology will be needed for not dis-
cussing this subject more exhaustively ; the quotations
given will be sufficient to indicate the channels from
which all desired information may be extracted, while
persons who wish to acquire fuller knowledge of a
mysterious phase of the world's religious development
will learn all that is certainly known in the elaborate
works of Fergusson, Squiers, Wake, Clarke, Inman,
Baldwin, Blavatsky, H. H. Bancroft, Lubbock, Prescott,
Tylor, and others.

CHAPTER XXI.

The Moquis Pueblos—Division into clans—Permitted degrees of marriage—Maiden accomplishments.

THE country inhabited by the Moqui Indians lies just west of the boundary line between New Mexico and Arizona (the 109th meridian), north and east of the Colorado Chiquito (Little Colorado or Flax) River, and some sixty or seventy miles south of the Grand Colorado. The villages or Pueblos of the Moquis are seven in number, each built upon the crest of a precipice of sandstone, impregnable to any assault to be expected from aboriginal foes. These villages are situated almost as follows : three very close together upon what is known as the eastern Mesa. The names of the villages in this cluster are, beginning at the eastern end, Tegua, also called Hano, Suchongnewy, and Hualpi.

A broad valley of seven miles of sand, interspersed with the corn, bean, and melon patches of these savage agriculturists, separates this mesa from the abrupt promontory upon which perches, first, the romantic Pueblo of Mushangnewy ; above that, looking for all the world like the stronghold of a mediæval German robber-baron, appear the masonry walls of Shupowlewy, and three miles away on the other wall of a wide and deep ravine the fortress of Sumopowy.

Oraybe, whose inhabitants studiously hold aloof from their blood-relatives of the other villages, occupies the summit of a lofty bluff, not quite ten miles, as the crow flies, from Sumopowy. What the meaning of these names may be we were unable to learn. Shupowlewy, it is allowable to suppose, means something equivalent to "peach orchard." It raises more and better peaches in the ratio of its population than any other Pueblo, and the word Shupowla, as we determined to our own satisfaction, means peaches. At least, when we resumed our studies in the villages, the word was useful in bringing all the half-ripe fruit we cared to purchase, and one of the Moqui young men, as anxious to ventilate his ignorance of Spanish as we were ours of Moqui, said that Shupowla was Dula-laz-no, which we took to be his idea of the pronunciation of Durazno (peach).

The name Moqui is not that by which they call themselves ; they have two names, one for ordinary use, the other for sacred or ceremonial occasions. The first is Opii, for which two interpretations were given ; the first that it referred to the manner of banging the hair common to this people ; the other, that it had some reference to the preparation of the bread-piki, which, in the shape of blue, banana-shaped cakes of corn-meal, can be found in piles in every Moqui house. The second, or sacred name, is Shumi, or something like that, which I learned from the Zunis

and also from the Moquis themselves.   Several of the
old men let me have it, but all the others with whom
I spoke professed a lamb-like innocence of the subject
which did not disconcert me in the least, as it was not
a matter they would be likely to confide to a stranger.

The Romans, we know, had some such sacred
name for their city which was never divulged save to
the initiate, lest a more widely-diffused knowledge
of it would enable their enemies to undermine the
defences by spell or incantation, in which the name
would of course figure.

The present dwelling-place of the Moquis is not
believed to have changed since the coming of Coronado
with the first Spanish expedition to this country in
1541.

It has never been conclusively demonstrated that
Coronado did enter the Moqui villages, but as he
made a very thorough examination of most of the
Pueblos, no violence will be done to historical accuracy
by assuming for argument's sake that the preceding
paragraph is strictly true.

They claim relationship with all tribes of Indians
who bang their hair, which would seem to affiliate
them with all peoples in the valley of the Colorado not
of Pi-Ute stock, *i.e.* all but the Chimohueois.   From
the number of deserted and dismantled houses on the
eastern mesa there is no reason to doubt that the
population of the first three villages has materially
shrunk within the past half century.   To how great
an extent this may be due to smallpox or some other

pest there is no means of judging; at present, the people on that mesa may be classified as healthy, and they certainly are prolific.

Turn where one will, he will be sure to bump against naked children, dogs, donkeys, chickens, goats, and sheep : the children, in some cases, show indications of scrofulous taint, of which more hereafter.

In former years the Moquis had outlying farming settlements and peach orchards at Muabe and Moyencopi, to the north-west, where they cultivated cotton ; and at Peach Spring, in the country of the Hualpais, now a station on the Atlantic and Pacific Railroad, where they raised much delicious fruit and grazed their herds of donkeys and sheep.

They are divided, as are all the American tribes, into bands or clans, each ruled by its own head or cacique, the general supervision of each village being entrusted to a " mungwee " or governor, elected by these caciques, and holding office for from one to two years. Each clan or gens, to give the name generally used, lives in its own section or ward, and in sending representatives to foot-races, dramatic dances, or things of that kind, will have them marked with totemic or gentile emblems. For example, if the clan or gens be that of the Eagle, the totem or clan-mark will be the eagle, and the dancer will be decorated on breast or back with some conventional symbol, recognised by the whole nation as the gentile emblem of the " Eagles." So with the Corn, Tobacco, Bear, or Badger representatives. The failing cases to this rule are to be found in such dramas as that of the snake-dance, where uniformity of decoration is insisted upon.

Upon this clan or gentile organisation of the American savage tribes depends not only much of their civic polity, but also their marriages and care of offspring.

It has been explained that a Moqui child belongs to the clan of the mother ; that all men and women of the same clan are *brothers and sisters*, between whom marriage is forbidden, although this contract is recognised between parties who come within our prohibited degrees.

For example, a young man of the Corn gens may be the son of a father belonging to the Eagle gens ; the sister of this father marrying will take to her own gens all children she may bear ; these children, Eagles, although first cousins of the young member of the Corn gens, will be regarded as perfectly eligible for marriage with him.

Schoolcraft says that—

"The totem of the Redskins is a symbol of the name of the progenitor, generally some quadruped or bird, or other object in the animal kingdom which stands, if we may so express it, as the surname of the family. It is always some animated object, and seldom or never derived from the inanimate class of nature. Its significant importance is derived from the fact that individuals unhesitatingly trace their lineage from it. By whatever name they may be called during their lifetime, it is the totem and not their personal name which is recorded on the tomb or adjetadig that marks the place of burial."

However accurate these remarks may have been

so far as regarded the tribes east of the Missouri, they must be taken with many grains of allowance for those of the south-west.

Among the so-called sedentary tribes or Pueblos of New Mexico and Arizona the totem or clan-sign is either vegetable or animal, while among Navajoes and Apaches it is simply geographical.

The method of tribal apportionment prevails among all savage races; the Negroes of Africa and the Aborigines of Australia, whose "kobongs," as minutely described by Sir George Gray, observe rules almost precisely like those of the clans or gentes of the Indians of North America.

Torquemada (quoted by H. H. Bancroft, vol. ii. p. 665) comments upon the peculiar principles governing marriages among the Aztecs. He tells us that they are divided into " linages " and " parentesco ;" that a child derives its parentage from its *father* (and not *mother* as with the tribes herein under discussion) ; and in another place he says that the respective " linages " lived in separate " barrios " or wards. A young man of any given lineage was prevented from marrying a young woman of the same lineage. Torquemada, and the other Spanish chroniclers, had hit upon this subject of gentile division, which is always to be understood when they make use of the expressions " linage," " parentesco," and " barrio."

The reader desirous of pursuing this topic farther, may consult with profit Morgan's *Ancient Society* and Lubbock's *Origin of Civilisation*. The writer has obtained complete lists of the clans of the sedentary tribes, —the Apaches, Navajoes, Apache-Mojaoes, Tontos, and others,—enough to demonstrate that this peculiar totemic or gentile organisation prevailed among all our native tribes, but he feels that the subject may not possess much interest for the general reader, and accordingly condenses within the limits of a paragraph matter which should for proper treatment be expanded into a distinct volume.

The Moqui child at birth is prayed over, and often rubbed with fine ashes, a custom observed also among the Zunis and, if history is to be trusted, among the Aztecs also.

"Ashes were rubbed on new-born babes to strengthen them and prevent bones from becoming loose."—Bancroft, vol. ii. p. 279.

The lot of the Moqui children is singularly free from trouble. They are not bothered with clothing or with daily ablutions. Until seven, eight, or nine years old, boys and girls run around totally destitute of covering, and scarcely less wild than the sheep and goats, whose sure-footed celerity, in jumping from rock to rock, they closely imitate.

Babies unable to walk alone are allowed to climb up and down the ladders which serve as entrance-ways to all the houses: clinging tenaciously to the rungs, they slide and climb down or up, assisted once in a while by watchful brothers and sisters. Dogs share in this accomplishment, and one of the most frequent, as it is one of the oddest sights to be seen in the Moqui towns, is that of a cur sedately making his way up or down this precarious mode of travel.

When a boy attains a suitable age he is drafted, so to speak, for the performance of such duties as watching the growing crops and ripening orchards, or herding the goats, sheep, and donkeys, which form such an important item of the wealth of this primitive people. The little girl is initiated at an early age into the mysteries of the kitchen, the fabrication of pottery and basket work, and, as she grows stronger, the operations of carding and dyeing wool, and the weaving of blankets, mantles, petticoats, garters, and sashes of cotton or wool. By the time she is fifteen, or even at an earlier age, she is considered nubile, and fairly entered in the matrimonial market. Her accomplishments are not very showy, but they are solid. She can bake, sew, dye, card, weave, and spin ; her nimble fingers fashion the plastic clays into every shape needed for use or ornament ; the tender shoots of the willow or the pliable roots of grasses respond to her fairy touch and round themselves into beautiful baskets, vivid with colouring, and repeating the sacred emblems of the butterfly, deer, or " thunder bird." In the number of stews, ragouts, and broths which she knows how to compound of the flesh of kid or sheep, and such vegetables as the onion, bean, and aromatic chile ; or in the endless diversity of hominy, mush, popcorn, and piki-bread, she will hold her own with the most ingenious American housewife.

If her house needs repair, without a moment's

delay she restores it to proper condition ; as the fervid sun of summer turns the velvety peaches to hues of scarlet and gold, or ripens to purple and blue the harvest of maize, the Moqui matron is constantly employed from early morn till dewy eve, drying fruit, husking corn, winnowing beans, or shredding pumpkins and melons. She has her faults,—the faults of her sex, of our common human nature,—but she makes a dutiful wife and a fond, affectionate mother.

CHAPTER XXII.

THE crusty old bachelor who hopes that in going
among the Moquis he will leave behind him the
fearful torture of "baby talk" with which civilised
mothers sometimes lacerate the ears of the unwary,
may as well disabuse himself of the fond delusion.
"Baby talk" is of rankest growth among Zunis and
Moquis, and perhaps, like the love of abusing the
neighbours, is a sexual peculiarity common to the
women of all races.

The children are well provided with toys and
games of all descriptions. Our little girls would find
in every house numbers of dolls, none of elaborate
workmanship, but all sufficiently good for their purpose. Often these are only the skin of a young kid
stuffed ; again, they are of wood, buckskin, or even
pottery ; and, lastly, the sacred images, after doing
duty as idols, are committed to the tender care of
the smaller children, who soon complete the work of
destruction.

Careful observations were made of everything seen

among them, and as these observations are supple-
mented by others taken at various times since 1869,
it is believed that a good general idea of their habits
and mode of life will have been obtained by readers
who have followed the course of this narrative.

They do not have the " convade," but, in common
with the Navajoes and Zunis, are strongly imbued
with the ideas of spiritual relationship between father
and child, upon which that curious practice depends.
To illustrate this, let me narrate an incident occurring
in my own experience, and although the hero was a
Navajo, yet in this vicinity (Keam's ranch) the
Navajoes and Moquis impinge so closely upon one
another in agricultural and pastoral lands, meet so
often in trade and at dances, and as they are to a
small extent intermarried, I make bold to assume the
existence of identical ideas upon this point in the two
tribes.   In Keam's store was a little iron figure representing a wrinkled old man smoking a lighted taper;
at this figure persons using cigarettes, pipes, or cigars,
were in the habit of getting a light without going to
the trouble of striking a match.   An old Navajo,
Ostin-Tzin-cle-he (Old man of the fire-stick or match),
who dropped in one morning, was offered a cigarette,
which he accepted, but when invited to light it at the
little statue lamp declined very emphatically. Curious
to learn his reasons, Keam asked for an explanation.
The old fellow said that it would be " bad medicine ";
his wife was expecting to present him soon with an
increase of family, and were he to light his cigarette

at that figure his wife would be sure to have a son just like it. Keam laughed heartily at the, to him, absurd notion, but the old Navajo was not to be driven from his opinions by ridicule. He reiterated what he had said, and appealed to several Indians standing near—Navajoes, with, I think, one or two Moquis; they all concurred in his prejudices.

The Moquis treat illegitimate children with the same consideration as is shown to those born in lawful wedlock. Their names refer to, but do not always indicate, the gens to which individual men or women belong. Very frequently it is not the gens of the Indian himself, but that of his father, which is preserved. An example of this has already been given in the name of the victorious racer, himself a member of the Cloud gens, but called Jushpoa or Badger, from the gens to which his father belonged.

The raiment of the Moquis is made of cotton and woollen goods, cut in the same general style as the garb of the Zunis. The best general idea of the attire of both sexes may be obtained by consulting the Plates.

The Moquis are much given to going about in their bare feet, an indulgence warranted by the clean, dry, level rock surface of the mesa upon which they dwell, where the friable sandstone has been worn by the attrition of generations six and eight inches deep in some of the trails.

The cotton mantles, petticoats, sashes, and kilts of the Moquis have already been sufficiently well

described.   They reproduce in our day the patterns
and materials in use at the time that Cabeza de Vaca
entered this region in 1540 (see Davis' *Conquest of
New Mexico*, p. 100), or which were in general
employment among the Aztecs at the time of the
landing of Cortes at Vera Cruz, a point upon which
Prescott and H. H. Bancroft may be consulted.

The royal robe of Montezuma was embroidered
with the sacred symbol of the butterfly, repeated in our
own day upon the mantles and skirts of the Zunis and
Moquis, or woven into their baskets in bright colours.

The standards carried by the Santo Domingo
Indians in the Tablet Dance [1] I know now were of
Moqui or Zuni manufacture.   No standards were,
however, seen among the Zunis and Moquis themselves.   The Shoshonees, in the heart of the Rocky
Mountains (Wyoming), have them elaborately made
of eagle feathers, and they were also of every-day
employment among the nations of Mexico.

Rabbit and coyote skins, principally the former,
are used in the preparation of coverlets, which,
according to demand, are made to serve as blankets,
mattresses, mantles, or even to suspend in front of
the doors should the wind blow with too great coldness and severity.

Feathers appear constantly in religious ceremonies
and dances, but are not in such ordinary use as among
the Plains' tribes farther north and east.   The Moquis,
Zunis, Navajoes, and Apaches have a common head-

[1] See Plate IV.

dress, a modification of the war-bonnet yet to be found among the last named.   It consists of a straw hat, surmounted by a plume of clipped feathers of the wild turkey, from amid which project two of the feathers of the eagle.   It makes a very effective decoration. Women use no head-dress of any kind, probably because their hair is puffed out so outrageously at the sides.   When exposed to the sun, they cover the head and face with the folds of their blankets in the same manner as Mexican women wrap themselves within the shelter of their " rebozos."

Masks are used in every dance and dramatic representation, and cover not the face alone, but the head and neck also.   These masks have various shapes, the favourite one being a cylinder of buckskin or cardboard, painted green, crested with feathers, and trimmed at bottom with a necklace of cedar.   Eyes, nose, and mouth are put in arbitrarily, the first being frequently bulging balls of buckskin set astride of a nose shaped of wood like a bird's beak; others again are altogether of sheepskin, the wool left on in the parts to cover head and neck, but denuded where the face is to be rudely represented by small circles for eyes, nose, and mouth.

While I say that these masks have various shapes, I must not be understood as asserting that the shape, colour, and arrangement of this disguise are left to the fitful fancy of the wearer ; on the contrary, each dance has its own special type of dress, to which the mask must conform.

Three or four of the masks found in the houses of
the easternmost towns had small horns affixed; in
one case they were a small pair of the horns of the
Rocky Mountain sheep, and in another a buckskin
cast of the heavy antlers of the same animal.

The breech-clout of the Moquis, constantly worn
by the men, is of white cotton cloth, six inches to eight
inches in width, and hanging down six inches in front
and rear. In their religious ceremonies they wear
them made of buckskin.

This garment of the Moquis is in strong contrast
with the pattern adopted by the neighbouring tribe,
the Apaches, who allow it to dangle to the knees in
front and almost to the heels behind, and sometimes,
though not frequently, decorate the borders with designs in scarlet thread.

The Moqui women seem to be, without cessation,
at work upon blankets and mantles, and yet the
supply has never equalled the demand. Boys and
girls of advanced age roam unconcernedly through
the streets of the different towns, especially of those
farthest to the west, in a condition repugnant to our
notions of modesty and delicacy. The traveller among
the Moquis learns as much of the customs of the
Garden of Eden, in respect to dress, as he is ever
likely to in any other part of the world.

Cradles of flat boards, with a semicircular screen
for the head, are swung from the rafters. They differ
in no essential particular from those used by all Indian
tribes; the little baby is wrapped up tightly in blan-

kets, with arms pinned close by its sides, and back straight against the hard unyielding casing, from which it looks out into vacant space for hours at a time. A lining of fresh cedar bark is placed within the cradle to add comfort and promote cleanliness.

The necklaces of the Moquis are of coral, chalchihuitl, sea-shell beads, bears' claws, olivette shells, hollow silver globes, and acorn cups. The silver beads are not in such plenty as they are among the Rio Grande Pueblos, and do not seem to be made by the Moquis. In a preceding chapter the question was mooted whether or not coral was known to the south-western Indians prior to the advent of the Spaniards. It may be worth while to insert here what is said upon this subject by Davis (*Conquest of New Mexico,* p. 100):

" The inhabitants in all this distance treated them (the party of Cabeza de Vaca) friendly, and gave them of everything they possessed, among which were deer, *blankets of cotton, corals that came from the South Sea,* and many fine *turquoises* brought from the north. They gave Vaca five emeralds made into arrow-heads, which were held in great esteem, and used in their dances and celebrations, which the Indians said they obtained from lofty mountains to the north, where there were populous towns and very large houses, in exchange for bunches of plumes and feathers of parrots." [1]

The turquoise here mentioned is the chalchihuitl, a stone held in high repute among all the aborigines of the south-west. Among the Aztecs it was considered almost sacred. Listen to what Las Casas has to say (see Bancroft, vol. ii. p. 458) :—

[1] See p. 26.

" He that stole precious stones, and more especially the stone
called chalchihuitl, no matter from whence he took it, was stoned
to death in the market-place, because no man of the lower orders
was allowed to possess this stone."

The Moquis do not possess the dexterity and skill
in working the precious metals which are evinced by
Navajoes and Zunis, some of whose silver work would
be no discredit to the best jewellers of New York.

Finger and ear rings and bangles of silver are to
be found in every family, the patterns following closely
those of the Zunis, if, indeed, the trinkets be not their
work.   Ear-rings are, with rare exceptions, made in
the form of a simple hoop, with two small silver globes
at lowest point.   But one hole is pierced in each ear—
a marked difference from the manner of tribes farther
to the north, which make as many as five holes in the
rim of each cartilage.

They display a great fondness for the iridescent
shell of the abalone, which they wear in all their
ceremonies as a pendant upon the breast.   This, they
told me, they obtained from the seashore, to which
they had been in the habit, at least until recently, of
making pilgrimages every four or five years.   These
stories I at first took with large doses of salt ; but the
Navajoes told me that the Zunis and Moquis both
used to go west on such pilgrimages, and an intelligent
Indian in the Pueblo of Jemez assured me that he
had worked for two whole years in the little town of
Santa Barbara, Southern California.

Very little, if any, face paint is used by them ;

all that I have ever seen used has been applied to
bodies, limbs, and countenance at time of dances.
They do not tattoo, do not use nose-rings or labrets,
and do not mutilate or disfigure themselves in any
way. The men bang their hair in front at level of
eyebrows, on the sides, at the level of mouth, and
gather all that is at back into a queue, which is carefully tied up with red yarn or narrow strips of cloth.
Young maidens wear their hair in two puffs, one at
each side above ears and back of temples, stretched
over a framework of worsted and small twigs.

A reference to the Plates will be of great assistance
in forming a correct idea of the methods in vogue.

The children are well supplied with toys. Among
these may be named bows and arrows, slings, toy
cradles, baskets, little household utensils of pottery,
tops of several kinds, and, lastly, doll-babies, either
regularly made as such, or else degraded to this
service after having served a tour of duty as gods.

The Moquis are dexterous in the manufacture of
baskets, of which there are no less than three or four
kinds. The simplest is of yucca shoots, plated without
ornamentation, and the other of tender willow twigs,
round, perfectly flat, and dyed in yellow, dark red
blue, and black; often these are interwoven with the
figures of the butterfly, deer, thunder bird, or other
sacred emblem.

Matting, also of yucca fibre, is another of the
Moquis manufactures.

The Moquis not only weave blankets and girdles of

wool and knit stockings of yarn, but they also make
mantles of cotton grown by themselves.   The borders
of these mantles are elaborately decorated with scarlet
and blue-black woollen embroidery in the pattern
known, I believe, as the Kensington stitch.   The
Moquis, like most primitive workers in wool, fix the
colours with urine.   They are almost alone in this
industry; in fact, if we consider the manufacture
from the growth of the staple to the appearance of
the cloak or blanket, they are without competitors.
The Zunis weave the same kind of cotton mantle,
but do not grow the fibre, preferring to buy this from
their neighbours the Moquis, whose fields, exposed
to warmer suns, have yielded the precious bolls from
generations long prior to the advent of the Spaniards.

Generally blankets or mantles alone are made, but
there are also to be found in each house beautiful petticoats and broad sashes, of the same material, similarly
ornamented and proudly displayed across horizontal
bars, swinging from the rafters of the living room.

These garments in our day command a very high
price—double and treble that of the corresponding ones
in wool alone, are invested with sacred qualities, and
used only on occasions of ceremony or of religious import.   Women are married in them, use them during all
the great festivals of their lives, and at death bequeath
them to their daughters; except in those rare instances
where an accumulation of wealth incites the surviving
relatives to an ostentation of grief, when they are
wrapped around the corpse and interred in the tomb.

Lieutenant-General Sheridan has one of these sacred mantles, made by the Zunis, and used by them in the winter festival of Fire : it enwrapped the figure of one of their gods called the Shálacu.   The Zunis told me that all the prayers and blessings invoked that day would fall upon that blanket, and those like it, and attach themselves to the persons of the owners.

Some notion may be formed of the value in which those garments are held by the Zunis and Moquis when it is stated that even with all the influence and persuasion Mr. Cushing could bring to my assistance, it was almost nine months before I succeeded in obtaining the one here spoken of.

The embroidery represents butterflies in rich scarlet and blue, and symbolical devices of a religious type.

The youngsters play ball, using globes of buckskin stuffed with hair, the game of " fox and geese," and derive much amusement from an odd kind of contest, which consists in seeing which of two sides can kick a small, smooth, flat stone to a certain goal.   They have something like our quoits, only instead of iron rings smooth, round stones are employed.   Races on foot or horseback are much indulged in, but cards are rarely to be seen among them ; a contrast to the partiality of the Navajoes, who while away whole days and nights, and bet the clothes on their backs in contests with the " paste-boards."

The musical instruments of this people are numerous. They have gourd rattles, rattles of tortoise-shells and sheep's toes, rattles of a T shape, horse-fiddles, made of pumpkins hollowed out and opened so as to admit of the insertion of a serrated stick, along which can be rapidly drawn a fragment of pine wood ; strings of shells, and strings of sheep bones. Whistles, flutes, and drums complete the list. The drums are made of large earthen ollas, covered with sheep-skin, or of hollow cottonwood logs, fashioned and painted like the drums described in the dance at Santo Domingo Pueblo.

Girls marry at almost any age beyond ten or twelve ; fifteen may be looked upon as the limit, but child marriages are frequent. The Moquis are mono-gamists ; they do not *purchase* their wives. The women, according to all accounts, have a powerful voice in determining their own future.

Bishop Hatch, a very intelligent, level-headed Mormon, who, when a boy, had been left among the Moquis, and had grown up among them, speaking their language and that of the Navajoes fluently, is authority for the following description of a Moqui marriage which he witnessed, and of which he gave me this account at " Sunset," Arizona, in August 1881 :—

" A feast was spread for the families of the bride and groom and invited guests ; in this figured blue corn-mush, " piki " or tissue bread, stewed peaches, and a ragout of mutton, beans, and chile.

" While the guests were paying their respects to the feast the bride and groom retired to an inner room, disrobed, and bathed each other from head to foot in clear water. Then they came back to the long room where the guests were assembled, were invested with their new cotton garments, the ends of which were tied together, and after listening to a brief homily from one of the old men were declared to be man and wife."

Let us compare this with the customs of the tribes farther to the south :—

"The ceremonies of the Pepiles were simple and unique. Matches were made by the cacique and carried into effect under his direction. At the appointed time the kinsfolk of the bride proceeded to the house of the bridegroom, whence he was borne to the river and washed. The relatives of the bridegroom performed the same act of cleansing upon the person of the bride.

"The two parties, with their respective charges, then proceeded to the house of the bride. The couple were now tied together by the ends of the blankets in which they were enfolded, and laid away married. After the ceremony an interchange of presents took place between the relatives of the newly-married couple, and they all feasted together."—Bancroft, vol. ii. p. 672.

Again, he says that "among the Aztecs the dresses of the bride and groom were tied together." The bride was placed on the left of the groom, and was dressed in a "cuatli or skirt, richly embroidered and worked."—Vol. ii. pp. 256-257.

After marriage the Moquis will speak to their mothers-in-law, or sit in the same room with them, which is more than the Apaches or Navajoes will do.

CHAPTER XXIII.

Status of wives—Reception of visitors—Weapons and instruments—
  Food supply—Characters and superstitions—Talismans and idols
  —Tobacco—No community of goods.

BOTH women and men in their way are extremely
industrious. The women have the management, control, and ownership of the houses. A man will never
sell anything in the house unless his wife consent, and
then she pockets the money. Often I have concluded,
as I fancied, a bargain with a husband, and have
been much perplexed by the arrival of the wife and
her refusal to ratify it. This feature of domestic
management is noticeable among the Pueblos generally.

The elevated place attained by women among the
Moquis is shown by the consideration accorded her.
No case of nose-slitting or other mutilation of a wife
can be put on record against the Moquis. Their
neighbours, the Apaches, were long known for the
brutal vengeance visited upon the women whom blind
jealousy led them to suspect of infidelity.

Among the most distressing sights to be imagined
is that of an Apache squaw with her nose cut completely off! And one of the very first, as it was one of

the noblest of the reforms instituted under General Crook's administration of affairs in Arizona (1871-1875), was the prohibition, under the severest penalties, of this inhuman torture.

The same frightful disfigurement was customary among the Iztepecs of Mexico. "The guilty woman's husband cut off her ears and nose."—Bancroft, vol. ii. p. 466.

The houses of the Moquis are of stone, in natural forms, gathered from the mesa upon which they live. This rubble is of all sizes and shapes from 3 inches to 8 inches cube, is laid in mud, plastered always on the inside, and sometimes without.

It makes a durable habitation. The houses are built upon the flat rock surface without foundations.[1]

The bedding of the Moquis is of sheep and goat skins, rabbit mantles, and blankets of Navajo as well as domestic manufacture. The Navajoes perhaps were the first to make blankets of *wool*. Their semi-nomadic life qualified them perfectly as herders, but incapacitated them for raising cotton.

Visitors among the Moquis are generally received with civility. Blankets and skins are spread upon the floor, upon which they are asked to seat themselves, and refreshments are in nearly every instance offered. Glancing about the living room, or at the exterior of the house, no totemic emblems are to be seen; but upon the baskets, pottery, and blankets, or

[1] See also pp. 114, 135, and 136.

mantles of cotton, as has been explained, the characters are very often symbolical.

For the treatment of disease they resort to sweating arrangements—"little sweat lodges" much the same as those with which the reports of travellers among other tribes have made the world familiar. They use emetics and clysters for simple troubles, but for obscure diseases invoke the aid of the medicine man.

The ventilation of their houses is in wretched condition, a fact which does not give them the slightest concern. The stench is at nearly all times sickening, and in the Estufas or Kibas, especially during the time of preparation for their dances, can almost be cut with a knife.

Their weapons of war are few in number, and not worth describing. Bows and arrows in no great quantity, and smoothbore muskets and shot-guns, dating back to the year 1, make up the inventory. It needs no second glance to assure the observer that he is among a people with whom agriculture, pastoral cares, and traffic occupy all the hours of the day, and who have neither time nor inclination for war, and but little for the chase.

These Indians have an instrument of wood, shaped like the letter L, with the elbow curved. With this they can do rapid and effective work against small game. As it resembles the "boomerang" of the Australians in all except returning to the feet of the thrower, I have always called this by that name.

They do not have the "macuahuitl" of the Aztecs. Careful search was made for such a weapon without success. But while at the Pueblo of Taos, in the summer of this same year, I noticed a "macuahuitl," or what might be taken for such. It was a heavy wooden club armed with projecting teeth of iron. The weapon was armed with teeth of stone, and when hurled with full force would cut off a man's head! When I drew a Moqui boomerang one of the old men said that they didn't use such things in Taos now, but their forefathers did.[1]

Stone hammers, axes, hatchets, adzes, shoes, berry-mashers, etc., are still plentiful in all the towns, more particularly those farthest to the west, but their use is rapidly fading away before the introduction of American steel and iron ware.

Mortars and mullers, each with pestles, and "metales" with the proper grinding stones, are in constant employment, many of them well made, but none with any attempt at ornamentation. These are, with scarcely an exception, of basalt, occasionally of compact sandstone, never of granite or steatite.[2]

The Moquis are skilled and laborious farmers, and make reservoirs and canals to store and carry water ; they do not irrigate, there being no necessity for this mode of applying moisture to the growing crops ; they protect their young harvests from tempests by build-

[1] The very same weapon was in use among the Indians on the Rio Grande in the latter part of the sixteenth century.—Davis' *Conquest of New Mexico*, pp. 248 and 262.   [2] See Plate XXXI.

ing on the windward side little walls of stone. Fish are not eaten, but rabbits are held in high repute, and field-mice, to speak from what was seen at Mushangnewy, are occasionally used. The last two articles of food are served to the eagles, which are still kept in cages in the Pueblos of Oraybe, Mushangnewy, Sumopowy, and Supowolewy, but in Suchongnewy, Hualpi, and Tegua (or Háno, as it is sometimes called), they are not to be seen.

Crickets sometimes figure in their messes, but their normal food is the product of their fields, orchards, and flocks. They raise corn, wheat, beans, tomatoes, chile, melons, squashes, peaches, and sun-flowers; all of these in quantity. A few apricots and nectarines are also grown. They also have fields of pumpkins, eating both fruit and seed, and expressing from the latter the oil for mixing such paint as requires it. In common with the Apaches and Hualpis they cut and roast the leaves of the mescal or century plant, of which they are extremely fond; and once in a while they come across a deposit of wasp honey, regarded as a precious delicacy.

Peaches and water-melons are dried; pumpkins cut into strips and desiccated, or, with ripe melons, stored away under mounds of hay for preservation until winter.

Bulbous plants furnish another source of supply, the wild potato being highly esteemed and eaten with clay [1] as a condiment. At a rough guess, it may be

[1] See p. 71.

asserted that they have no less than thirty varieties of farinaceous food; corn, in the ear, roasted and boiled, hulled, popped or ground, made into mush with water or milk, and into cakes with the flour of pumpkin and sun-flower seeds, spread as a thin gruel over hot plates of sheet-iron, and baked at once into crisp sheets delicate as tissue paper, and then rolled into the form of bananas, or patted between the hands into tortillas, which taste too much of mutton suet to commend themselves to an American palate; or finally, assuming the shape of small rolls which are far from unpleasant to the taste. These are a few, and a few only, of the multifarious devices of the Moqui cuisine.

Not satisfied with the bountiful tribute of fruit yielded by their orchards, they levy assessments upon the wild plants of their country. The Spanish bayonet and Indian fig furnish fruits much in favour with the Moquis, and used by them in the raw state or baked in ovens.

Sheep and goats supply the greater percentage of their meat diet, but they are by no means averse to a good mess of stewed pup. They have great flocks and herds of sheep, goats, and donkeys; an inconsiderable number of cows and horses; a sufficiency of hogs, some chickens and turkeys, and a superabundance of growling, worthless dogs.

Ovens, shaped like bee-hives, are to be found in every street, and also upon the roofs. They have two kinds of fuel—cedar branches for ordinary purposes, and compressed sheep and goat manure for "firing" pottery.

Silver money is used exclusively, and nickels are regarded with ill-concealed distrust.

But such a determinate value is attached to buckskin, eagle and wild turkey feathers, pelts of the Rocky Mountain lion, chalchihuitl, abalone, olivette shells (unpierced), the perforated sea-shell beads, silver necklaces, and other ornaments common to themselves, the Zunis, Navajoes, and the Pueblos on the Rio Grande, blankets of Navajo manufacture and their own cotton mantles and girdles, that it would not be going far out of the way to dignify some or all of these commodities with the title of circulating media.

Among their manufactures may properly be placed those of saddles and bridles ; table ware is made of pottery, but spoons and ladles of horn, wood, and gourds, are in every house.

Another industry is the making of idols, which in scores and scores adorn or disfigure the living rooms. These are generally of wood. A fuller description is reserved for the appropriate place.[1]

They are a hard-working people, superstitious to a degree, and devout pagans, possessed of an elaborate theology and ritual.

Intimate commercial relations are maintained with the Cohoninos or Ava-Supais on the west, the Navajoes to the N.E. and S.E., the Apaches and Zunis to the

[1] See p. 257.

south, the Pi-Utes to the north, and the Pueblos along the Rio Grande, Puerco, and Jemez rivers.

They make no stimulants, but a ready market exists for all the native wine and brandy the people of Isleta can supply, as well as for any " tizwin " the Apaches can spare from their own needs.

They are avaricious in the extreme, vacillating and timid, and generally do not impress one as being so reliable as their immediate neighbours, the Apaches and Navajoes.   They have not been known to engage in hostilities with whites or Indians since the date of American occupation.

At the present day they bury their dead in the ground at the foot of the mesa ; corpses are interred with heads to east and wrapped in blankets.   There are no funeral processions, and there are no professional " keeners " or mourners.

Their religion is indeed a curious mixture, something worthy of a life-study.   There are to be noticed in it, even upon superficial examination, traces of all the devotional aberrations of which the human mind is capable.

To begin with, the worship of ancestors is well-defined.

No well-bred Moqui, Zuni, or other Pueblo Indian will eat of food without throwing into the fire a small crust that the spirits of their dead may not suffer.[1] The elements come in for their share of adoration, as

---

[1] The Aztecs threw food into the fire in honour of the God Tlalte-cutli.—Sahagun and Torquemada, quoted by Bancroft, vol. ii. p. 285.

do the plants and stars generally. Upon the walls of their Estufas are rudely scratched and painted the symbols of sun, moon, morning and evening star, and Pleiades.

They have the same sacred animals as the Zunis, prominent among which are the snake, mountain lion, bear, mole, and eagle. There are truly more gods than there are Moquis ; the uglier and more mis-shapen the deity, where all are hideous and distorted, the more venerable in the eyes of the worshipper. Being an agricultural people, the Moquis naturally bow at the shrine of the power which dispenses or withholds the rain ; this god of the clouds, Omá-a, was decidedly in the ascendancy at the time of the snake-dance, but it would be idle to assume that he was chief of the Moqui pantheon. In twenty-four hours the propitiatory offerings might be laid at the shrine of a rival. They have a vague feeling of rever-ence for As-sun-nut-li, the Woman in the Water of the West, from whom come beads, grains, fruits, and flocks.

Sacred springs and fountains dot their country ; many of these are walled up with masonry, and, as in the case of one not far from Supowlewy, have placed on the steps going down to them votive presents of eagle feathers tied to twigs, of small pieces of willow sapling painted green, of petrified wood, and of other materials which the experience of the untutored savage has assured him will be most certain to placate or propitiate.

Each Moqui is provided with a talisman or amulet, constantly worn, and believed in with the same abiding faith displayed by the African towards his fetish. These are arbitrarily assumed to represent the deer, bear, eagle, lightning, phallus, or other sacred principle by which the Moqui is guided and protected. The efficacy of these talismans is increased tenfold when smeared with the blood of the animal represented ; in such an event the happy possessor goes forth confident that should bear, deer, or antelope cross his path it must yield to his fleet arrow or unerring bullets.

Idols of large size, fifteen inches high, exist, and are much reverenced. Attention has been called to the peculiar sacredness apparently attaching to the concretionary sandstone " torsos" bearing a fanciful resemblance to human or animal forms. These have been found deposited in the ground, surrounded by a circle of globular sandstone pebbles ; one dug up by the writer not far from Oraybe, in October 1881, had been thus honoured. It bore a crude likeness to a headless four-footed animal, either the bear or mountain lion.

We here found a form of idol different from any before described. This may have been simply a corner-post of the field belonging to one of the clans, but the human lineaments depicted upon the surface, and the small sacrificial plumes buried at its feet, warrant the conclusion that it too was an idol.

The Romans had a god " Terminus," who guarded

their boundaries, and in whose honour they observed
sacred ceremonies called "Terminalia." The Zunis
have similar ceremonies every year, and as they insist
that they possess the same religion as the Moquis,
there is less obstacle to the assumption than there
might otherwise be. Human sacrifices are no longer
indulged in, nor indeed were there found any traces
that they ever had been. The averment of Pedro
Pino that all the Pueblos had maintained this horrid
rite in secret down to a comparatively recent date
will be found on pp. 196, 197, and is worthy of consideration.

The Moquis have an implicit belief in witches and
witchcraft, and the air about them is peopled with
maleficent spirits. Those who live at Oraybe exorcise
the malign influences with the chanting of hymns and
ringing of bells. While with General Crook at that
isolated and scarcely-known town, in the fall of 1874,
by good luck I had an opportunity of witnessing this
strange mode of incantation. The whole village
seemed to have assembled, and after shouting in a
loud and defiant tone a hymn or litany of musical
sound, emphasised by an energetic ringing of a bell,
advanced rapidly, in single file, down the trail leading from the crest of the precipice to the peach
orchards below.

The performers, some of the most important of
whom were women, pranced around the boundaries of
the orchard, pausing for a brief space of time at the
corners, all the while singing in a high key and get-

ting the worth of their money out of the bell. At a signal from the leader a rush was made for the trees, from which, in less than an hour, the last of the delicious peaches breaking down the branches were pulled and carried by the squaws and children to the village above. In the early days of spring, when the fields are to be tilled, the devout Moquis prepare the sacrificial plumes of eagle down attached to little sticks, which are buried in the corners of their lands.[1]

Tobacco smoking plays an important part in all the religious celebrations of the south-western Indians. They have among them two kinds : that known to us as tobacco, and another called bunchi on the Rio Grande and piba by the Moquis, which latter is a low, squatty plant, with thick, broad, dark-green leaves, which have an acrid taste. Pipes are used in sacred ceremonies, as are hollow canes, similar to those once employed by the Aztecs.—V. Bancroft, vol. ii. p. 284.

No women appeared in the snake-dance, at least not as active participants. The great numbers present confined themselves strictly to the throwing of the cunque or sacred meal, which figures so prominently in every solemn rite, and to the muttering of prayers whose purport was not learned.

Inquiry developed the fact that women are admitted to a full share in many of the devotional ceremonies, which in nearly every case have a dramatic character.

[1] " Oviedo observed certain bundles of sticks planted at the corners of each field " (in Nicaragua).—Bancroft, vol. ii. p. 719.

The last, but by no means the least, division of the rites of this ever-strange race, cannot well be discussed in a publication of this kind, which may find its way into general circulation. Allusion is made to phallic and obscene worship, which has a deep root in all the towns of the sedentary Indians, especially those of the Zunis and Moquis, and it may briefly be said that no part of the world has more to present that is repugnant and disgusting to the sentiments and judgment of people brought up in the schools of a Christian civilisation.

Two topics have been left untouched until this moment. One is the question of community of goods among the Indians of this country. There is not at the present moment, and I doubt if there ever was, at least among the tribes of the south-west, such a mode of accumulating, preserving, and distributing property as the Miri or Commune as it exists among the Russians in our day, and which is the typical exponent of this theory.

In taking this stand I know that I am antagonising the position maintained by Morgan, one of the ablest writers upon the subject of aboriginal government; but for all that, I have not the slightest hesitancy in affirming that no such system as Communism is recognised by our native tribes, and no such system would be tolerated by them for a moment.

They are co-operative in all their labours, whether as hunters, herders, or tillers of the soil ; but each man gathers the spoils of his individual skill and daring, or the fruits of his own industry. The Moquis and Zunis, as a general but by no means absolute rule, plant by clans or gentes, but each farmer has his own patch of corn, beans, and melons, and each matron her own little plot in which to raise onions, beets, chile, and other vegetables. Regular details are made in the different villages for such duties as herding, patrolling, guarding the growing crops from crows, or constructing the little ditches which allow superfluous rain to escape; but the crops are not turned into a common store, nor is their distribution under any one's superintendence.

Each family puts away its own supplies, preserves them in bins which generally hold enough to last them through a bad harvest, and cooks and eats *ad libitum*, without reference to the wishes of any other persons.

But, on the other hand, an Indian never acquires real estate according to our knowledge of the term. He has a possessory right in any strip of land he may cultivate, so long as that cultivation continues, and no longer. The moment he vacates any other member of the tribe may put in seed and gather the resulting harvest.

As an Indian expressed himself, "We don't own the ground any more than we own the air and water."

CHAPTER XXIV.

THE following brief description of the pottery of the Pueblos was originally prepared to accompany the small cabinet of specimens collected for Lieutenant-General Sheridan during the time that I was on duty among the tribes of the south-west compiling the ethnological notes and memoranda of a fractional part of which this work is a condensation.

It is hoped that the description, incomplete as it is, may afford some idea of the progress attained by our aborigines in the ceramic art, the knowledge and practice of which, once widely diffused among the inhabitants of our country, are now confined to the sedentary Indians of New Mexico and Arizona.

A short description of the mode of fabrication, purposes, and uses of this pottery may prove of interest, and is submitted for the information of readers, who are cautioned that only the faintest outline of the subject is attempted.

The material employed is the marl and clay found in the immediate vicinity of most of the Pueblos:

this is carefully freed from grit or other extraneous particles, mixed with water and tempered to a paste of the consistency of dough ; in this are incorporated fragments of old pottery, crushed to the fineness of saw-dust, the object of the addition being apparently to increase the porosity of the general mass, and permit the free escape of air-bubbles during the process of firing.

Where a fine " biscuit " is desired, the squaw from time to time samples the mass by putting it to her tongue.   In the coarser varieties, minute pebbles are always to be found, and, in the work of the Hualpi Indians of Northern Arizona, pounded granite or mica schist.

The entire manufacture is monopolised by the old squaws, many of whom evince a dexterity and artistic skill which excite admiration and wonder when the meagre facilities at their command are considered. They employ neither wheel, lathe, nor mould, but frame each article by hand alone, commencing with a small lump of paste, in which a depression is made by a rapid twirl of the thumb, addition and shape being given with the eye alone as guide, the material being constantly damped and patted with a small paddle of pumpkin rind.

The desired size and shape having been obtained, the pottery is first exposed to the warm rays of the sun and thoroughly dried, and is afterwards, frequently although not always, rubbed and polished with a small smooth flat stone.

The fuel employed is sheep manure pressed into compact cakes, which are preserved in stone bins or other sheltered places until needed.

This fuel supplies a strong but equable heat well suited for the purpose of firing, and it may be remarked that the inhabitants of the elevated valleys of Thibet make a general use of the same fuel, which they call Argol, and which the eminent French missionary priest, the Abbé Huc, assures us is held in the highest repute for the qualities mentioned. The pieces to be fired are carefully placed upon small stones, and covered with cakes of the fuel, which is then lighted, and in the course of an hour or less the baked pottery is sufficiently cooled to be withdrawn and laid aside until required for use.

An exception to the kind of fuel here mentioned is to be found among the Apaches, living near Abiquiu and Tierra Amarilla in the northern part of New Mexico, who occasionally make a very crude pottery, which is fired by means of the pitch or turpentine of the piñon tree: its inferiority in design and manufacture alike is apparent at a glance.

While making an examination of Indian ruins, in the Vude valley, Arizona, in December of last year, I came across a stone bin filled with what was evidently the chewed fibre of the century plant or mescal. For the information of those unacquainted with the subject, it is fair to say that but little of this plant can be eaten; by roasting, much of the starchy matter it contains is changed into syrup, which is sucked out

and the filamentary mass thrown away. The reason
for saving these dry wads was not apparent ; a plausible explanation, which will answer until a better be
devised, is that they served as fuel for burning the
pottery of the pre-historic inhabitants, who had neither
sheep nor goats.

Such a fuel might not be greatly inferior to the
straw burned by the Russian Mennonites in Dakota,
or the corn cobs consumed in the kitchens of our
Western farmers.

The designs are applied in red, yellow, white, and
black, and more rarely, as will afterwards be specified,
in green ; as the squaw had no need of a model for
giving shape, so also she gets along with without
pattern or drawing from which to trace the totemic
or other symbols with which she decorates her work.
These are painted on with small brushes or pencils,
made sometimes of the fur of the rabbit and at others
of the fibre of the yucca. Red and yellow are furnished by ochreous earths, white from kaolin, and
black from carbonaceous matter.

Some of the manufacture to be found in the
Pueblos on the Rio Grande, near Santa Fé, has a
semi - crystalline lustre due to the presence in the
earth of small particles of half-disintegrated mica
schist.

The colours are applied before firing, which incor-
porates them thoroughly with the body of the pottery
itself. While full rein seems, at first inspection, to
have been given to individual taste and fancy in the

matter of decoration, a closer examination will show
that besides the designs of a purely ornamental type,
such as checker - work or flower forms, there are
two general classes of ornamentation—the totemic,
reproducing such clan marks as the deer or other
animals, and those in which the symbolism is of a
more pronouncedly religious character, as the sun,
snake, or the sea-serpent, frog, and tadpole, the last
to be seen on the sacred pottery baskets in which are
kept the sacred corn-meal and the holy water used
during their religious ceremonies and dances. Animal
figures occur with great frequency in all the pottery
ornamentation, flowers and plants being delineated
only at comparatively rare intervals.   Several of the
examples of floral ornamentation purchased at Acoma
and Laguna discovered artistic abilities of a very
high order, and would have been no discredit to
our best American ceramists : unfortunately, these
prized specimens were crushed into fragments in
packing.

Di Cesnola (*Cyprus*, p. 94) speaks of finding vases
of bright red or black varnished ware of globular
form, upon which the decorations consisted of zigzag
lines and other simple geometrical patterns "incised
deeply into the clay, and afterwards filled in with a
white substance, probably plaster."

Two fragments of this ware were found by Mr.
Schliemann in his Trojan excavations (engraved in
Troy and its Remains, p. 135), and "there seems
to be little doubt of the great antiquity of this

class of pottery." No pottery answering to this description is to be found among the Moquis in our country, or in the ruins of Arizona.

Animal figures are not only delineated upon the various earthen vessels made by the Pueblo Indians, but the vessels themselves are shaped into animal forms which are sure to attract attention from the grotesque exactness with which the characteristics of the animal represented are adhered to.

The potters of Zuni, Acoma, and Laguna surpass all others in this class of work, those of the first-named Pueblo excelling most in the figures of owls and tortoises, and those of the last two in fishes and oxen. It is noticeable that earthenware owls, almost identical with those now made in Zuni, have been exhumed from ruins in Arizona, in districts inhabited by the fierce Apache for hundreds of years.

Small figures of animals half-baked or unbaked are from time to time placed in the Estufas of the Moquis, and similar ones have been excavated from the ruins near Prescott, A.T.

The Pueblos nearer to Santa Fé display more of an inclination to reproduce misshapen and distorted "figurines," which are most generally obscene—and probably at one time served as idols, much as the painted wooden " rain-gods " (so-called) of the Moquis do at this day. This, however, is mere conjecture.

Prince, in his work on *Pottery and Porcelain*, p. 93, gives a description which may apply to this case.

"Small statues and figures were in favour and common among the Romans, representing a great variety of subjects, mythological and real. Actors, buffoons, dwarfs, portrait figures abound. Wherever the Roman power extended in Europe, these figures were found in quantity. They were called Sigillia or Sigillaria, the last days of the Saturnalia, called Sigillaria, being the time when it was customary to make presents of these images."

It may possibly be that this custom was transplanted from Spain, but another and more plausible explanation would be that these originally were intended for cinerary urns or mortuary vases, and that when cremation, if it ever existed along the Rio Grande, was superseded by burial in the earth, these figures were still manufactured, no longer for service, but first as emblems and at last as toys. Such a custom obtained in Yucatan. "Cremation in Yucatan was reserved for the higher classes. An image of the dead person was made;—of wood for a king, of clay for a noble. The back part of the head of this image was hollowed out, and a portion of the body having been burned, the ashes were placed in this hollow, which was covered with the skin of the occiput of the corpse."—Bancroft, vol. ii. p. 801. In another place (same volume, pp. 612 and 614) he says that statues were made in honour of the dead Mexican kings, and cites Duran to the effect that the bones of a certain king were placed inside of a pottery statue. He tells us also (p. 608) that the Aztecs and other Mexican tribes cremated. Davis (*Conquest of New Mexico*, p. 169) says that the people of Cibola burned their dead. Cibola is supposed by some to be the Moqui, by others the Zuni villages.

Herbert Spencer, *Principles of Sociology*, c. xxi., gives the following information, which may be of service :—

"The Mexicans, according to Gomara, closed the box (in which some hair and teeth of the deceased king were present), and placed above it a wooden figure, shaped and adorned like the deceased. Then they made great offerings, and placed them where he was burned and before the box and figure. . . .

"So also the Egyptians often worshipped mummies in cases shaped and painted to represent the dead man. The Mexicans practised cremation, and, when men killed in battle were missing, they made figures of them, and, after honouring these, burnt them and buried the ashes."

Vases in forms of animals,—fishes, dogs, chickens, ducks, etc., exhumed at Dali, are represented on p. 98 of Di Cesnola's *Cyprus*. Schliemann says (*Mycenæ*, p. 260), "Vases of terra-cotta in forms of animals were frequent at Troy." It may be added that, according to his own writings, they must have been frequent at Mycenæ also.

The purposes for which this pottery is made are too numerous to mention ; they include an answer to almost every demand in the domestic economy of this singular people, such as receptacles for the preservation of various foods, platters and pots in which to cook it or set it upon the floor when ready for consumption, spoons, cups, plates, ladles, the sacred dishes already spoken of, paint and salt holders, and last, but by no means least, *drums* and *chimneys*. To make the drums, a large olla is selected, one that will hold from five to ten gallons, and covered tightly with a sheepskin, upon which the performer beats with a curved stick. The music extracted seems "to sooth the savage breast," but in nearly every case gives civilised people a violent headache.

The chimneys of most of the Pueblos are constructed of ollas which have passed the heyday of their youth and usefulness for other purposes. The bottoms are carefully knocked out and one pot placed above another until the necessary height is reached, the whole structure being held in place by a plaster of mud.

No well-defined example of glazing has yet been found in the pottery of the American Indians of the south-west. That to which the term glazed has in time past been applied without due consideration, is now conceded by the most careful thinkers to be nothing more or less than fragments of vessels used for cooking purposes, and in which a partial vitrification of the siliceous or saline particles present in the clay itself had been accomplished by the long-continued application of heat. The polish upon these fragments may also have been occasioned by attrition with corn cobs and sharp pieces of slate, which are used by the squaws in cleaning all culinary vessels.

Prince (*Pottery and Porcelain*, pp. 17 to 35) defines glazed pottery as pottery covered with a thin coating of glass. Different mixtures are used to form

this glaze, the practical result being the same that
when the pottery covered with the glazing mixture is
baked, the mixture fuses and forms a thin transparent
glass, covering the ware and any painting which has
been placed on it. Schliemann (*Mycenæ*, p. 284)
refers to the discovery of a "very large quantity of
hand-made or very ancient wheel-made pottery. To
the former category belongs a vase which has been
wrought to a lustrous surface by hand-polishing."

The black polished specimens of modern manufacture so frequently designated as glazed, should
more properly be called "varnished." They correspond
in description to the specimens unearthed by Schliemann at Mycenæ, and by him called "monochromatic
black lustrous."

This variety is much prized by the Indians for its
power to withstand sudden extremes of tempera-
ture. It is found in greatest plenty in the Pueblos
on the Rio Grande, notably in that of San Juan.

Squiers (*Nicaragua*) quotes the remark of Mr. W.
W. Edwards, *Voyage up the Amazon*, to the effect
that this black lustre is there "produced by a resinous
gum found in the forests, which was gently rubbed
over the vessels, previously warmed over a bed of
coals."

The Indians of Acoma and Laguna make use of a
bright green pigment applied in circular blotches to
their pottery before firing, which fixes it to the surface
in such a way that it may almost be called a glaze ;
the composition of this pigment was not learned :

there is some reason to believe that it is of modern
introduction.

The strongest pottery of modern make is to be
found in the Moqui villages. These are situated on
the crests of vertical sandstone bluffs, from 500 to
800 feet above the springs and reservoirs yielding
their supply of water. All that is used for culinary
or drinking purposes has to be carried on the backs of
squaws who patiently trudge up and down the steep
and giddy paths traced in the faces of the precipices,
each bearing upon her shoulders an olla, holding from
three to six gallons, a weight of which the strongest
man would soon grow weary.

The antique pottery of North America differs
from that of modern manufacture in being firmer
in texture and generally simpler in ornamentation.
The necessities of their surroundings made the
Pueblo Indians of the past more careful in the preparation of their biscuit and its firing; checker, and
right line decoration in black, white, and red,
are the typical forms of its ornamentation, a rule,
however, honoured as much in the breach as in the
observance.

The colouring upon most of the fragments of
antique pottery strewing the hills of Arizona is as
vivid as the day when applied. Analogous to this is
the pottery of Tyrius, which, although "exposed for
2300 years to sun and rain, has lost none of its fresh-
ness."—Schliemann, *Mycenæ*, pp. 15-16.

The important part played by pottery in the

domestic economy of the Moquis and other sedentary
Indians causes us to marvel why, in the long course of
centuries during which they have been acquainted with
its manufacture, they have not invented some such
labour-saving appliances as the wheel, which has been
known to the world from the highest antiquity. Tylor
(*Anthropology*, p. 275) states that "in the wall-
paintings of the tombs of the kings, Egyptian potters
are represented at work."

Wheel-made pottery was exhumed by Schliemann
at Mycenæ and Troy (*Mycenæ passim*). And yet
hand-made pottery is still made in our own day in
the Hebrides (Tylor, *Anthropology*).

The forms of the ancient pottery of Arizona and
New Mexico are various; small animals, of terra-cotta,
are occasionally unearthed. A very large well-baked
and well-shaped owl, was excavated from the ruin close
to the ranch of Mr. C. E. Cooley in Cochise Co., Arizona.
It was, according to his statement, an exact duplicate
of those made by the Zunis at this day. Some of the
specimens found are painted, some void of all decoration; and the painted vessels are decorated on the
exterior or interior or both. There are specimens
which would seem to indicate that they had been made
by laying strip upon strip of moist clay; others are
marked as if they had been pressed in the damp state
into a basket which was afterwards burned away,
and many again are plainly indented with the finger-
nails of the makers.

Pitchers are by no means uncommon, with and

T

without lips and handles; the mass of perfect pieces fall under the classes of large ollas, holding from two to four gallons—medium, of a capacity of one gallon, and bowls or basins of all dimensions, from those of a small cup up to those holding one gallon and more.

Small ladles, with hollow handles through which to suck the broth contained in the bowl of the ladle itself, occur in the ruins along the Verde River, and are the prototypes of the dippers used by the Moquis at this time.

In a monograph upon the *Antiquities of New Mexico and Arizona*, Dr. H. J. Hoffman falls into the error of supposing that the Zunis and Moquis do not use the polishing stone. This must have been stated without due consideration, as the polishing stone can be seen in use whenever the squaws put the finishing touches to their pottery.

A determination of the specific gravity of several specimens (antique) made by myself was, for the coarse real variety used for cooking utensils, 2.07, and for the finely kneaded, compact yellow and blue-gray biscuit, 2.24, a slight difference from Dr. Hoffman's results, which may, nevertheless, be more trustworthy than my own, as my facilities were not of the best.

The fine-grained specimens absorbed 6 per cent of their own weight of water, and the coarse 10 per cent in twenty-four hours. I will close this long article by saying that Mr. F. H. Cushing, who has lived among the Zunis for several years, has given much attention to the study of aboriginal ceramic art and decoration, and an authoritative work from him may soon be expected upon this important topic.

CHAPTER XXV.

Bead work—A sudden storm—The cliff-dwellers.

No description has been given of the bead-work of the Moquis, for the reason that they manufacture this on a small scale only.

They do make beads out of shells, but these they wear in strings about their necks. The Moquis, and in fact all the Pueblo Indians, have cylindrical buckskin cases, encrusted with beads, in which they insert their side tresses. These are but seldom used, and very likely have been obtained from the Utes on the north. Neither do they do any work in porcupine quills, unless we dignify by such a name the few anklets of that material to be seen in some of their dances.

We were compelled, by reason of constant storms, to remain at Keam's ranch for several days. We killed time by conversations with the Navajoes, which, if they gave no data beyond what had been obtained at Fort Defiance early in the spring, at least corroborated all that had then been learned.

The first evening after our arrival, as the sun was setting, the mist thickened suddenly, and a fearful cloud-burst broke upon us; in less time than it

takes to write these lines it had flooded the creek-
bed, raised the water to a depth of three inches on
the level ground around the house, carried away the
dam, which was built of ponderous sandstone slabs
two feet on a side, and then subsided as quickly as it
had come.

Inside of half an hour the whole tempest had
come and gone. Eight to ten feet of water had swept
like a solid wall down the narrow channel of the creek,
and the stars were again shining!

A rumour came that one of the Navajoes had been
killed by lightning; a rumour discredited at first, but
accepted when a messenger came in to tell Garryowen that it was his uncle, and that he must go
home to "sing" over the corpse.

Before going to bed we had a visit from Ostin-
Nalihe, a Navajo verging on old age. He confirmed
previous reports concerning As-sun-nut-li (The
Woman in the Ocean).

This goddess is of double sex, and has dispensed
many favours to the Navajoes. She sent blue corn
to the men, and white corn to the women. She also
sent them sea-shell beads. The Navajoes formerly
obtained beads from the Moquis and Cohoninos, who
used to get them from As-sun-nut-li (i.e. used to
make pilgrimages to the Pacific Ocean) and bring
back shells to be worked into beads).

When property is stolen there are men who will
sing to As-sun-nut-li, and learn from her who the
culprit is.

Years ago, before they had seen the Moquis, the
Navajoes used to live over on the other side of the
Sierra la Plata, and there they hunted the buffalo;
did not know whether the Moquis ever hunted the
buffalo or not.   The Navajoes " came up out of the
ground " on the other side of the Sierra la Plata, and
lived there for a number of years.   At that time the
Moquis ranged around here, and had plenty of horses,
sheep, and cattle.

The Navajoes in those days used to raid upon the
Moquis.

The Apaches once were Navajoes ; they still speak
the Navajo language.   They came here first, " a long
time ago," but how long he could not say, only it was
before the time of four old men (*i.e.* his father, grandfather, great-grandfather, and great-great-grandfather).
His ancestors told him this.   As-sun-nut-li had something to do with this ; exactly how much he did not
know.   (This may be a vague tradition of a migration
by water.)

When I told him that away up in the north, where
the snow and ice cover the ground for months at a
time, there were large bands of Indians speaking the
Navajo language (alluding to the Tinneh and Kutchin
tribes in British America), Ostin-Nalihe replied,
that when the Apaches left two other bands left also,
and went north.   This last tale I gave no credence
to : the old man's manner showed that he made it up
on the spur of the moment to impress me with his
ability to answer every question.

He confirmed all that I had been told of the Navajo clans, who make over forty.

He merely gave me the names of the Tutsoni or Water gens, the Todichini or Alkali gens, the Topa-au or Near the Water's Edge, the Tohanni or Close to Water, the Tzinachini or Wooded Mountain gens, and a few others.

The Navajoes do not marry in their own clan ; if they did, "their bones would dry up and they would die." There are many descendants of the Pueblos among the Navajoes. Ostin-Nalihe went so far as to assert that whole bands of Pueblos had run away from the "Mexicans" long ago, and joined the Navajoes ; among these were the Maydishkishdi or Mountain Cayotes, who used to live in the Pueblo of Jemez, the Klogni, the Kiajanni, and others.

The Navajoes say that the cliff-dwellers were carried off from this country by a bad wind. He repeated this statement without explaining his meaning. Was this bad wind a pestilence or an epidemic? Such a supposition is not altogether unreasonable. Famine, syphilis, and pestilence from filth constantly threaten the Moquis in our own day.

In front of Keam's store, high up on the opposite side of the cañon, in a niche in the vertical face of the rock, is a pyramidal pile of stones, placed there by the ancestors of the present Moquis, so they say. It is not now possible to approach it, the trail which formerly must have run along the face of the cliff, and portions of which are still visible, having been carried away by a landslide or something of that kind.

CHAPTER XXVI.

Fate of a missionary — Mushangnewy — A natural fortress — Poor
accommodation — Use of American implements — The first
vehicle.

August 15, 1881.—The morning hours were bright,
and gave rise to hopes of fair weather, but as the
afternoon advanced we were again disappointed at
seeing great banks of black and brown vapour massing
right over the house. A few drops pattered on the
dirt roof, a scattering fusillade followed, and then the
flood poured down, covering the ground for a couple
of inches in depth, and bounding over the walls of the
cañon in muddy cascades of varying volume. Of
these one, tawny as the mane of an African lion,
sprang from bench to bench, pausing upon each long
enough to send a cloud of muddy spray high in the
air, and then, with a roar to appall the stoutest heart,
descended to lower levels in a torrent sweeping everything before its path.

Seeing only in such a case is believing. No description could do justice to one of these Arizona
cloud-bursts. Mr. Keam's house lies in a narrow gorge
only 100 yards wide, and the receptacle of every drop
of water falling within an area of ten miles square.

It does not take much calculation to show the power of one of the storms prevailing here during the rainy season.

We succeeded in hiring as guide Nahi-vehma (the Peacemaker), who spoke Navajo and Moqui fluently, and had a frail knowledge of English and Spanish. He told us about the Spanish missionary who "long ago" had come among his people preaching with a cross in his hand. He said that God had a Son, but couldn't tell who God's wife was, so the Moquis threw him over the precipice.

The next morning (August 16), to our great joy, we were able to resume our journey. Within four hours we had passed round the corner of the first mesa and the spot where we had left our ambulance while at the snake-dance. Shortly after this we became entangled in a series of high sand-dunes, rippled by the winds as are the sea-beaches by the waves.

Here the labour became very severe upon our mules. The valley between the eastern mesa and that upon which stand the Pueblos of Mushaugnewy, Supowlewy, and Sumopowy, is from five to seven miles broad, sloping down in a gentle grade to the middle, where, during the rainy season, is to be found a stream flowing from the north and joining that which issues from Moqui cañon. At the moment of our passage this brook was 20 feet wide, 3 to 6 inches in depth, and flowing with a swift current, the result, as we thought, of some one of the countless storms then deluging the hills and valleys.

In this valley and along the trail we pursued were many fields of corn, melons, pumpkins, squashes, and sun-flowers, the last being from 8 to 10 inches across the disk, and between 12 and 14 inches from tip to tip of petals.

Every half mile or so a startled Moqui boy would jump up from the ravine in which he lazily sprawled at full length watching his goats and sheep. Scarcely less wild than his flock, his flight would be stopped only by the reassuring voice of Nahi-vehma.

Each revolution of our ambulance wheels drew us nearer and nearer to the promontory upon which could be descried the outlines of Mushangnewy; promising corn-fields increased in number, each guarded by its double line of scarecrows—the animate and inanimate, —the former the glittering-eyed Moqui children sheltered in lodges of branches.

A heavy mass of clouds hung overhead, threatening another visitation of rain and cold; the force of its fury was, however, spent upon the valleys and peaks around about us, but we had a taste of its power at the moment of attaining the foot of the mesa of Mushangnewy.

This mesa is a precipice several hundred feet in altitude, rising out of a sub-structure of clay, which slopes away at an angle of forty-five degrees from a point midway between the crest of the "mesa" and the plain. This clay, *talus,* is slashed and wrinkled in all possible directions by ravines and arroyos, ranging from 2 feet to 200 feet in depth, across and between which runs a maze of sheep and goat and donkey trails. In every available nook are gardens protected with laborious care : these are not more than 15 feet square, and are enclosed with rough masonry walls, under which pass at suitable points little canals of wood, stone, and clay, to carry off any superfluous water.

I examined all these gardens, and saw onions, corn, chile, beans, and other vegetables, all growing finely. I formed the impression that many of these were seed patches, but the greater number were for the purpose of raising onions and chile.

Above the gardens, around a bend in a deep ravine, were springs and reservoirs, which determined our bivouac for the night. The mules were unhitched on the summit of a small rounded clay knoll, which would shed water almost as fast as it fell.

While Gordon and Smallwood were getting everything ready for the night a deputation of Indians— men, women, and children—descended the trail from their village above in the rocks, greeted us kindly, shook hands, made us a present of two green peaches, and asked for tobacco. One of the men had an unsightly protuberance on the inside of the right knee-joint, and varicose veins in both legs. One of the little boys had long woolly hair like a Hottentot. Another of the men had in his hand a bunch of field-rats, which he made signs that he was going to eat, saying that they were "lolamai" (good). We afterwards discovered that they were to be given to the caged eagles in the village.

I returned with them to their houses, climbing a very steep trail, which first took us across a series of small hills of sand and clay. We passed five or six pyramidal piles of sandstone, identical in appearance with those in the niche in the wall of the cañon opposite Keam's ranch.

That these had a symbolical purport I suspect very strongly without being ready to assert it. It is very probable that they are reminiscences of a former age in which stone worship prevailed, and of which other suggestions constantly obtrude themselves upon one's notice in travelling through the villages of this people.

This surmise was not weakened by finding that only 15 or 20 feet distant was a sacred spring, a pretty little source of cold water, dug out and walled up with masonry, and having steps of stone running down to the bottom, where the respect and venera- tion of adoring Moquis were typified by sacrificial plumes of eagle feathers, and by the little green- painted sticks so frequently noticed as votive offerings in all niches and in front of all idols.

From the sacred spring a long flight of steps, built into the scarp wall of the precipice, conducted us to a flat bench a little below the rim of the mesa, but about 150 or maybe 200 feet above the clay and sand hummocks upon which the piles of sandstone were arranged. Here the upper extremity of this staircase

was spanned by a heavy bold archway of sandstone
boulders, and, in all respects, was one of the most
impregnable approaches I have ever seen or read of.
To attempt to carry Mushangnewy by direct assault
would be madness and an impossibility, unless the
commander of the attacking forces should be willing
to water each step with the choicest blood of his
bravest men. We stepped out from this stone staircase into one of the small peach orchards of the Pueblo.
The fruit-bearing trees were protected by palisades of
cedar branches, and the tender shoots were surrounded
by walls of rocks, partly, as I inferred, to afford protection from the severe winds, and partly to keep
them from being nibbled or trampled by goats and
donkeys.

At the end of the orchard several trails converged
upon that which we had followed. These must be
easier of ascent and descent, because upon them were
seen a great many " burros " laden with cedar branches
for fuel. It by no means follows that these donkeys
could not and would not run up and down the stone
stairs I have just been describing. They go anywhere that a man can ascend or descend without
hanging on by his hands, and on this very staircase
were hoof-prints to show that donkeys had passed by.

Loaded animals could not well force themselves and
cargoes through the narrow stone archway, for which
reason, and which reason only, more circuitous routes
of travel had to be adopted.

I have never yet seen a donkey climb a tree. The

feat perhaps is impossible, but if any donkey ever does succeed in doing it, it will be a donkey from Mushangnewy.

One of the Moquis coming close enough, I stopped him and made signs to our ambulance and then to his wood, and lastly to some money in my hand. He understood me, and for two silver dimes started down the precipice to deliver to Gordon and Smallwood a sufficiency of fuel for cooking our supper and breakfast.

On the outskirts of the town are great dump-piles. In these are compactly pressed the garbage, ashes, and offal of departed generations. The filth and vileness of the present day have been left to cast their fragrance upon the air of the town, which has as disgusting an appearance as some of the slums and purlieus of New York.

While I was writing my notes, seated upon this indurated mass of prehistoric offal, half a dozen Moquis drew near—one of them an Albino—and asked if I was Mo-mo-nee (Mormon). A score of paces farther led me into the town of Mushangnewy, a small affair, containing not much—if any—over 200 people. The houses are of two and three stories, built of sandstone rubble laid in mud. They surround a small plaza or public square not more than fifty paces on a side. In the centre of this plaza is an underground Estufa. The general make-up of Mushangnewy is modelled so closely upon the pattern of Hualpi and the other towns on the eastern mesa, that a more particular descrip-

tion is not called for. The villages or towns on the
eastern mesa are much cleaner and in better order,
their proximity to the edge of the mesa making it
easy for them to get rid of all decaying or noxious
matter.

Their houses, too, are of more commodious size
than those of Mushangnewy, where the rooms are
quite small and low, mere dog-kennels, I might say,
and of the average dimensions of 10 by 8 feet on the
floor and 6 feet high.

Moqui houses generally, on the ground-floor, have
a depth of at least three rooms. The first will be a
living room, the next a store-room for food and dishes,
and the third will be a receptacle for farming utensils,
but there is no certainty in this any more than there
would be in our own houses.

From the provision made for winter, one would be
led to suspect that the storms of snow and wind and
rain attacking Mushangnewy must be very severe.
Upon the roof of every house were nicely stacked
great piles of cedar wood, and, in juxtaposition with
these, strings of corn were hanging from every wall.

I took a seat in an empty room to shelter myself
as well as I could from the chilling rain which had by
this time soaked through my clothes, and was running
down my spinal column in a cascade of imposing
dimensions.

The Moquis had secluded themselves in their
apartments, and as no one had come up to offer me
the freedom of the city, I was compelled to make

myself at home. I helped myself to a wooden stool, and was prospecting around for a nice ripe melon, when the shrill whistling scream of a caged eagle startled me so that I looked to find that I was the focus of a dozen pairs of eyes, all of men and boys— the women and girls having betaken themselves to places of concealment, from which, I have no doubt, they scrutinised minutely my every movement. It was an indescribable sensation, that of being "a stranger in a strange land," an object of curiosity to the men and of apprehension and fear to the women and children.

The Indians who had come down to our ambulance and those encountered on my way up to the Pueblo had acted in a perfectly friendly manner, as indeed did those who were now gathering about me. But it was absolutely certain that very few strangers had ever reached the "penetralia" of Mushangnewy. I spoke pleasantly to those who were nearest, and succeeded in making them understand that I wanted to look through their houses ; no objection was interposed, and one or two of them even accompanied me. They seemed greatly perplexed by my unaccountable behaviour in stopping every few steps to note any item of consequence.

We saw plenty of cats, dogs, burros, and chickens : the roosters crowed defiantly, the cats humped themselves in readiness for hostilities, and the mangy dogs snarled and snapped at our heels at every corner.

Only the donkeys gazed upon us with an expression of benignity, born of sympathy and fellow-feeling.

The town was decidedly filthy. There were the usual piles of vegetable garbage and animal offal and ordure to be expected in places as small and poor and low in the social scale. There were great bundles of green corn-shucks and water-melon rinds lying round loose for the delectation of peaceful burros and naked children.

An assortment of agricultural implements, hoes, spades, and shovels, of American manufacture, was to be seen in every dwelling. The rain suddenly ceased about 6 P.M., after Moran, who had come up to join me, and I had been thoroughly soaked. We descended into an Estufa, which in all respects was the duplicate of those described on the eastern mesa, especially those in poorer condition. In size, position, and filthy smell it is their counterpart.

There were no designs on the walls. It possessed at date of our entry three or four stone stools, a couple of fine stone mortars and pestles, with fresh green paint still adhering to them, and the customary et-ceteras of sacrificial plumes, buckskin masks, gourds, and tortoise-shell rattles.

The people of Mushangnewy have the ordinary large earthenware olla, but also use large gourds for holding water.

They have abalone shells for neck pendants and for ornaments in their dances. Their houses contain pottery of the same patterns as made on the eastern

mesa, and also " boomerangs," rabbit-skin mantles,
sheep-pelts for couches, with coverings of coarse,
domestic blankets woven in narrow, transverse blue,
black, and white stripes.

String after string of cut and dried pumpkins hang
from the rafters; baskets of their own make, both
plain and coloured, or with symbolical figures interwoven; Navajo blankets, gourd and earthenware
ladles, Navajo lariats of buckskin, ollas and jugs of
all sizes, and rows of coarse, wooden, and nearly
always unpainted, idols.

Besides the Estufa in the centre of the plaza
there were three others on the outer line of the Pueblo,
built along the crest of the precipice, whose vertical
face serves them as an inner wall.

The timber in these Estufas had been cut with
blunt, perhaps stone, implements, and the ladders
were held together with raw hide. They were all
dank, noisome dungeons; each had stone stools and
mortars and pestles for grinding paints. In one was
a number of tablet head-dresses, closely similar to
those exhibited at Santo Domingo. In another was a
blanket, just commenced upon its frame, and two
rabbit-skin mantles lying on the stone pavement.

At the foot of the precipice, which goes down 75
feet without a break from a vertical line, are the sheep
and goat corrals; and below these, on a broad, flat
shelf, a reservoir of water.

The summit of the mesa we could now make out
to be about 500 feet above our ambulance.

We examined every house in the town, and found in each the articles specified above. Stone hammers were seen in common use.

Going back to our bivouac for supper, we carried with us two fairly-ripe water-melons, for which we paid a nickel each.

The women and girls evinced less fear, and when they perceived that we were in the market as purchasers of melons and any other garden truck they might want to sell, they became very friendly.

We walked back with our purchases, pausing long enough on the edge of the precipice to notice that, under the steep cliffs of sandstone and on the flat surface of the clay slope, reservoirs had been laid out to receive and store all the water draining from the heights above.

The people coming down from Mushangnewy to our bivouac were intensely interested in the ambulance, which they examined attentively in all its parts. For reasons which could not be learned, they painted snakes on the felloes.

I have not a doubt that many of them had never seen a wheeled vehicle of the kind before, certainly not so close to their own homes.

The sun sinking behind the western clouds threw a rosy and golden flush upon the battlements of Supowlewy ; the salient angles stood out bold and prominent in the brilliant light, relieved by the gloom of the re-entrants.

Perched upon the summit of its impregnable crag

of sandstone, both it and its neighbour Mushangnewy might have stood for types of feudal castles,
and we for poor benighted travellers wearily trudging
along the king's highway, fearful of attack from the
wicked knights whose home was above with their
kindred spirits the predatory hawks and eagles.

Another deputation of Moquis arrived as we
squatted down on the ground to eat our supper.
Their ostensible mission was to see Nahi-vehma.
They expressed great pleasure at meeting us, and
insisted every few moments upon shaking hands
and calling out lolamai. Suspecting what was the
matter, I ordered Smallwood to open a can of preserved pine-apples and to give them also a couple of
handfuls of hard tack from the stores we were now
obliged to watch with such jealous care. We had
already used up about two-thirds of the supplies, and
unless we found Mormon settlements on the Colorado
Chiquito would suffer before reaching Fort Apache.
That night we slept undisturbed, and upon awakening next morning were delighted with the prospect of
the first absolutely clear day for nearly a month.

There were yet a few lingering battalions of sullen
clouds, the rearguard of a broken, retreating army,
making as bold a front as possible, but from these we
did not fear much ; even as I wrote the blue spaces
in the sky were enlarging, and the sun, in the full
majesty of his golden light, was ascending the
eastern horizon.

CHAPTER XXVII.

A return to the Pueblo—Goats and donkeys—A wealthy woman
—The children of the village.

LONG before day-dawn we received our first detachment of visitors—men, women, children, dogs, and
"burros."

The men of Mushangnewy wear the same dress as
the men of the eastern villages, when they wear any
at all. This appears to be a matter of individual
taste and discretion; numbers of them, both inside
their own houses or while visiting us, had worn
absolutely nothing except a breech-clout. Each,
however, kept a coarse blanket in which, when so
disposed, he wrapped himself up with the stolidity of
a Sioux and the dignity of a Bedouin.

One of the visitors in the first detachment was an
Albino boy, the second we had seen belonging to this
town.

We made these visitors a present of the two
water-melons purchased last night. These melons were
a dark green on the outside and looked ripe, but upon
being opened their hearts and seeds were discovered
to be perfectly white, and their pulp *cucumbery* in
taste. We had a golden opportunity to get up a

reputation for generosity, even if we bestowed upon our neighbours a first-class attack of colic. The Moquis relished the gift extremely, and left nothing beyond a thin green rind.

Mr. Moran was much better this morning. Last night he refused to eat any supper, and complained of headache and general debility. I conjectured that he was threatened with a slight typhoid attack, which we both had every reason to apprehend from exposure to rain and chilly winds, burning suns, irregular and at times poor food, dirt, discomfort, and rotten Pueblo Estufas and houses.

The only thing in the shape of medicine or stimulant with our party was a bottle, half-used, of Brown's Jamaica Ginger. This I administered on the old woman's principle, that "if it didn't do him any good it wouldn't do him any harm," wrapped him up as warmly as possible in our damp blankets, and let him go to sleep.

Before breakfast we walked together a little distance up the ravine to the "seed-beds," which numbered by actual count twenty-seven, and then to the walled reservoir with stone steps leading down to the water. Near by was a hillside covered with fragments of pottery, also a half-obliterated trail, which we followed until it led to an old ruin, traceable by the lines of sandstone blocks, fragments of pottery, and obsidian flakes scattered over the ground. The identity of this hill can readily be established by the outcroppings of coal which occur on its flank.

Coming down to the reservoir and "seed-gardens" were a half-dozen or more children, without exception pretty and bright. The men and women, on their part, impress one as good-natured but stupid. They evinced no fear of us at our own bivouac, which they could approach after deliberate reconnaisance. Doubt and apprehension were uppermost in their minds whenever we pounced out upon them from behind a sheltering rock, or disclosed ourselves in some abrupt bend of the deep and narrow ravine. None of them ran, not even the children, but they hurried by, impelled by motives of prudence to get as far away from us as possible.

Breakfast was hurriedly swallowed, and then we began an ascent to the Pueblo, taking a different path from that followed last evening. The one chosen this morning was nothing but a sheep and goat trail, and as we slowly made our way upward, among, between, and around weather-beaten sandstone boulders, or under sentinel crags whose grim heads, reaching cloudward, bore the marks of many a Titanic struggle with the winds and rains of eternity, herds of goats skipped nervously past us, the leader giving his rammy bleat of warning that it would not do to go too near us. The attending herders saluted, with friendly nods and smiling faces, "lolamais," and vigorous thumpings, the last applied to the ribs of their burros, which became greatly frightened whenever we attempted to draw near.

A score or more of particularly old rams assembled

in cabinet council upon the walls of their corral, 50
or 75 feet above us, to determine what manner of
creatures we were.

Their beards wagged philosophically to and fro, as
if to assure us that their deliberations were to be calm
and impartial. Their heads were put close together
in brief consultation. There was a short interval of
suspense, succeeded by a prolonged baa-a-a-a of distrust, which notified all the flocks and herds within
earshot of the echoing cliffs that the decision had
been adverse, and no communication was to be held
with us.

Every little while an awe-struck herder would
come up close to me, glance in stupid wonderment
at my swiftly-moving pencil and the written characters left in its trail, or go to Mr. Moran to examine
his drawings, which were invariably looked at *side-
ways*.

This was so marked that Moran called my attention to it, and from this on we noticed that every
Moqui, when asked to look at a picture, would first
do so in the manner mentioned. They could not be
made to comprehend what our business was, and we
were really too busy to make much of an effort at
instructing them.

These people stink atrociously; their garments
and skins emit the foulest of smells. Their poverty
has much to do with this; their clothes are worn
until they drop off in pieces, and their skins, although
I believe they wash with commendable frequency,

cannot fail to be constantly sullied and saturated with the filth of their confined and ill-kept quarters.

Mr. Moran made excellent sketches of this romantic trail, as he had already made of everything of interest seen on our trip. Wind and rain had carved the faces of the cliffs into weird and fantastic shapes, which fancy readily assumed to be massive buttresses, outlying towers, or frowning battlements. Wherever a projecting ledge afforded a foothold a corral of stone had been built for sheep and goats. These frisky animals skipped from rock to rock with an agility rivalled only by the sedate sure-footedness of the burros; all alike looked at us with fearful eyes, or nervously ran from the trail as we drew near. Flitting shadows, darting furtively behind the rocks overlooking our position, revealed the presence of men and boys keeping our movements under the closest surveillance.

I have been using the terms trail and path with many misgivings of the correctness and propriety of so doing. From this point onward there can be no reasonable excuse for ambiguity; the pathway became a step stairway of stone clinging to the precipitous cliff.

Although Mushangnewy, like the rest of the Moquis towns, has every symptom of decay, with ruined and abandoned houses, yet the number of children to be seen is something remarkable. In one group I counted eleven, splashing bare-footed and bare-legged in the reservoir; the boys almost entirely naked, the little girls clad and their hair dressed in the picturesque manner of their people. We entered the Pueblo, and climbed up the ladder into one of the houses. It had no windows, no doors, and no lights, either of glass or selenite.

A woman, kneeling down upon a sheepskin, was winnowing a small pile of wheat, which she afterwards ground in a "metale." We could find no bow-drills in this town. We saw a wooden idol, marked with these figures, ⊕ ⊥ The matrons wore their hair loose and parted in the middle from nape of neck to forehead, and then plaited in two tresses, concealing the ears. In this house I came across fresh (hens') eggs, corn, pumpkins, peaches, and melons, both green and dried; pumpkin flowers and seeds; soap-weed (for washing hair and clothes), peach and apricot kernels; wooden idols, abalone shells, "wyavi" or piki bread, baskets of Moqui, Apache, and Cohonino make, and all the incidental filth of a Moqui dwelling.

The old woman showed me a small stone bear or mountain lion talisman, exactly like those seen in the snake-dance. I failed to persuade her to sell it. In another house, evidently the property of a very rich woman, were great stores of blue and white corn, piled up separately; dried pumpkins in long twisted strings hanging from the rafters; hominy, corn-bread, a small piece of American bacon, mutton-

tallow in bladder casings, gourd water-jugs, yellow
and blue flat baskets of Moqui make, stone mortars,
sheep pelts, rabbit-skin mantles, some excellent pottery
and blankets, a row of wooden idols, fastened to one
of the largest beams, and a supply of tortoise-shell
and gourd rattles, masks, head-dresses, sashes, and
other appurtenances of their dances.

And in a back room a pile of American hoes and
of wooden forks for use in the fields.

Mushangnewy has all the appearance of a very
old town ; the few doors to be seen are of the crudest
forms and archaic patterns.   While I was writing in
this house, to which I was driven for shelter by a
totally unexpected shower of rain, the old woman
who owned it hurried over, summoned to her domicile
by the screams and cries of a squad of women and
children, who, from the roofs on the other side of
the square or court, were watching the stranger with
mingled fear and distrust.

The old hag had her fears allayed after seeing that
nothing had been molested, and learning from the
signs made that I wished to exchange silver for pottery
and baskets.

She disposed of specimens of each at fair prices,
and then I bade her adieu to resume my stroll about
the Pueblo.

Mushangnewy is built in form of a double, narrow,
rectangular court, connection being made by a low,
dirty arcade.   The windows, more especially those
facing outward from the first-floor rooms, are simply

loop-holes, 4 inches square; upon the second and third stories they are as much as 8 inches square. The sills are of stone; the lintels of riven cedar branches and twigs. Walls are roughly made of rubble laid in mud, the fragments of masonry being of all shapes and sizes, exactly as picked up on the mesa.

The angles are "slouchy," and the workmanship crude but strong enough for its purposes. Around each wall, on top, is a line of well-laid stone coping.

The roofs are of earth. The rafters are poorly cut, the implements used being, beyond doubt, axes of stone.

The Pueblo Indians, generally, when constructing a new house, or rebuilding an old one, utilise all material on hand, none of which is of more importance than the rafters. These require much labour to fell and haul, in the first place, but once in a house, ought to survive long after the other component parts have commenced going to pieces, as they are not subjected to any great strain, and are fully protected from the inclemencies of weather. The walls are plastered with mud laid on with the hands. Deer horns are inserted as pegs for clothing, etc., but blankets, mantles, and other raiment dear to the feminine eye, are carefully displayed across horizontal poles swinging from the rafters.

No trouble was experienced in communicating with the old woman, who readily sold stone hammers, axes, pottery, baskets, and such other truck as I fancied.

Far different was the behaviour of the children, who scampered like squirrels whenever I betrayed the slightest anxiety to approach. For a short interval after my arrival the braver and more venturesome spirits remained in either of the little rectangular courts, darting from cover to cover behind my back. The danger of seizure became too great when Moran, having finished his sketching below, joined me, and accordingly there was a general flight to the coping of the upper stories, whereon they perched, boys and girls, like a line of crows.

I counted thirty-two looking down at one time—twenty-two in one cluster, the older children half-dressed, but the younger, of both sexes, without a vestige of clothing, not even so much as ear-rings.

While at Mushangnewy I was much surprised to observe humming-birds darting swiftly through the air.

CHAPTER XXVIII.

FIVE hundred yards from Mushangnewy stands the Pueblo of Shupowlewy, capping a sandstone pinnacle of very small superficial dimensions. The trail to this neighbouring town jumps down the northern face of the Mushangnewy precipice for 250 feet, then points straight for Shupowlewy, keeping close to the crest of the sandstone mesa, in whose flanks, in every suitable nook, are groves and orchards of peach-trees, and upon attaining the base of the pinnacle or crag of Shupowlewy affords the ambitious traveller all the opportunity his soul can desire for gaining distinction as an Alpine climber.

The path or stairway is nearly vertical, in places absolutely so, but so well-defined and, like all the Moqui trails, so well worn by the feet of generations, that a feeling of security is imparted to him who first essays the ascent.

The name Shupowlewy means peaches, or peach orchards, in the Moqui language — a distinctive appellation fairly won by the large groves and clumps of trees yielding this delicious fruit. All the ravines were dark-green with the waxy foliage of the

peach, and there was also a range of fine gardens laid
out on a flat promontory, with a southern exposure,
which juts out from the precipice 200 or 300 feet
below the houses.

On the little bench, a hundred feet below the crest
of the precipice, were tanks and reservoirs of rain-
water, in which naked children splashed gleefully
until one turning round caught sight of me prowling
among the rocks, and raising a yell of fear and alarm,
started the whole gang to scampering away as fleetly
and nimbly as a herd of their own goats. A boy,
posted as a sentinel on the top of one of the highest
houses, sang out at the top of his voice that the
stranger was coming; such at least was the idea of
his meaning supplied by its effect, since immediately
after the shout had ended groups of curious and
excited men, women, and children gathered behind
the copings of the walls. Little girls, young men,
and boys, ran away frightened at first view of the
terrible intruder.

Curs snarled and snapped, and might have proceeded to more effective hostilities had it not been for
the uplifted stone axe which suggested prudence in
attack. This style of reception was not very grateful
to my feelings, and being alone (Moran was behind
in Mushangnewy sketching), I felt ill at ease, thinking that some intemperate or ill-disposed young men
might be tempted to insult or assail me.

This was no time for turning back. I reflected
that if disposed to injure me nothing could prevent

their doing it where I was. I had no arms of any sort, and could do nothing to defend myself, but I felt pretty well satisfied that the Moquis at the worst would forbid me to enter the town. The Pueblo of Supowlewy, like Hualpi, is on one side built flush with the face of the precipice, the stone stairway by which I had tediously climbed coming out close to one of the angles of the plaza.

Above me I counted twenty-three children, naked and three-quarter naked, who awaited my approach, and upon my arriving near the top steps dashed away at full speed as their comrades had done. How many more children there were I suppose I shall never know; I do know that as I passed the houses, from every dark hole and corner above me gleamed one pair or more of black, snaky eyes, which retreated into darker and more inaccessible seclusion, as I began to climb the house-ladders. I looked about me and saw that I was in a narrow and gloomy quadrangular court, surrounded by houses the counterpart of those in Mushangnewy. Chickens and dogs were plentiful, and the second rather too warlike for my notions of comfort.

I moved up a ladder into the first of the houses which struck my fancy; four women, two naked children, and a cat, were the occupants. The women were plaiting baskets of the yucca fibre, which is used green, but is first split in two from butt to tip.

There were many rabbit mantles, a few blankets and girdles of wool, still fewer of cotton, and a decent equipment of pottery. The women were busy, but not too busy to keenly watch me, and all I was doing. One of the naked babies, clasped tightly to his mother's breast, paused for a moment to gaze with big, black eyes upon the new-comer, and, having satisfied his curiosity, resumed with redoubled vigour his search for nourishment.

Refreshment was placed before me in a basket, the corn-meal tortillas of the Mexicans. Of these I ate a small quantity for the sake of politeness, but they were so strongly flavoured with mutton-tallow that I could not enjoy them very much.

In the adjoining house I saw two Albino children; they had different mothers, but the mother of the larger one had a younger child in her arms of the normal *yellow* colour of the American Indians. These children were naked, completely so — a fact which gave me great pleasure, because I could so much the more readily examine them; their mothers were delighted also, fancying that I was admiring the youngsters. They certainly looked perfectly healthy, and were finely formed. The absence of colouring matter from the iris made the pupils of the eyes a greenish gray, if they had any tint at all; the sclerotic coat was pink, probably from extravasated blood, and the eyes themselves weak and constantly blinking under exposure to the sunlight.

The skin upon their bodies was soft, but of a bright pinkish hue, like that of an American child

X

which has been badly sun-burned. Their hair, long, white, and towy, confirmed their general resemblance to the brats of the "poor whites" of the mountain regions of Georgia and the Carolinas.

On this mesa the inhabitants, if less cleanly in their surroundings, were more devout in their aspirations than the dwellers in the three Pueblos to the east.

No house so poor that it did not possess from fifteen to thirty, and even more, of the grotesque wooden idols, painted in gaudy colours, of which so much has already been said. These were usually to be seen tacked in a long line to the rafters, or attached to one of the walls. When from long service they become broken or faded, the children welcome them as playthings, and complete the work of demolition by first sucking off the rest of the paint and then breaking them to pieces exactly as white babies would do.

Shupowlewy emulates Mushangnewy in the number of its burros. They plod pensively up and down every set of stone steps, munch with melancholy mildness the succulent corn-fodder considerately spread for them in the plaza, or trudge with philosophic meekness from point to point, bearing loads of colic - dealing green melons, or great bundles of dry cedar fuel for the use of the good housewives of the Pueblo.

The gentle burro has but one fault. He has a fine voice, and he knows it, and will often fall into a doze while composing a symphony with which to vex the ear of night. His driver, always a stout and un-feeling, full-sized Indian, grown callous to anything like sentiment, arouses the faithful beast from his reverie by the application of a stout club as thick as a man's wrist. Whenever this rattles down upon his hindquarters, with the melodious energy of a bass drum in a beer-garden, the donkey infers that, like poor Joe in "Tom All Alone's," he is to keep moving on.

We descended into an Estufa. It adhered to the generic type of all the Moqui Kibas, being dirty, damp, foul, and smoke-begrimed. Set in the walls were pegs for hanging clothes; in the floors were mortised beams to receive the upright posts of the loom whenever a blanket was to be woven. There were the usual stools of stone, buckskin masks and head-coverings, with collars of cedar and corn-husks, and in a niche in one of the walls a collection of offerings to Omá-a. Stone mortars, with green paint still fresh, and a number of the blackened willow wands, having one end inserted in clay globules, and the other tipped with small eagle feathers, made me believe that here, as in Hualpi, where I had noticed and sketched the same paraphernalia, the snake-dance was celebrated, although not perhaps openly.

In the construction of this Estufa, and of all the buildings at Shupowlewy, but little, if any, help had been obtained from steel axes or saws. There were

no designs on the walls. The banquette following
three sides of the room, the dais on the fourth, the
hearth or ash-hole in the centre (full of ashes),
were, in the minutest particulars, duplicates of the
corresponding appointments of the Estufas in
Hualpi and Suchongnewy. The entrance to the
roof was covered with a mat of yucca fibre to exclude rain.

Twenty yards off in the door of a house was
a young mother talking "baby talk" to a pretty
infant, which bore the infliction with the same expression of disgusted resignation to be seen on the
countenances of American infants under similar
circumstances.

We made a very thorough examination of this
town, going into every house and descending into
every Estufa, but finding nothing new to us. In
the course of my stroll I purchased numbers of beautiful
baskets, one or two wooden idols, and a goodly array
of stone implements and some toys.

Having finished the examination of this small but
extremely interesting locality, I climbed down the
trail to Mushangnewy and beyond, and after a short
but exhausting walk, passing immense sandstone
monoliths, struck the trail running down to the
"seed-beds," and a moment or two afterwards had
reached the ambulance, where "Nahi-vehma" was in
readiness to take us to Sumopowy.

Before leaving the foot of Mushangnewy we
bought a handful of peaches, blushing red under

the warm kisses of a loving sun. These were as yet too hard to be eaten uncooked, but Gordon and Smallwood thought they could "make a mess" by stewing them in the coffee-pot, an experiment worth a trial.

While Gordon was hitching up the mules Smallwood set out our lunch of warm tea, canned cranberries, and hard tack.

Moran and myself, with appetites whetted by toilsome climbing, set on like a couple of half-starved Comanches, and did royal work upon the bill of fare mentioned, and upon an allowance of breakfast bacon, daintily broiled in the ashes.

Our appetites received the cordial approval of the surrounding Moquis, to whom as a parting gift we left the remains of our lunch, or to speak with more exactness, they attacked it the moment we desisted. One of the older Moquis, who did not seem to get an even share of the plunder, had his feelings appeased with a couple of handfuls of tobacco.

This made them all grin a new expression of thanks, and gave us an opportunity to inspect their teeth, which cannot compare with the fine ivory of the Apaches and Navajoes.

Moran had succeeded in getting an excellent sketch of the stone staircase and stone archway of Mushangnewy. While working he was approached by half a dozen Moquis, who, by signs and words, informed him that the Navajoes had once made an attack upon their Pueblo, hoping to carry it by storm. They penetrated to this staircase, and were allowed to rush half-way to the summit, when from front, flank, and rear a hail of rocks, stones, and clubs poured down, sweeping the unfortunate savages off their footing.

CHAPTER XXIX.

Sumopowy—Another storm—A deserted village—Cordially received—
Moccasins—General details—Enlightening the natives—A nasty
place.

AFTER getting down into the plain we turned north,
going up the valley between the two mesas, passing
a dry spring excavated to some depth and walled up
with rubble masonry. Close to this Nahi-vehma
showed a child's grave, which may be ˙described as a
rectangular crypt of sandstone slabs, without head or
foot stone.

Above our position Mushangnewy and Sumopowy
loomed grand and impregnable like the eyries of eagles.
The crest of the precipice upon which they are built
is fully 750 feet above the plain in which we now were,
and not less than 150 feet above the level of Hualpi.

A long line of Moqui corn-fields filled this valley,
the greater part of them bordering a little stream
which entered it. These were all guarded by small
boys naked, or nearly so. As our ambulance slowly
pulled through the sand one of these youngsters ran
after us, calling out for the driver to stop. Nahi-
vehma made a sign to Gordon to check his mules to
let the boy catch up.

The object of his visit was to effect the sale of a nice-looking melon, held in his hand, for which he asked in eager tones, "metchi, metchi" (matches, matches). We gave him a few matches, a handful of smoking tobacco, and a nickel. This unexpected generosity tickled the youngster. He shouted lola-mai, and ran off at full speed.

A score of rods farther on two other naked boys ran over to examine our ambulance, every detail of which afforded them interest and pleasure.

They followed us for almost half a mile. One of them had very pronounced Hebrew features. Other Moquis also drew near, but we saw no women nor girls. These men and boys spoke cheerily to Nahi-vehma, or when desirous of making a favourable impression upon strangers, treated us to their customary lolamai.

This valley might be described as of sandstone covered with shifting sand thinly grassed, into which our wheels would have sunk deeply had it not been for a welcome shower which lasted long enough to pack the ground and make progress easy.

The grass and cedar, which were very poor near the towns, improved in quantity and quality as we receded from them. The herds and flocks had, beyond question, eaten and stamped out the herbage, and the demand for fuel had caused the cutting down of much timber.

Nahi-vehma employed an old Indian (Tobi-Moqui, a member of the Butterfly gens) working in a corn-field to conduct us by the nearest available route to the summit of the mesa upon which stands the Pueblo of Sumopowy.

The old fellow comprehended in a minute what was wanted, and did not pause or hesitate in the movement which he took under his charge, and got us to the top of the mesa without accident.

Oraybe and its farms and gardens were visible on another mesa on the right, through the thick coat of cedar covering this portion of the hill upon which we were travelling.

When we reached the top we saw that a fearful tempest was deluging the country in a great semi-circle around us, but leaving us unharmed.

Immense rolls of cloudy vapour, having a decided resemblance to ink-stained or smoke-brown cotton, dipped down nearly to the horizon, and from them poured solid cataracts of water, behind which boomed Heaven's dread artillery.

We did not have much leisure for admiring this effort of angry nature. Snap went our ambulance tongue, and we saw, unless we could improvise repairs, staring us in the face a sojourn of at least a fortnight in this miserable region. To make these, we set at once to work, unravelled a rope and wound the twine as tightly as it could be pulled around the fractured parts, getting a fairly good splice. The accident was not without compensating features. While Gordon and Smallwood were splicing the tongue Nahi-vehma and the old Indian with him

called me to the edge of the precipice, and there, in
a pretty little gulch leading up from the valley we
had just left, pointed out a well-defined trail, which
Nahi - vehma said was the "camino" (road) from
Hualpi to Oraybe.   When I looked along it, with my
feeble recollection of the landmarks, I was yet able to
recognise the line of travel pursued by General Crook's
party which I accompanied in 1874.   On examination we discovered a feasible mode of descent, requir-
ing, it is true, considerable patching here and there,
and especially at the top, where a vertical ledge, 18
by 20 feet high, interposed.   The facilities at hand—
sand, clay, boulders, and dead timber, supplied all that
was needed to make a respectable waggon road, so that
when we returned from Sumopowy we should not
have to descend by the long trail up which we had
come, and could thus save close on to five or six miles
of heavy sand and bad rocks.   We went into bivouac
on the mesa a few miles out (as we understood it)
from Sumopowy, in a situation affording plenty of
rain-water in pools in the sandstone, and an abundance of grass and firewood.

The storm still raged and roared on all sides ; the
flocculent, inky cloud-masses were tipped with white
and gold from the last rays of the expiring sun,
and an exquisite bow of promise spanned with its
many-hued semicircle a broad expanse of clouds,
reaching half-way to the zenith.

The old man, Tobi-Moqui, who had guided us so
cleverly, left after supper to run over to his house at

Mushangnewy, which in a straight line could not be over five or six miles from this point. His eyes snapped with joy at sight of the stipend of a shining dollar, and a double handful of our best smoking tobacco. The last words from him were lolamai! lolomai! lolomai!

With this one word and its negative, " ca-lo-lamai" (not good or *bad*), Moran and I constructed a small-sized language of our own which thus far, when used with various modulations for inquiry, assent, negation, wonder, and approval, constituted a satisfactory working medium of communication with Nahi-vehma and his friends.

During a vicious storm of rain and wind which plagued us for an hour, our mules and Nahi-vehma's plug pony stampeded, leaving us in the dark and in the lurch at the same moment. In the pitchy blackness of night, without a star to guide, nothing could be done but wait patiently for the first ray of dawn.

Some hours before morning I was awakened by a distant rumbling of thunder. Looking up at the sky a sight was witnessed never to be forgotten. The " sable curtains of night "—the theme of the poet— had become a tangible reality.

A powerful current of wind was clearing the sky of clouds, and as these passed over us they dropped almost to the ground like so many festoons of crape looped up with gems. The stars were gathered together in clusters, which shone like masses of burnished silver, and ocular illusion brought about, I suppose, by the vapour, with which the atmosphere was saturated, acting as a lens. Take it altogether, it was the most magnificent display of the kind I have ever witnessed, and excelled anything that the bold imagination of Doré would ever dare to depict upon canvas. I was badly frightened for a while, thinking that a cloud-burst was gathering above. With the first faint flush of light of the next morning (August 18, 1881) Gordon and Nahi-vehma started to hunt for the animals which had been stampeded by the lightning of the previous evening. They found them five or six miles back, grazing near an old ruin. When they returned, and before breakfast was quite ready, Nahi-vehma took me to see a ruin, not over 100 yards from our ambulance. We passed through a thick growth of scrub cedar, and near to many pools of rain-water accumulated in the rocks.

With such an annual rainfall as visits Arizona, it has for years been a matter of surprise to me that no organised effort has ever been made for the storage of water. A few thousands of dollars, judiciously expended, would blow out of the sandstone or granite tanks and reservoirs capable of holding millions of gallons. Innumerable small ravines and box-cañons could be dammed and walled up, and add their store of the precious fluid to the uses of the farmer, miner, and grazer; and this great district, so much of which is now allowed to lie barren and idle, could be made to rival the fertility of Egypt and Northern Africa in ancient times.

The ruin to which Nahi-vehma led me corresponded closely to the scores of others traced and noted in my journals, and to those already alluded to in this narrative. There was a staircase of stone, in fair preservation, leading down by 75 or 100 steps to springs and reservoirs in the face of the cañon, and below the reservoir a half-obliterated trail ran to flat pieces of farm land, once cultivated. Nahi-vehma was unusually communicative this morning. He told me that our old guide of last evening belonged to the Butterfly gens, that in Oraybe we should find the same clans as in the other Moqui towns, except that the Oraybe people had another clan—the Crane— but did not have the Oak or the Road-runner. Nahi-vehma then spoke in fond terms of his boy, who was a wonder, as he thought. He had been all the way to Saint George, Utah, to trade with the Mormons, who must have given him the elements of an education, because the proud father maintained that he could "lead" and "lite" all the same as a "Melly-cawno" (American).

Continuing his remarks, he said that the Moqui houses were "woman house" (*i.e.* belonged to the women, who, as we have seen, build and keep them in repair). The sheep were "man sheep" and "woman sheep" both ; the horses "man hos"; the blankets "woman pisala" (*i.e.* the women's *frisada*, the Spanish for blanket).

The Moquis have but one wife, the Navajoes "a heap."

We passed children's tombs of stone, and also came to a pile of stone, four feet high, at the corner of what had been a small, square stone house. The stones had been piled up in the same way as those seen near the sacred spring near Mushangnewy, and fragments of pottery strewed the ground. Nahi-vehma said that the Moquis came here to pray to the sun.

We left our ambulance at this point, which was not more than half a mile from Sumopowy, and walked on to the town, letting the vehicle follow more slowly over the rocks.

Just outside of the town we met two barefooted women approaching an altar of stone, semicircular in form, and containing the customary god or fetish of petrified wood, with the invariable tribute of painted twigs, pottery, eagle-down, etc.

We inquired for the house of the "Mungwee" (Governor), and climbed the ladder leading to the roof of the first story. This building was somewhat superior to those to be found in Mushangnewy or Shupowlewy. In the principal room seven wooden idols in the stereotyped form of wood, painted in red, green, yellow, and black, were attached to the middle one of the smoke-blackened rafters, and there were also pottery, vases, and utensils of all shapes and sizes. Stone mortars and pestles, finely made, but uncarved and undecorated, Moqui and Cohonino baskets and American sieves, axes, and spades, and, finally, planting-sticks of Moqui make, were the first things claiming our attention. Sheepskins were spread on the floor, on which we were invited to be seated.   A basket of piki bread was brought in by one of the squaws and laid at our feet.   This bread, despite its tallowy taste, was sweet and palatable.

The old " Mungwee" expressed himself as glad to see us, and offered every courtesy in the prosecution of our work.

We made the best use of our time, and sought for every item of novelty or interest worthy of record. We found spindles stuck in the ceilings of willow twigs above the rafters, necklaces of the shells of domestic fowls, water-jugs of wicker ware made by the Cohoninos filled with seeds of the squash and melon, cylindrical wooden boxes containing feathers for making sacred plumes, and, in general, all the features of the internal economy of the other Moquis, with the exception that scarcely any silver ornaments were to be seen.

Our ambulance, after much pounding over the rough rocks, had reached the Pueblo, and was now surrounded by a throng of curious and daring youngsters, while others, less bold, remained with the women and babies upon the house-tops.

Sumopowy had its complement of rain reservoirs, which afforded the young boys and girls, donkeys and pigs, a congenial wallowing-place.

This town covers a rectangular plat 175 paces in length by 80 paces in width, my pace being 30 inches.   There are two small courts, connected at one end by a very small alley, and at the other by a low arcade. The longer sides of the bounding rectangle lies east and west.

No notable differences exist between the dimensions, structure, and arrangements of the houses of this town and those already described in the others. There are many three-story buildings here, but the general average is only two. Many buildings are in a state of hopeless dilapidation, some indeed have been abandoned, and, on the other hand, during the time of our visit not less than half a dozen were undergoing alteration, enlargement, and repair. There are no selenite or glass windows, and no doors that are well constructed, unless we call by this designation three or four which from their peculiar appearance led me to suspect that there had been a mission church in the neighbourhood which had been robbed of them after the Spaniards abandoned the country. This conjecture would chime well with what I learned at a later date from Bishop Hatch of the Mormon Church, who asserted the former existence of such an edifice, and also that the Moquis had made free use of the rafters and other material in the construction of their own houses.

Sumopowy boasts of four Estufas or Kibas, one of them a hopeless wreck, and all patterned in the same mould made so familiar in these pages.

The population cannot be far from 350, and is superior by at least 100 to that of either Mushangnewy or Supowlewy.

Very few grown men were visible, and the women, with whom we gradually put ourselves on a footing of kind treatment, when asked by Nahi-vehma where their husbands and brothers were, pointed to the north-west beyond Oraybe, and said that they were hunting antelope.

Children and donkeys were plentiful. The children were all naked, none of those of either sex under seven or eight years of age bother much about fashion in dress ; a thick coat of mud on legs and bellies was the closest approach to a full-dress toilet that could be detected on any of them. The few men who remained in the Pueblo wore no clothing beyond the breech-clout, and a short cotton shirt coming down to the hips, with the exception of two or three who aspired to the *rôle* of dandies, who added to this costume loose cotton drawers reaching to mid-calf, and split up to the knees along the outer seam.

In the manner of wearing hair and clothing both sexes closely followed the styles set by the Moqui towns more to the east, but in the moccasins I detected a change.

The moccasins worn here, when worn at all, are turned up in front, almost like the toe-shields of the Apaches, and no doubt for the same reason—to protect the toes against injury from thorns and rocks.

On the outskirts of the town are garbage-piles, receptacles for such of the filth as the inhabitants are

Y

content to spare from the vicinity of their houses, where large quantities still remain.

Children, dogs, chickens, burros, sheep, and goats roam at will about the courtyards and along the streets, each contributing freely a quota to the common filth.

There also were to be seen, inside the houses, a respectable number of cats, none of which appeared upon the streets.

The first fears of the squaws and children gradually wore off, aided by the stimulus of curiosity to learn something about our ambulance, the first wheeled vehicle of its size, and perhaps of any size, which had been brought to this town. Nahi-vehma said that the women denied that any wheeled conveyance had ever before been near their houses, and certainly the intense interest with which they clustered round to examine it proved that here, as well as in Mushangnewy, the great bulk of the population knew but little, if anything, about such contrivances.

The old squaws saw a good chance to do a little trading in peaches, of which we purchased a quantity, almost ripe. Smallwood, without delay, began to stew them in the coffee-pot.

While he was preparing our lunch, Moran and myself strolled through the town, entering every house, and making purchases of idols, baskets, pottery, and other manufactures, which cost a trifle for each piece, but in the aggregate depleted our pocketbooks most wofully.

There were many mantles of rabbit fur, and one of cayote skins, sewed together with sinew, sheep pelts for rugs and bedding, and skins of cayote and fox, which appear with such constancy in the sacred dances.

Firearms were not seen, and there were no bow-drills.

Bows and arrows were abundant. The bows were painted roughly in red, yellow, green, and blue.

In the centre of one of the courtyards was an altar, two and a half feet high, and the same in thickness and depth, covered on top with a slab of sandstone. Inside was a collection of water-worn rocks, and the customary votive offerings of painted twigs, eagle-down, and petrified wood.

The children finally conquered their aversion or fears and scampered about in twos, threes, and half-dozens, ascending and descending from plaza to house-tops with the recklessness and agility of goats.

The chimneys in Sumopowy are of ollas, or of small stones set in mud and capped at top with an olla, the bottom of which had been knocked out. Cottonwood troughs for holding the food of the burros lay at different points in the streets and plazas. It goes without saying that each house was under the protection of from three to thirty idols, whose grotesque faces leered at us from the largest rafters.

There were numbers of boomerangs, some ornamented with cabalistic figures, and others without decoration.

Burro saddles of home manufacture were hanging from pegs, while slung across horizontal beams were women's petticoats, mantles, and girdles of white cotton; the mantles and skirts embroidered in blue-

black and dark green wool, with the symbol ⌐⌐⌐⌐,

which may possibly be a prayer for fertility. Almost the same symbol occurs on the walls of the Estufas when these people are interceding for abundant harvests.

In an inner room of the house of the Governor were piles of American hoes, axes, and spades, and suspended from the walls were two batons of office.

A squaw showed us a musical instrument made of a pumpkin hollowed out. Across an opening in the rind had been fixed a stick with serrated edges, and the symphony with which our hostess regaled us was played by running a second stick along these indentations; a sheep's shoulder-blade was used in the more pathetic passages. In general arrangement it was not unlike the horse-fiddle of the American schoolboy, which, in the hands of an energetic and conscientious performer, can destroy the peace of a whole neighbourhood.

Sheep manure, pressed into cakes, was laid up in houses built to screen it from the weather. This is used as fuel for burning pottery.

Cedar-wood covered a large portion of every roof and terrace. The people of Sumopowy do much of their cooking in holes in the ground near their houses. They have no ovens, at least I saw none. There was much corn in store ; every house has from two to six piles of corn in the ear, each pile 8 feet by 4 feet by 10 feet. There was also a liberal supply of the blue-flake or piki bread, but none in form of our loaves, and plenty of sheep and goat meat, peaches, squashes, and melons. The people were very dirty, not in dress alone, but in person. Although the population was so small (350-400), there were three or four persons blind of one eye, nor were the teeth nearly so regular or indicative of such a fine state of physical health as those of the Plains Indians, or the Apaches and Navajoes nearer to them.

Smallwood had lunch ready by midday, and after satisfying our own hunger, distributed the remaining stewed peaches and a can of pine-apples to the Moquis who had drawn near, and taking the sweet mess in their paws, swallowed it at one gulp, licking their fingers and smacking their chops, like a drove of hogs at a swill tub. Our popularity was enhanced by the further donation of a little smoking tobacco to the men and older boys. Mr. Moran attempted to explain to Nahi-vehma the locomotive followed by a train of cars. He made a rough sketch on the sand, and I furnished the motive power and the necessary puffing and whistling. Nahi's face brightened ; he said he " saveyed," but wanted to know where the " horses " were. Moran pointed to the engine and said that *that* pulled the whole train. " Oh," said

Nahi, " me savey now! *Hoss* behind push um ; dat's
all lite."

We moved back from Sumopowy to the place
where we had broken our ambulance tongue, and
where we were to attempt a descent to the valley
hundreds of feet below.   There was, at the brink of
the precipice, a " jump-off," or rather a double " jump-
off," of twenty or thirty feet, *vertical*, which had to be
repaired before we could think of moving an inch.
" Nahi " was first sent down the trail on foot, pulling
his pony after him.   I wanted him to investigate the
country ahead and see if there was anything else of
a serious character to obstruct us, because I feared
to be caught in a bad situation half-way down the
mountain, where we might be compelled to abandon
the ambulance.   Our guide returned with a smiling
face and the cry of lolamai.   He reported that
the camino was lolamai, except in this one spot,
which he thought we could easily repair.   We had
been expecting just such a report, because our position gave so extended a command of the country
beneath that the eye could follow the trail in all its
bearings, save only where it was hidden by a projecting hill or steep ravine.

Coats and vests were " peeled," and all hands set
to work with a will.   Stones of large size were
plentiful, and with dead cedar trees, covered over with
clay and sand, soon made a ramp of great steep-
ness, but according to Gordon's ideas, good enough
to descend.   The lead mules were taken out, wheels

locked and braked, and the thrilling drive commenced.

The angle of the grade was not far from 60 degrees
or 70 degrees, and none of us but Gordon had much
hope of the ambulance getting to the bottom in
safety. The mules were powerful and well-trained;
Gordon a brave and skilful driver; the running gear
stout; and the sand so loose that the wheels sank too
deep to let them roll very much.

Gordon simply said, " Let her rip, Lootinint ;"
and in a few seconds we saw him and his trusty
mules, with the ambulance, safe and sound at the
bottom of our improvised grade.

The rest of the descent offered no serious obstacle ;
that is, none that we were afraid of ; but it was a long
time after sunset before we struck the trail in the
valley made on our upward trip.

In a pretty recess in the mountain-side was a
large field of " frijoles " (black Mexican beans) growing finely ; and upon the crest of the mesa overlooking
it could be discerned the ruins of an old Pueblo, of
stone laid in mud, the walls averaging 10 or 15
feet in height. Nahi-vehma said that the Navajoes
had at one time been very bitter enemies of the
Moquis, and especially of the people occupying this
ruin ; that the Navajoes could not get into the Pueblo,
but harassed their flocks and destroyed or carried off
their harvests, and long ago, when Nahi's father
was a very small boy, the survivors concluded to
abandon their home and incorporate themselves with

some of their relatives living in the Pueblo of Sandia, on the Rio Grande.

(There are at this day, in the Pueblos of Sandia and Jemez, people called "Moquinos," who claim to be of Moqui derivation.)

CHAPTER XXX.

THE seventh and most important of the Moqui towns
—Oraybe—was not reached by Moran and myself on
this trip, the ground around Mushangnewy being so
cut up by rain that our ambulance could not advance.

Personally, I have made several trips to Oraybe ;
the first in October 1874, with General Crook, and
the last in October 1881, with Mr. Stroul of Santa Fé,
New Mexico, an ambulance driver named Mullan,
and two Moqui boys about eight or ten years old,
from Mushangnewy.

A condensation from my notes of these several
visits will be all that is necessary, the general resemblance between all these villages being so great.

Oraybe lies north and west from Mushangnewy,
the distance as nearly as we could estimate being
twenty miles, and the trail generally sandy and
stony.

Approaching the town indications and outcroppings of coal are frequent. The position of Oraybe is
different from that of its sister Pueblos. Instead of
being on the crest of a hill it is on the side, and is

about as inaccessible as any of them. The trail leads through corn and melon fields, guarded sometimes by what I took to be idols. These consisted of a heap of sandstone slabs, the central one vertical and painted with white marks for nose, eyes, and mouth.[1]

Closer still to the town are peach orchards of considerable size, having passed through which one has to ascend a long flight of stone steps leading up the face of the bluff.

The houses are identical in material, size, height, etc., with those on the mesas farther to the east.

The population of Oraybe cannot be far from 1500. From the moment of our first arrival we were surrounded by a throng of not uncivil Indians, who had been told by the two young Indians whom we had hired as guides that we were Mormons. The Mormons have great influence over the Oraybe Moquis, who decline to have any relations whatever with other Caucasians. It was some time before I knew what had induced this cordial treatment. In the meanwhile I was busy making purchases of pottery, fine baskets, and one or two very old drums, made of small, hollowed cottonwood logs, covered with the hide of some animal, apparently the horse.

A number of half-ruined and abandoned houses would seem to attest the gradual diminution of population, but there was nothing to strengthen such an idea if one turned to the herds of burros, goats, dogs, and naked children.

[1] See Plate XXX.

Of the last, we saw and counted eighty-five on the roofs of one street. The advent of such intruders had stirred this community to its depths, and every one who had eyes with which to see was gazing at us.

Looking back into the broad valley, we scanned an expanse of broad acres of corn, melons, beans, and pumpkins, and in every house store-rooms, piled high with these products, spoke of plenteous harvests.

The atmosphere of the locality is rare and dry ; were it otherwise, a pestilence would surely result from the garbage and filth, animal, human, and vegetable, coating the streets.

Outside of the town limits was a great reservoir, 50 to 60 yards in diameter and 3 feet deep, wherein children splashed, and "burros," dogs, goats, sheep, and chickens slaked their thirst.

Chickens were seen in great numbers, and made the air resonant with their incessant cackling.

One of the houses had an iron lock upon the door, two or three panes of glass in one of the windows, and a couple of atrociously poor lithographs in colours.

The old woman was delighted to have us notice her riches, and withdrew from a recess in the wall three or four cheap cups and saucers of American china-ware. Her house was abundantly provided with onions, chile, corn, melons, pumpkins, and squashes, in all the modes of their use by the Moquis. The children had gathered outside, peering through the open door when possible, or taking secure positions upon the adjacent roofs to critically observe us as we passed out.   Stroul quietly peeped through a window, and counted over 150 of tender years.

In front of this house a squad of twenty-two women were dexterously husking corn; the chip, chip, chipping of the husks sounded like the clicking of hammers in a stone quarry.

There are ten Estufas in Oraybe, each of which was visited.   Upon the walls of several were designs of a religious or symbolical character; one of these represented a procession of thirteen figures, eight holding bows in right hands, and five with crosses upon their breasts.   Another was decidedly phallic in character, and still another represented a double or twisted snake.   This last was carved upon a stone stool.

The Oraybes pay some attention to hygienic matters, as we observed pits dug for and filled with garbage.

Their dogs go down ladders *head first* almost as rapidly as the men do.

Melons and peaches are abundant, cheap, and of exceptionally fine qualities.   The fruit is eaten and the seeds also, which are dried and mixed with those of the sun-flower.

One of the men of Oraybe was a Cohonino Indian, who came here three or four years ago, and became blind, since which time he had remained.   He was, when we saw him, a tall, well-formed man, past middle age.

In one quarter of the town a band of women were rebuilding their house and plastering the mud on the inside with their hands. The men were bringing beams and stones for use in the construction.

The mothers of Oraybe have a curious way of putting their children to sleep. They stand first on one foot and then on the other, giving themselves a swaying motion, which corresponds to the rocking of a cradle.

We saw no Albinos, but did see several *semi-Albinos.* Their hair was light brown, skin white, complexion ruddy.

If they were full Albinos they did not manifest the peculiarities of their class. We watched a couple of old women making the pretty Moqui baskets frequently alluded to in these pages. The construction was rapid, and the only thing worrying the old crones was the drying out of their willow twigs, which they kept carefully imbedded in wet sand to prevent such an accident.

Altogether Stroul counted 203 children, of both sexes, between one month and eight years of age. The count was made with great care and under the best advantages, and I am persuaded is somewhat under the real number in the town. We did not see many horses, but there were numbers of burros and good-sized herds of sheep and goats. Saddles and bridles for horses and donkeys were in every house. Some of these may have been from the Navajoes, with whom

the Oraybe Moquis trade constantly.   During our
stay there were not less than thirty Navajoes in the
town, who, in spite of finding a ready market for
saddles, fine blankets, and silver necklaces, looked
down with undisguised contempt upon the purchasers, much as Norman pirates were wont to despise
the Saxon hind.

A pound of smoking tobacco, half as much loaf-
sugar, and a heaped up handful of blue and scarlet
beads, put us on the best footing with the Navajoes,
and none too soon.

An Indian, much inflated with his own importance, came up to Stroul and myself, and asked if we
were Mormons; the young boys who had come over
with us from Mushangnewy had, unknown to us,
started such a story.   We told the old duffer we
were Americanos from Washington.   He at once
ordered us to leave the town.   This invitation we
were compelled to decline, and continued our promenade, with a body-guard of Navajoes, gay as pea-
cocks in their bright-coloured garments.   The old
fellow's impotent rage was amusing to see, but he
finally simmered down enough to take a little smoking
tobacco, and bring us in return a couple of melons
good enough for anybody.

The clans or gentes of the Oraybe Moquis are
almost identical with those of Suchongnewy. Nahi-
vehma said that in Oraybe there is a Crane gens, but
the Oak and Road-runner gentes are both extinct.

Bishop Hatch of the Mormon Church insisted that

while he was in Oraybe there was a sacred family among the Moquis : he said that there was a widow, whose infant son, not over four years old, was upon every feast-day or occasion of ceremony loaded down with beads of sea-shell, chalchihuitl, abalone, and everything else precious in the eyes of the Moquis.

Concerning the clans or gentes of the Moquis I give the following lists, obtained at different times, and varying slightly from the inability of different Moquis to give the correct Spanish for each clan name, or my own inability to understand them.

The first list, obtained from Tochi, has already been given.

Surgeon Ten Broeck, U.S. Army, in 1852, compiled the following list :—1, Deer ; 2, Sand ; 3, Water ; 4, Bear ; 5, Hare ; 6, Prairie Wolf (cayote) ; 7, Rattlesnake ; 8, Tobacco Plant ; 9, Seed-grass.

Tegua Tom, in October 1881, gave me the following names :—1, Water ; 2, Toad or Frog ; 3, Sun ; 4, Snake ; 5, Rabbit ; 6, Butterfly ; 7, Tobacco ; 8, Badger ; 9, Corn ; 10, Cottonwood ; 11, Clown or Dead Man ; 12, Bear ; 13, Coyote ; 14, Deer ; 15, Lizard ; and 16, Road-runner.

The Tegua Indians living in the village of Hano or Tegua with the Moquis have : 1, Sun ; 2, Corn ; 3, Snake ; 4, Tobacco ; 5, Cottonwood ; 6, Pine ; 7, Cloud ; 8, Bear ; 9, Parrot.

Tom himself was of the Corn gens, his father of the Frog, and his wife of the Bear. Nahi-vehma, Tom said, was a Road-runner.

Nanahe, a Moqui Indian living among the Zunis, told me at Zuni, in November 1881, that " in the days when the world was created, God gave to His children certain things ; such things as they wished for and cried for He gave them, and these became their gentile or clan emblems."

TRANSLATION MADE FROM ZUNI INTO ENGLISH BY MR. FRANK CUSHING, AND FROM ZUNI INTO SPANISH BY PEDRO PINO.

1. Parrot	Go together (*i.e.* form a pluatry).	13. Bear	Go together (*i.e.* form a pluatry).	
2. Cottonwood		14. Hemlock[1]		
3. Macaw		15. Rattlesnake	Do.	
4. Corn	Do.	16. Dove		
5. Frog		17. Tobacco	Do.	
6. Turkey	Do.	18. Cotton-tail Rabbit		
7. Eagle		19. Olla-jocue or Blue seed-grass.		
8. Sun		20. Bunch-grass	Do.	
9. Badger	Do.	21. Deer		
10. Butterfly		22. Yellow Wood	Do.	
11. Coyote	Do.	23. Squash		
12. Skeleton				

Of these lists the last is the most correct.

Our ambulance excited almost as much interest in Oraybe as it did in the three middle towns ; but it should be remarked that in Oraybe was a small two-wheeled cart, badly broken and unserviceable, left behind possibly by a party of Mormons going through to the Little Colorado.

Not far from Oraybe may be found sacred springs like that near Mushangnewy, and a phallic shrine, to which reference only can be made.

[1] Hemlock may be Kúga (Firewood).

Our return trip from Oraybe was one of the coldest and most uncomfortable I have ever experienced. When the start was made the weather was still open and fair, and notwithstanding it was almost the last day of October, not too cold for our clothing, which had been worn all through summer and was almost worn out. A bitter wind blew down from the north the night after we had left the town, and very nearly froze us to death. We did everything with the means at hand that a long frontier experience suggested : dug a long trench in the ground in a sheltered depression, and piled up earth, rock, and brush on the windward side; covered the bottom with sage-brush and corn-stalks from the fields next us ; built fires which did but little good ; put the two Moqui boys in the middle, and, huddling all in a pile, spread over us the insufficient supply of blankets and great-coats. But the cold became so intense that our humble couch was vacated, and we crouched over the half-dead embers hours before the genial sun had lazily crept above the line of hills in the east and thawed and warmed our benumbed limbs.

CHAPTER XXXI.

Bogged—Crossing a stream—The trail found—Across the plain—A
Mormon road—A dreary waste—A sand-storm—A Mormon
settlement.

WHEN the preceding brief digression was made the
ambulance was in bivouac at the foot of the Mushangnewy mesa, from which place we thought it could be
taken across country to the line of the Atlantic and
Pacific Railroad, but to what particular place we could
not say, as the road was still uncompleted.

My recollection of the country, feeble as it was,
satisfied me that the plan was feasible, and a long con-
ference with Nahi-vehma brought out the fact that
there was a "heap" of "Mo-monee house" (Mormon
settlements), where we could expect to buy forage for
our mules and food for ourselves. Nahi then added
that some distance to the south of us was a "camino"
(waggon road), which he knew he could find. This
occurred late at night on the 18th of August; the
next morning, by five o'clock, coffee had been made
and swallowed, mules harnessed, and we were on the
move.

We halted for a few moments at a clump of cottonwood, where the Moquis had dammed up an arroyo ;

here was a great abundance of good rain-water, with which we filled our five-gallon keg and the canteens.

The day opened bright and beautiful, and our hearts were glad with anticipations of a journey without further hardship. Scarcely had we gone a mile from last night's stopping-place when we ran into a miry "alkali" flat full of mud "chuck-holes."

The mules struggled bravely through the first half-dozen, but at last succumbed to one in which the ambulance sank more than axle-deep in a viscous "adobe" mud, and they themselves were immersed shoulder-deep. They became frantic, and plunged and tossed, entangling themselves in the harness, and exciting our fears to the utmost.

Our practice had been to give all the aid in our power to the animals; to walk up every hill, through all deep sand, and in every wallow or bog where water had collected and mud formed. To our absence from the ambulance should be ascribed our escape from very grave peril. Smallwood and Nahi-vehma threw themselves flat upon the heads of the leaders and kept them from tossing or kicking, while Moran, Gordon, and myself unhitched the traces. We were much worried about the poor animals and the ambulance, scarcely crediting the possibility of the escape of either from serious injury. Examination revealed the soundness of the vehicle and the safety of the mules, with the insignificant exception of a deep scratch on the breast of the near wheeler. But there the ambulance was, axle-deep in the stickiest kind of clay. Nahi-vehma was sent ahead to spy out firm ground, of which there did not seem to be much left in the country, while we unloaded everything, even the seats, dug two feet of clay from about the wheels, harnessed the wheelers to the hind axle, and then, with the assistance of Nahi, who had returned, and of two other Moquis, who, seeing our predicament, had run over from a corn-field, we pulled and pushed and lifted clean on to dry ground.

In a few minutes more we had repacked and re-harnessed and resumed the journey.

We turned to the west, moving parallel to the banks of the quagmire (it would be an abuse of terms to call it a stream), to the locality which Nahi had designated as the most favourable for attempting a passage. The situation was not especially encouraging; the banks were vertical, ten feet high, but fortunately of a crumbling mixture of sand and clay, yielding freely to the vigorous attacks made with our solitary shovel and with pieces of cracker boxes.

A grade was made in less than no time. Gordon was left in charge of the mules on the hither side, until Moran, Smallwood, and myself had waded across to determine where there was the least danger of get-ting mired.

By this time we were joined by half a dozen Moquis, including our two assistants at the previous break-down. One of these youngsters had a hoe, which I borrowed for a quarter dollar, and with which some energetic service was done. Moran, Smallwood, and Nahi working with the spade, turn and turn and turn about, I with the hoe, and two of the Moqui volunteers with pieces of cracker box, caused the farther embankment to crumble into the stream, thus making a grade to Gordon's perfect satisfaction.

A startling crack of the whip and a series of yells, shrill as the war-whoop of an Apache, wakened the mules to the advisability of pulling with every muscle in their bodies; the passage was effected without much trouble, Gordon giving an extra yell "just for luck," as he expressed it, the rest of our little party of white men cheering, and the Moquis ejaculating in a hearty pleasant-voiced way, lolamai, lolamai.

We gave a small present of coin to each of those who had worked and scraped with the shovel, as we had not forgotten to do to those who had come to our help in the previous predicament.

This liberality pleased the recipients greatly. They squeezed our hands to the tune of lolamai, lolamai, while the idle lookers-on who had not done anything at all came up with a petition to be included in the distribution.

Probably they thought that they deserved pay for their sympathy. We declined to give them a cent. They abated their claims to a humble request for matches. This was not unreasonable, so we made an apportionment of smoking tobacco and *good* matches to those who had worked, and of *bad* matches alone to those who had not.

The *good* matches were those which would ignite

when rubbed on anything, the *bad* ones had to be scratched against the box containing them. The Moquis could not understand this. They tried to light one or two of those which Moran had given them, but of course unsuccessfully, and pronounced the gift "ca-lolamai" (no good).

Moran, affecting the greatest surprise, took the matches back, rubbed them against the box in his hand and produced a brilliant illumination. The Moquis were mystified. They tried another and another without result, while Moran, with a simple touch of the wrist, caused the same matches to strike the box (concealed in his sleeve) and to blaze fiercely. They scratched their heads and looked askant at all of us. What thoughts passed through their minds I know not, but suspect that they considered we had put bad medicine of some sort on the fire-sticks.

Nahi-vehma, proud of his superior knowledge, smiled with complacency upon his ignorant relatives, whose wonderment he did all he could to increase. The party followed the ambulance to see where we were going; a fortunate curiosity, it proved to be, because within less than 250 yards we came to another and more troublesome ravine, where all our new-made friends, assured of reward, pitched in and helped with might and main, digging with hoes, and spade, and sticks, or even with hands alone, carrying rocks and branches or clods of sod, or when the grade was ready, pushing with their shoulders at the wheels.

We settled our obligations to their gratification, and drove off amid a chorus of lolamais.

The hair of one of these Moqui boys was very peculiar; I inferred that he must be a half Albino, although his skin was dark. On the crown the hair was the colour of corn-silk,—a dirty yellowish white; at the bottom it was a jet black.

At 9 o'clock Nahi-vehma, then riding a short distance in advance, gave a whoop and threw up his hand; he had struck the trail for Sunset Crossing (of the Colorado Chiquito).

He followed this almost due south, going up grade, and getting into a country well grassed with "grama"; at noon we had reached a small arroyo, full of rain-water, where we unhitched the mules to give them a chance to roll and rest, as well as rid themselves of the stings of pestiferous gnats which annoyed them beyond endurance. Here we examined what, from surface indications, was a good coal-measure.

In the afternoon the trail ran through a fine pasture-land, mantled with vernel green. We saw on all sides a broad grassy plain, sloping back towards the Moqui villages. This plain we estimated to be seven miles broad, covered in its whole extent with the choicest "black grama" grass, and in area could not have been less than 20,000 acres. It was succeeded by a hilly formation, and we were then surrounded by buttes of odd and picturesque shapes. When the skirt of these hills was reached a prolific growth of sage-brush and grease-wood asserted its

dominion.   We crossed the first range of hills without
serious bother, and descended into a second broad
expanse of refreshing green grass running for miles
in every direction.   Herds of Navajo ponies were
discernible on the flanks of the small knolls enclosing
this lovely meadow on the south, and sheep trails
without number, leading hither and thither, showed
unmistakably that the Navajoes were sensible of the
value of this grand pasturage.

The sun was almost below the horizon when we
drove up alongside of two or three deep pools, where
we watered the mules and filled what little was lacking
in our keg and canteens.

Near this tank was a deposit of fine-grained clay,
very plastic, drying readily in the sun, tenacious,
susceptible of a beautiful polish, and destined some
day to become an important article of commerce.

The various hills and buttes, blue in the distance,
changed as we drew near to peaks of black basalt,
covered at base with a thin *talus* of reddish earth, the
result of their own disintegration.   Where the grama
grass, as it sometimes did, grew in and upon the black
basalt itself the combination of colours was peculiarly
effective, and in the rays of the sinking sun the mounds
looked like moleskin.

Nahi left us this evening at our bivouac in the
hills, some twenty miles south of Mushangnewy.   We
did not need his services, as the country was no longer
strange, and we could not be more than forty miles
from the Atlantic and Pacific Railroad.

The next morning we moved out long before day-break, not having any breakfast, as our previous bivouac had been made after dark, and was without water. Three miles out on the trail we came to an "arroyo" full of tiny, trickling springs, dammed up by the Navajoes. The reservoirs thus formed were protected from mules, ponies, or burros which might desire to enter, by framework of cedar branches inclined across the water.

Here we stayed only long enough to water the animals and prepare for ourselves a cup of hot coffee. Ten miles farther we again halted, still in a country full of lava and basalt hills of small elevation, but comely in contour and proportions. In the early gray of the morning they peeped above the horizon, hazy and ill-defined, assuming shape and tone as we slowly diminished the distance between them and us, showing grassy bases and rugged lava crests, seamed and hacked with ravines and gashes of all sizes.

The only signs of animate creation were a vicious badger, which eyed us suspiciously from a hole into which it retreated precipitately as a bullet whistled alongside its head; a lordly eagle sailing lazily in mid-air; a scared jack-rabbit jumping and doubling wildly over and behind sage-brush, its white feathery rump showing at one instant, and the next its delicate, long pink ears, tremulously erect in the sunlight as it paused for breath and to watch our strange vehicle; and lastly, in a pretty green valley, herds of Navajo sheep and goats, a "bunch" of their ponies, three or four petty corn patches, and as many "hogans" (houses). In this beautiful nook, at the foot of a sugar-loaf mesa of black and green, and in face of another which might be mistaken for its twin brother, we rested for two hours, an indulgence appreciated by the mules, which ate ravenously of the succulent herbage.

Before Gordon had unharnessed a Navajo woman and a little girl rode up and examined our team with studious, half-satisfied eyes, and then without a word stolidly rode away. Two hundred yards from where we rested the Navajoes had dug out a spring and made a reservoir and drinking-place for their herds. This reservoir was full of tadpoles and the *fish-reptile* of Arizona, a peculiar creature, formed like a fish, but having four legs as well as fins. It corresponds closely to the "axolotl" of Mexico.

Not a mile below this spring began what are known as "the breaks of the Little Colorado," an elevated plateau, in two benches, the crest of the upper 1200 feet and that of the lower 600 feet above the level of the stream. For a distance of fifteen miles back from the river is a desert unsurpassed for aridity by any equal area in the whole world. Wind and water in the rainy season have eroded the faces of the benches into thousands of odd forms, in which the neutral tints of bluish-gray, reddish-brown, and sage-brush green vie for prominence, and are blended in a confusion as pleasing as it is bewildering.

A few shrivelled sprigs of grease-wood, a speck or

so of sage-brush seen at great intervals, and in one or two shady nooks a solitary leaflet of green which may be grass, or something else, constitute the sole verdure, the sole covering for these hills of burnt, baked clay and sand.

While on the incline leading down from the upper bench a thunderstorm arose without a moment's notice, and gave us all a good drenching. Here could be made out the grade of what must at one time have been a very respectable piece of engineering, a road down into the valley below, or rather down to the lower bench, following the best curves, avoiding points where clay or rock would have been likely to interfere with wheel or pack transportation, or crossing chasms demanding a great amount of hard labour and the exercise of the best judgment in the construction of retaining walls and buttresses of stone.

This we had no doubt was the work of the Mormons, who had been trying to make a road to connect their Arizona settlements with those north of the Cañon of the Colorado.

Whoever had done the work had done it well, but fruitlessly. A fearful cloud-burst must have swept over this place lately, and with immense power had hurled great cubes of rock from their positions or gnawed out awful gaps 5 and 6 feet deep and 8 and 10 feet wide in the path we were to descend.

We set to work with a will; took off our coats, rolled up our sleeves, dislodged the biggest boulders we could find above each gap, and let them slide down so as to fill them sufficiently. The retaining walls made convenient quarries,—a succour almost providential, as we had no axe strong enough to fell trees had any been near.

We lifted the greatest boulders, many of them so heavy that they required the combined efforts of our whole party of four, and after getting them into the worst gaps in the line of travel, laboured with renewed energy to fill in with smaller stones or clay scooped up in handfuls.

The leaders were unharnessed, and led to the foot of the repaired road, and then the cool and skilful Gordon managed the wheelers, while the rest of us held for dear life to the straps and wheels on the upper side to keep the ambulance from overturning.

Upon reaching the bottom of this horrible " washout " our hands were covered with blood, oozing from scratches and cuts received in the struggle with stubborn rocks, and our clothes were wet with perspiration from exhausting work under so burning a sun.

At the foot of the mesa a pretty little valley, or " cañada," as the Mexicans would call it, spread out, where in the shadow of high bluffs green grass and young sage-brush grew with luxuriance.

The cloud-burst by which such havoc had been wrought at the upper end of the grade must have been unusually potential in its energy, but restricted in its area, and had left no traces of its violence in this lovely glade which we followed down a short distance until it opened out upon the broad and unhappy-

looking valley of the Colorado Chiquito. It was not
less than twelve or fifteen miles from the base of the
bluffs upon which we were to the thread of the stream
—a distance not great in itself, but made apparently
interminable by being nothing but a perfectly flat
expanse of sun-baked clay, above which, at rare intervals, projected hummocks of sage-brushes, looking like
little islands in a vast ocean of mud. Such they must
be whenever the pigmy current of the river swollen
by mountain rains becomes a raging sea and covers
the low country for miles along its banks.

The rays of the sun, reflected back from the
polished surface of the plain, dazzled and pained our
inflamed eyes, and made us regret the cool, green
glade in the hill-skirts.

For fifteen miles we pulled over this unwholesome
and exasperating desert, our weariness aggravated by
a mirage reflecting with tantalising distinctness the
limbs and branches of the young cottonwood along
the banks of the distant river.

There was no change in the formation until we
approached the immediate vicinity of the banks, when
we encountered low bluffs of sandstone and shale and
a beach of water-worn pebbles, and passed through
a grove of petrified trees, lying on the ground in
fragments, the average length of the pieces being
from 5 to 10 feet, and the diameter from 12 inches
to twice that dimension. Moran called to me to
look back at the mesa we had descended. We
saw that it was a regular "bad land," for all the

world like that at Green River, Wyoming, and no doubt a continuation of it. The combination of neutral tints was so harmonious, and the stratification of red clay, yellow sandstone, buff clay, marl, and shale, so regularly and horizontally banded and striped, that it suggested the idea of man's handiwork.

Our course had turned up-stream, going nearly east, from which direction a faint and refreshing breeze was blowing.

Dead in front of us two or three perfectly vertical, symmetrical, and well-defined whirlwinds lazily whisked across the plain, pirouetting gracefully about their axe.

While our eyes admiringly followed their movements the breeze rose into a gale; the gentle murmur, which at first had so pleased us, gave way to a harsh scream, the forerunner of that meanest of afflictions—the Arizona sand-storm.

The sky became overcast, assuming a dull-gray colour, which soon changed to a yellowish-brown from the mass of sand and dust held in suspension in the atmosphere; on the higher hills, in the distant horizon, purplish-black, hour-glass-shaped water-spouts were wreaking destruction upon the fair face of Nature. The sand-storm blew with savage fury for the remainder of the day, filling the ambulance with a drift of dust, and so covering our clothing that we could have been mistaken for millers.

The irritating particles settled in eyes or hung

upon lids, lashes, moustaches, or in ears, and upon lips and mouth.

We did not care much for our own distress and discomfort, but the poor mules, so severely strained all day, were beginning to show signs of speedily giving out.

We could barely make out their heads, and could not tell whether or not they were following the road. I determined to abandon the effort to reach Sunset that night, and directed Gordon to halt upon reaching a low sandstone bluff, then a short distance ahead.

My plans changed when we reached there. The tempest lulled for a moment, enabling Gordon to look forward and descry what he felt confident was a farmhouse of unusual size surrounded by stacks of hay. This he thought could be reached in a very little while, and by so doing we could help the animals by getting them hay and perhaps grain.

The river, which was not very far away on our right, was separated from us by a tract of overflowed ground, the breeding-place of malaria and mosquitoes. So, all things considered, we thought we could not do better than trudge on at snail's pace to the farmhouse, or whatever it might prove to be.

The progress made was wretchedly slow, and I do not think that our leg-weary mules would have been successful had we not run upon five or six cows, with full udders, jogging complacently to the barnyard, to yield up their rich tribute of fragrant milk.

The sight of these domestic animals had a most encouraging effect upon the mules, which pricked up
their ears and threw themselves into their collars
with fresh courage.

We were all—animals and men—badly " tuckered
out " as we drew rein in front of the row of hay-
stacks and the long palisade of one-storied log-houses,
which in the gloom of approaching night were all that
we could distinguish of the Mormon settlement of
Sunset.

Our arrival occasioned a great deal of surprise to
the Mormons. They had learned a week previously,
from a party of Moqui Indians who had seen us at
the snake - dance, that we purposed making the
trip, but they believed it to be impossible with an
ambulance. Three or four of their men had gone out
to examine the condition of the grade down which we
had come. They had gone as far as the summit of
the mesa—the terminal point of the completed road,
and had there found the wash-out, which they considered would be impassable for any wheeled vehicle.
The tracks of the animals ridden by these men had
given us some uneasiness. We saw where they had
circled and twisted round in the vicinity of the road
and were unable to conjecture what their business
might be. We saw that they were not "estrays,"
the boot-tracks alongside the road showing that the
animals had been ridden, and by Americans; but if
Americans, they might be horse-thieves—a surmise
which made us uncomfortable.

The Mormons plied us with questions, and expressed astonishment and gratification at our successful descent into the valley; one of our interrogators, who had been out with the road-viewers, said that he would have been willing to bet $10,000 that an ambulance could not get down that fearful place without going to pieces. "You can bet $10,000 more," I replied, "that *this* ambulance will never do it again, at least if I have anything to say about it."

My conversation with the Mormons was interrupted by the rapid approach of three or four men, whose dress was as dirty as our own, and whose untrimmed hair and beards and burned countenances betokened severe exposure to sun and wind and rain. Under all these forbidding externals they had the manner and bearing of well-bred gentlemen. They introduced themselves as members of the U.S. Geological Survey, and gave their names as Gilbert Thompson, Topographer in charge; J. A. Hillers, Photographer; James Webster, and Levi Bootes,— the last the son of Colonel Bootes of the army.

No welcome could have been more cordial or more generous. Moran had known Hillers in days gone by, but that did not make any difference in the treatment accorded to either of us or to our men. Thompson had his drivers unharness our played-out animals and turn them loose upon a bed of hay.

They were soon watered, provided with all the hay and grain they could eat, and were gently flapping their ears and whisking their tails in the dreamy delusion that they had reached the mule's paradise. After we had seen them thus bountifully provided for we followed Thompson and the other gentlemen to the tents of the surveyors. Jack, the cheery-voiced cook, had done wonders in the short time since our arrival.

He had spread a canvas upon the ground and covered it with everything his larder afforded, and we feasted heartily on mush-melons and clabber, a combination which ought to have killed us, but did not.

Hillers reappeared with a mixture of ginger and whisky. The ginger was all right, but the whisky, from the Mormon town of Brigham, was as vile as Arizona could produce, and, to judge from its taste, was compounded of equal portions of camphine, cayenne pepper, and carbolic acid.

But Hillers meant well, and, in all seriousness, did us a great deal of good.

CHAPTER XXXII.

WHEN we awaked and dressed we learned that it was Sunday, the 21st of August. We made our ablutions in the " acequia " flowing behind the tent, and as we looked up saw that we were the focus of the glances of an irregular group of sturdy Mormon boys, all barefooted, all freckled, all in shirt-sleeves, all with one brace drawn tight across the right shoulder, and all, I must admit, manly and bold in appearance.

They looked as if cut out by the one die, or, at least, as if patterned after the one model. This was the result not of common parentage, but of the co-operative system of supply prevailing in Utah, by which all the towns and villages receive their clothing in gross, and all the children, one may say, are clad in uniform. This idea grows into conviction when one turns to describe the hats, heirlooms dating back to a generation prior to the coming of Columbus. These hats are of coarse straw, grown yellow in the sun; each is deeply voluted at the rim, except at the segment bitten out by dogs at play.

There are no such ornaments as hat-bands or hat-ribbons to be seen among the Mormon youngsters in these outlying settlements, or " stakes," as they designate them, and how they manage to keep this wonderful head-gear on during the prevailing sand-storms is something which passes comprehension.

These boys are near enough of a size to be twins, but all sizes may be had for the asking, from the moon-eyed baby at its mother's breast to the brawny youth driving home the herds.

They are all nice boys, guiltless of the impertinence to strangers one would be sure to encounter in our own small villages.

Indeed, they are more noticeable from their astounding uniformity in the way of shocking bad hats and shocking bad freckles than from any disagreeable peculiarities.

The most unpleasant feature in their talk is the monotonous drawl of their words, which in themselves are amusing enough.

" Any centipedes around here, Bul ? "

" Qui-i-i-ite a fe-e-e-ew."

That boy was right; there *were* centipedes in and around Sunset, and one which Mr. Thompson had captured that very morning was over five inches long, lusty, and square-shouldered.

The Mormons courteously invited us to attend Divine service in their school building, an invitation which I was glad to receive and accept.

Before the hour for the religious exercises there was time for a stroll about town, which I made along with Moran and Thompson, and a chatty, convivial old gentleman named Shutt, who had come down from Salt Lake with the survey party, and had borne the hard knocks with unfailing good humour.

I found him bright, amusing, jolly, good-natured, and with the bland, affable, but sometimes self-important, air so common with gentlemen past middle age, who are getting to be, as the small boy said, " hump-backed in the stomach."

In appearance he was the personification of Falstaffian good-fellowship : his head bald and shiny, the result, according to his own story, of early piety ; his nose, peeled by the sun, bulbous and spongy, and emulating the colours of the dahlia ; and his eyes scalded out of all colour by the fierce sand-blasts.

Take him in his entirety he was certainly the worse for wear, but he had lost none of his good-humour, and added much to the life of his party.

" Sunset" consists of a long building, one story high, built around a hollow square, to which there are two entrances,—open spaces in the line of palisade buildings,—each wide enough for the passage of farm vehicles. It is constructed of upright cottonwood trunks, chinked with mud, and covered with an inclined roof of pine planking. The square is fifty yards on a side, and amply commodious for all the present needs of the community. All windows and doors face upon this square, a feature in the construction induced by fear of roving bands of hostile Apaches or Navajoes.

In this one building over two hundred men, women, and children reside, although at that time numbers were absent for various reasons. Families were separated by partition walls, but messing was communal, all the inhabitants eating together in the large dining-hall in the centre of the square.

We did not arrive very early at the service for a very good reason,—a feast of red-ripe luscious watermelons caused us to forget Mormons, church, and everything else.

The fruit was delicious, equal to anything of the kind I had ever tasted, and, according to the boys who sold it, did better than any other product of the valley.

The Mormons have had to contend against the most appalling obstacles in the establishment of this "Stake of Zion," and deserve all the credit which can attach to energy, patience, and industry.

They have proved that cattle will do finely in the foot-hills, where they can secure plenty of nutritious grasses, spring or reservoir water, and a perfect immunity from their worst enemy, severe cold.

The value for agricultural purposes of the lands at Sunset was still undetermined, but a little farther up the Colorado Chiquito, along the line of the railroad, at the towns of Saint Joseph, Holdbrook, Woodruff, and Saint John, good crops of cereals, fruits, and vegetables can be counted upon yearly. At Sunset the well-water is impregnated with salt, but at the other towns named it is free from every deleterious or unpleasant ingredient.

Not only melons, but onions, peas, beans, beets, corn, and wheat are raised in quantities sufficient to excite great hopes for the future prosperity of all these young settlements. They have numbers of cows, all fat and in excellent condition, which keep them supplied with milk, of whose richness and delicious flavour I shall always testify with the greatest willingness.

Sunset, I was told by a lame Mormon, was garrisoned by the Order of Enoch, a sort of communistic society pertaining to the church of Latter-Day Saints.

Divine service was held in the building, which, during week-days, served as a school-house. The congregation was composed of from seventy-five to eighty persons, the men in their shirt-sleeves, and one-half the grand total children. The presiding elder or bishop had delayed the opening exercises on our account; the first hymn, chanted by the whole assemblage, began as we took our seats on the benches reserved for us.

The theme was one of praise to Almighty God, who had watched over and guided His people through storms, tribulation, and persecution, confounding kings and dukes and counts.

I judged it to be a favourite with the singers, nearly all of whom had left Europe to escape oppressive and iniquitous laws.

After the hymn came a sermon by " Brother " Savage.

This old gentleman was a study, and an interesting one.

He was a grizzled old Englishman from the humbler walks of life, whose early educational advantages had been but slender.

His unkempt hair hung in tangled, gray masses, down his shoulders; his complexion, sanguine, sunburned, and weather-beaten, was badly freckled; and his snaggled teeth, projecting tusk-like from an unnecessarily large mouth, helped, with the matted locks, to conceal and disguise the acute and astute mind, of which an occasional suspicion was aroused by the quick flashes of humour and intelligence shooting from the bright blue eyes, almost covered up under shaggy brows.

He was innocent of coat, collar, or cuffs, and his raiment ran the gamut of dilapidation and dirt, from the old and filthy vest to the older and filthier shirt, and the oldest and filthiest of pantaloons; each bearing, as a veteran his scars, a full complement of patches—souvenirs of hard and honourable service.

" Brother " Savage, I thought, must be one of those people of whom we frequently read, who feeling the " power of the spirit," yield to the holy impulse, and throw themselves with fervour into the work of evangelising souls by " orating " to their neighbours upon " Scripter." Such self-appointed ministers may become bores—frequently they become nuisances; yet in some instances, and " Brother " Savage, I take it,

was one, they develop oratorical and polemical powers
not to be underrated, and command the fullest respect
of the little flocks that hearken to their ministra-
tions.   At the commencement of his discourse
" Brother " Savage was certainly timid, embarrassed,
perhaps " stage-frightened," in presence of so many
strangers ; these feelings rapidly disappeared as he
warmed to his theme, and we were soon compelled
to acknowledge that he possessed a fund of shrewd,
logical common - sense, and had made the best use
of all opportunities of study thrown in his way.

To criticise his sermon in all fairness, I have given
an outline of his personal appearance, his uncouth
manners and rustic apparel, and have also referred to
the impressions to which these gave rise ; but it is
simple justice and nothing else to concede that his
discourse was one of the best I had ever listened to,
and far superior to many I have had inflicted upon
me by high-salaried clergymen of greater pretensions.

One had to forget or ignore a few grammatical
solecisms and peculiarities of pronunciation like
" brethring," " sistern," " traditionated," and others of
that type, and to attend only to the logical perspicuity
with which he laid down for the information of the
visitors an exposition of the Mormon doctrine, based,
as he claimed, upon the " sacred Scripter." He outlined the belief of his co-religionists in all that Christ
taught : baptism by immersion, the imposition of
hands, etc., but carefully excluded from his disquisition
any reference to polygamy.   His manner was gentle

but earnest ; his diction unlettered but forcible ; and his argument subtle and cogent within the limits assigned them.   He made a very forcible impression upon me, and I was sincerely glad that I had attended the services and heard him.   Mr. Shutt dosed placidly on the " anxious bench " during the whole sermon, his nose gleaming like the head-light of a locomotive. He indignantly contradicted our opinion that he had not followed the preacher's arguments, and claimed that he was satisfied from the explanations made that Mormonism, except in the one phase of polygamy, was as clearly an evolution—an outgrowth from the spirit and teachings of Puritanism—as any other of the creeds enunciated on our continent in the last one hundred years.

When Brother Savage had concluded communion was celebrated.   This was after the simplest of models—a distribution of wheat-bread in great chunks and of water in pitchers, every one who so desired helping himself as the attendants approached him.

The congregation did not have much to commend them in the matter of intellectuality, as expressed upon their countenances.   The men were of ordinary mental calibre, and the women coarse, clumsy, unrefined, and from the down-trodden castes of Europe. Some of the little babies were comely, but only one grown woman could be included in such a category ; this was a young girl, just budding into maturity, whose correct anatomical outline was rather suggested than concealed by her clean calico garments, and whose countenance had much that was modest, gentle, and refined.

Next to her in beauty, although this term is rather too strong for its present application, came three Navajo-Mormon half-breed girls, whose black, flashing eyes, long lashes, aquiline noses, and olive complexions recalled to mind the physiognomies of the women of Judea.

Among the men at Sunset was Bishop Hatch, in my opinion the shrewdest and brightest person in the community. His name has already been cited as an authority in these pages, and I enter it again to say that in a long conversation I received a corroboration or explanation of the inferences and conclusions drawn from my personal observations of the Moquis. Bishop Hatch had once lived among them for years, speaks their language with fluency, and although not highly educated, is shrewd and intelligent.

It is now time to awaken the gentle reader, and tell him my task is done and his martyrdom ended.

I should be pleased to have had him remain with Moran and myself while we completed the tour of the other Mormon villages on this stream, or pressed down to Camp Apache, and noted the manners and customs of that fierce, brave race, the Apaches ; or returning, remarked upon the quaint peculiarities of the Indians of Zuni ; but this would be too much of a tax upon his patience. It is better we should part now before

he is thoroughly worn out.   I leave him at the advance
station of the Atlantic and Pacific Railroad, whose
locomotives are shrilly whistling as I write.

I do not know to what railroad centre he may
wish to be carried ; to the young one of Albuquerque,
the older of Kansas City and Omaha, the bustling
activity of Chicago and Saint Louis, or the far-distant
cities of New York, Boston, or Philadelphia, but
whithersoever it may be, I wish him God-speed and

FAREWELL.

INDEX.

VIEW OF THE MOQUI PUÉBLO OF HUALPI, N. E. ARIZONA.

State Dinner of the Madhi Dervishes of Fantee Asuanta August 19th 1881

A.F.HARPER.

F Hall Photo Litho London. E.C.

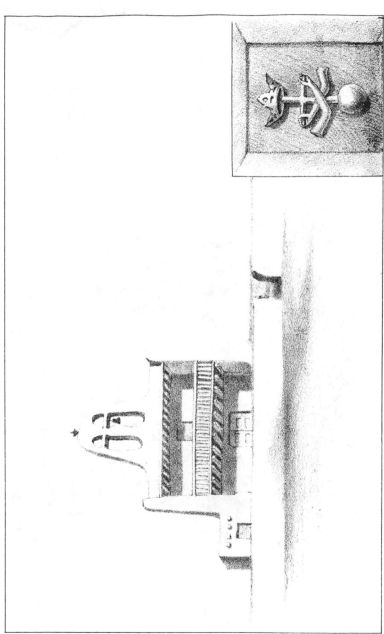

Pl. III.

CHURCH, NEW MEXICO, AND ARCHIEPISCOPAL COAT OF ARMS CARVED ON DOOR.

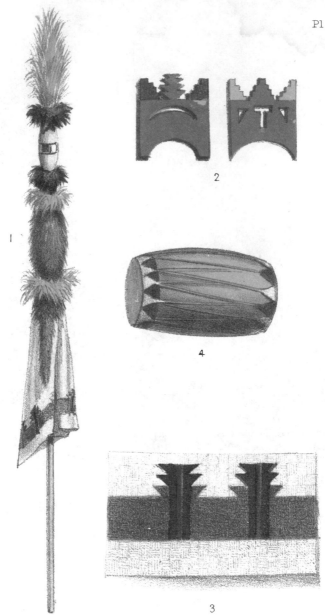

Pl. IV.

I, SACRED STANDARD. 2 HEAD DRESSES.
3 BORDER OF STANDARD. 4 DRUM.

Pl VI.

MALE DANCER, DANCE OF THE TABLET, PUEBLO OF SANTO DOMINGO
NEW MEXICO.

Pl VII.

CLOWN DANCER. DANCE OF THE TABLET. PUÉBLO OF SANTO DOMINGO,
NEW MEXICO.

Pl. VIII.

NAVAJO BOY, "GARRYOWEN".

Pl. IX.

NAVAJO WOMAN.

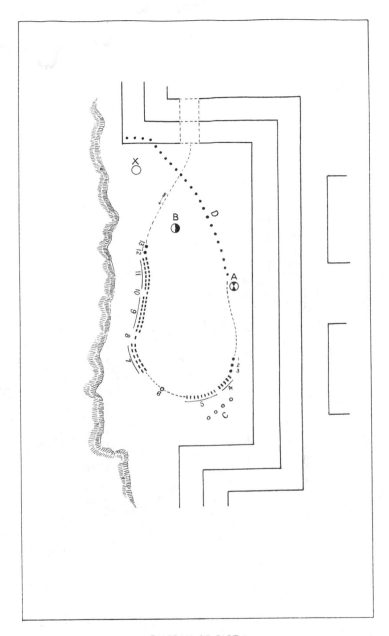

DIAGRAM OF PART I.

A. SACRED LODGE, B, SACRED ROCK, C & D, SQUAWS, I, HIGH PRIEST,
2 & 3, MEDICINE MEN, 4; FIVE MEDICINE MEN WITH T SHAPED RATTLES,
5, NINE CHILDREN DITTO, 6, OLD MAN WITH WHISTLING SLING, 7, 8, 9,
AND II, BANDS OF DANCERS, 12 & 13, OLD MEN WITH BOWS, X, ESTUFA.

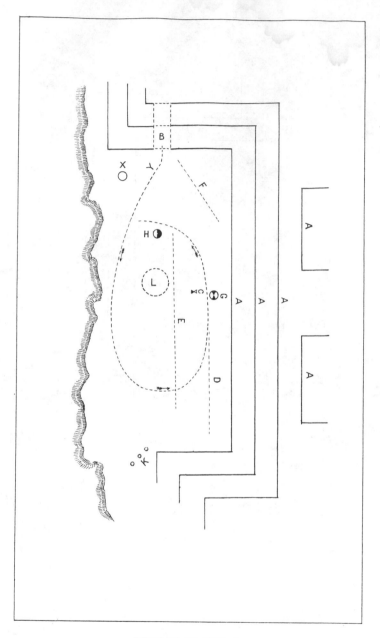

DIAGRAM OF PART 2.

AAAAA, LINE OF HOUSES, B, ARCADE, C, HIGH PRIEST, D, LINE OF
CHORISTERS, E, OF DANCERS, F, OF SQUAWS THROWING MEAL, G, SACRED
LODGE, H, SACRED ROCK, K, SQUAWS THROWING MEAL, L, SACRED CORN RING.
M, EDGE OF PRECIPICE, N N N GOAT AND SHEEP CORRALS, Y, LINE OF
MARCH, INDICATED BY ARROW, X, ESTUFA.

Pl. XII.

MEDICINE MAN WITH BOWL OF SACRED WATER.

Pl. XIII.

MEDICINE MAN WITH SLING AND MEDICINE BOW.

Pl. XIV.

DANCER HOLDING SNAKE IN MOUTH.

Pl. XV.

ATTENDANT FANNING SNAKE.

Pl. XVI.

YOUNG GIRL THROWING SACRED CORN MEAL UPON SNAKES.

Pl. XVII.

C. F. Kell, Litho. Castle St. Holborn E.C.

SACRED LODGE

Pl. XVIII.

ALTAR, REPRESENTING SNAKES AND MOUNTAIN LION.

Pl. XIX.

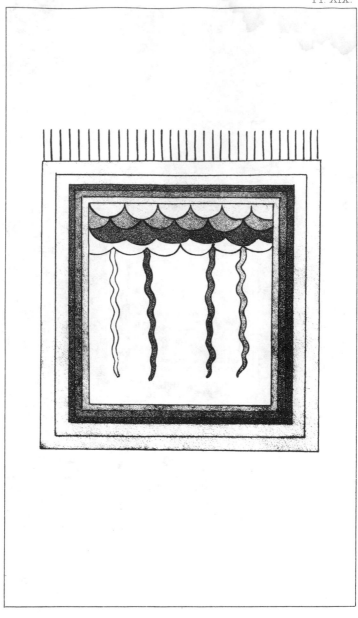

ALTAR REPRESENTING RAIN CLOUDS AND LIGHTNING.

Pl. XX.

STONE IMPLEMENTS SEEN IN SNAKE DANCE.

Pl XXI.

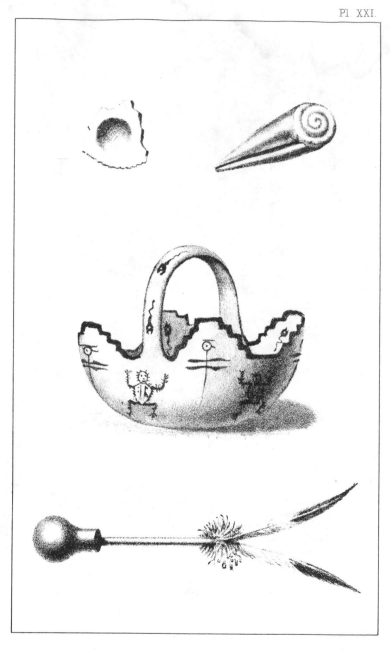

SEA-SHELS, POTTERY BASKET, AND FEATHER WAND.

Pl. XXII.

Pl XXIII

DECORATION UPON WALL OF ESTÚFA

Pl. XXIV.

DECORATION UPON WALL OF ESTÚFA.

Pl. XXV.

DECORATION UPON WALL OF ESTUFA.

Pl. XXVI.

DECORATION UPON WALL OF ESTUFA.

Pl. XXVII.

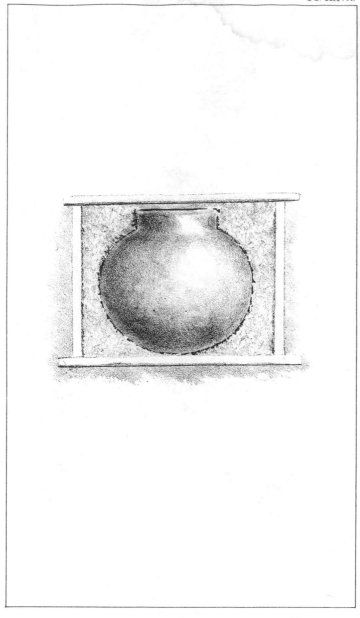

MOQUI METHOD OF PREPARING MUSH IN UNDERGROUND OVENS.

Pl. XXVIII-I

PUÉBLO POTTERY. I FROM SAN ILDEFONSO. 2 MUSHANGNEWY.
3 HUALPI. 4 SPOON, SUCHUNGNEWY. 5 LADLE SUMOPUWY.
6 CONDIMENT STAND. 7 TOY MOCCASIN. 8 WATER JAR. 9 CANTEEN

Pl. XXVIII-II.

PUEBLO POTTERY. 10 PITCHER, 11 BOWL, 12 WATER JAR, 13 WATER JAR,
14 LADLE, 15 BOWL, 16 BOWL, 26 PITCHER, 27 PITCHER.

Pl. XXVIII-III.

PUÉBLO POTTERY. 17 & 19 ANIMAL FIGURES, 18 BOWL, 20 JAR,
21 & 22 ANIMAL FIGURES, 23 BASKET, 24 WATER JAR. 25 PITCHER.

Pl. XXIX.

1 MORTAR and PESTLE, 2 STONE MILL 3 WATER JUG,
4 MASK

Pl. XXX.

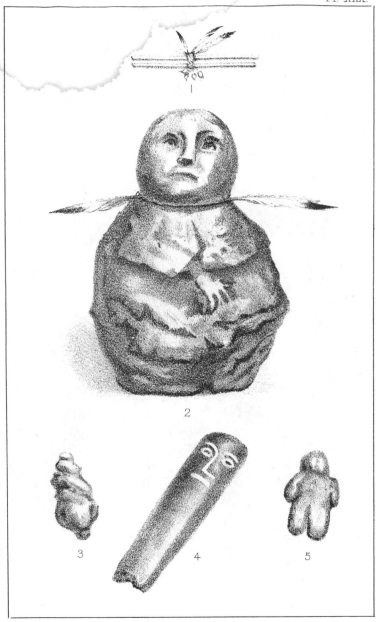

IDOLS. 1 VOTIVE OFFERING OF TWIGS, 2 OF BASALT,
3 & 5 OF CONCRETIONARY SANDSTONE, 4 SANDSTONE SLAB.

Pl. XXXI.

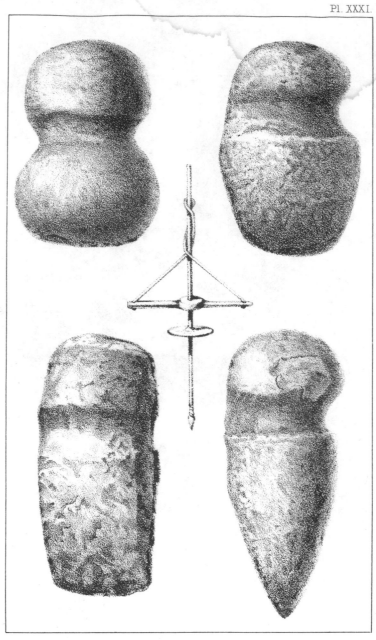

STONE IMPLEMENTS. HAMMER, HATCHET, BOW-DRILL,
AXE AND PICK.